Mornings *with* JESUS

2017

DAILY ENCOURAGEMENT *for your* SOUL

365 DEVOTIONS

SUSANNA FOTH AUGHTMON

GWEN FORD FAULKENBERRY

GRACE FOX

TRICIA GOYER

TARICE L. S. GRAY

SHARON HINCK

REBECCA BARLOW JORDAN

ERIN KEELEY MARSHALL

DIANNE NEAL MATTHEWS

CYNTHIA RUCHTI

SUZANNE DAVENPORT TIETJEN

Guideposts
New York

 ZONDERVAN®

ZONDERVAN

Mornings with Jesus 2017
Copyright © 2016 by Guideposts. All rights reserved.

Requests for information should be addressed to:
Zondervan, 3900 Sparks Dr. SE, Grand Rapids, MI 49546

ISBN 978-0-310-34713-2 (softcover)

ISBN 978-0-310-34715-6 (ebook)

Acknowledgments: Every attempt has been made to credit the sources of copyrighted material used in this book. If any such acknowledgment has been inadvertently omitted or miscredited, receipt of such information would be appreciated.

Scripture quotations marked (AMP) are taken from *The Amplified Bible* and *The Amplified Bible, Classic Edition.* Copyright © 2015 by The Lockman Foundation, La Habra, CA 90631. All rights reserved. Copyright © 1954, 1958, 1962, 1964, 1965, 1987 by The Lockman Foundation. Used by permission. www. Lockman.org. Scripture quotations marked (CEB) are taken from *Common English Bible.* Copyright © 2011 Common English Bible. Scripture quotations marked (ERV) are taken from Easy-to-Read Version Bible. Copyright © 2006 by Bible League International. Scripture quotations marked (ESV) are taken from the Holy Bible, English Standard Version, copyright © 2001 by Crossway Bibles, a division of Good News Publishers. Used by permission. All rights reserved. Scripture quotations marked (GNT) are taken from *Good News Translation.* Copyright © 1992 by American Bible Society. Scripture quotations marked (GW) are taken from *God's Word Translation.* Copyright © 1995 by God's Word to the Nations. Used by permission of Baker Publishing Group. Scripture quotations marked (HCS) are taken from the Holman Christian Standard Bible. Copyright © 1999, 2000, 2002, 2003 by Holman Bible Publishers, Nashville, Tennessee. All rights reserved. Scripture quotations marked (ICB) are taken from *The Holy Bible, International Children's Bible.* Copyright © 1986, 1988, 1999, 2015 by Tommy Nelson, a division of Thomas Nelson. Used by permission. Scripture quotations marked (ISV) are taken from *The International Standard Version of the Bible.* Copyright © 1995-2014 by ISV Foundation. All rights reserved internationally. Used by permission of Davidson Press, LL. Scripture quotations marked (KJV) are taken from *The King James Version of the Bible.* Scripture quotations marked (MSG) are taken from *The Message.* Copyright © 1993, 1994, 1995, 1996, 2000, 2001, 2002 by Eugene H. Peterson. Scripture quotations marked (NAS) are taken from the *New American Standard Bible,* copyright © 1960, 1962, 1963, 1968, 1971, 1972, 1973, 1975, 1977, 1995 by the Lockman Foundation. Used by permission. www.Lockman.org. Scripture quotations marked (NCV) are taken from the *New Century Version.* Copyright © 2005 by Thomas Nelson, Inc. Used by permission. All rights reserved. Scripture quotations marked (NIV) are taken from two editions: *The Holy Bible, New International Version, NIV.* ® Copyright © 1973, 1978, 1984, 2011 by Biblica, Inc.® All rights reserved worldwide. *The Holy Bible, New International Version.* Copyright © 1973, 1978, 1984 by Biblica, Inc.® Used by permission of Zondervan. Scripture quotations marked (NKJV) are taken from *The Holy Bible, New King James Version.* Copyright © 1997, 1990, 1985, 1983 by Thomas Nelson, Inc. Scripture quotations marked (NLT) are taken from the *Holy Bible,* New Living Translation. Copyright © 1996. Used by permission of Tyndale House Publishers, Inc., Wheaton, Illinois. All rights reserved. Scripture quotations marked (NRSV) are taken from the *New Revised Standard Version Bible.* Copyright © 1989 by the Division of Christian Education of the National Council of the Churches of Christ in the U.S.A. Used by permission. All rights reserved. Scripture quotations marked (RSV) are taken from the *Revised Standard Version of the Bible,* copyright © 1946, 1952, and 1971 the Division of Christian Education of the National Council of the Churches of Christ in the United States of America. Used by permission. All rights reserved. Scripture quotations marked (TLB) are taken from *The Living Bible.* Copyright © 1971 by Tyndale House Foundation. Used by permission of Tyndale House Publishers Inc., Carol Stream, Illinois 60188. All rights reserved.

Cover and interior design by Müllerhaus
Cover photo by Shutterstock
Indexed by Indexing Research
Typeset by Aptara

First printing August 2016 / Printed in the United States of America

Dear Friend,

Welcome to *Mornings with Jesus 2017*!

Whether you are new to *Mornings with Jesus* or are a returning reader, know that there is a blessing reserved for you within each day's reading: wisdom within each Scripture verse, reassurance within every devotion, and encouragement within every "Faith Step."

Mornings with Jesus is written by eleven faith-filled women who tell their engaging stories in accessible one-page devotions for every day of the year. They chronicle their day-to-day experiences to reveal the peace and promise of Jesus and His undeniable grace. Best-selling authors Tricia Goyer, a mother of ten, and Cynthia Ruchti, a doting grandmother of five, as well as Gwen Ford Faulkenberry, a caring teacher, and Grace Fox, a devoted missionary, convey how they better understand the true value of friendship and family, the courage to endure after a deeply felt loss, how to grow in wise counsel, and how to graciously receive and embrace lessons in humility. *Mornings with Jesus 2017* will allow you to look at life through Jesus's prism of light and know that you are loved. "As the Father has loved me, so have I loved you. Now remain in my love" (John 15:9, NIV).

Our shared yearlong journey includes two special series: "Advent" written by Erin Keeley Marshall and "Holy Week" written by Faulkenberry. Throughout these seasons and every day of the year, *Mornings with Jesus 2017* will remind you that Jesus is always with us and that He carries us through the challenges of life. Through the loss of a loved one or the end of friendship, through the struggles of raising children and even answering Jesus's call in your life, His boundless love will help you carry on. You'll be refreshed by the promise that He says: "I am gentle and humble in heart, and you will find rest for your souls" in Me. The wondrous love of Jesus makes us want to know Him more, embrace His teachings, and walk with Him every day of our lives.

It is our hope that *Mornings with Jesus 2017* will fill you with peace and reassurance of His grace and love for you. We want you to be encouraged by Jesus's promises that He holds your fears, doubts, and heavy burdens each step of the way. This is a simple blessing that we hope will live in your heart and carry you through in Jesus's love today and always.

Faithfully yours,
Editors of Guideposts

P.S. We love hearing from you! Let us know what *Mornings with Jesus 2017* means to you by e-mailing BookEditors@guideposts.org or writing to Guideposts Books & Inspirational Media, 110 William Street, New York, New York 10038. You can also keep up with your *Mornings with Jesus* friends on Facebook.com/MorningswithJesus.

Especially for You!

Now you can enjoy the daily encouragement of *Mornings with Jesus 2017* wherever you are! Receive each day's devotion on your computer, tablet, or smartphone. Visit MorningswithJesus.org/MWJ2017 and enter this code: faith.

Sign up for the online newsletter *Mornings with Jesus* through MorningswithJesus.org. Each week you'll receive an inspiring devotion or personal thoughts from one of the writers about her own devotional time and prayer life, how focusing on Jesus influenced her relationship with Him, and more!

SUNDAY, JANUARY 1

As they were talking about these things, Jesus himself stood among them, and said to them, "Peace to you!" But they were startled and frightened and thought they saw a spirit. And he said to them, "Why are you troubled, and why do doubts arise in your hearts? See my hands and my feet, that it is I myself...." Luke 24:36–39 (ESV)

HAVE YOU EVER FACED something new in your life and been confused about what Jesus was doing, how much He was really involved in your circumstances?

These days I'm confused about some new things Jesus is doing with my family. My husband started a new business and we've relocated to a new neighborhood, and frankly, life feels foreign, as if I landed in the middle of someone else's life and am supposed to take it from here. It's unfamiliar territory, and at any given moment I feel more unsettled than peaceful.

But I've got enough history with Jesus that even when my feelings speak otherwise, I know who holds today and the future. He's the same One Who has held me to this point. When I quiet myself, I can recognize Him. I have to look for Him, just as He invited His shell-shocked followers to do when they struggled with fears and shaken peace at the new way He was showing up in their day-to-day lives. They'd never seen Him appear suddenly like that. They were uncertain and scared about how to respond or even process what had just happened.

Jesus is Lord of the new, and I need to be ready for Him to do something new in my life. —ERIN KEELEY MARSHALL

FAITH STEP: *Think of a time when your life changed. Name the emotions you felt. How did you sense Jesus's presence in your circumstances? Ask Him for eyes to look for Him and a heart to see and respond to Him.*

MONDAY, JANUARY 2

"I am the Lord your God, who teaches you what is best for you, who directs you in the way you should go." Isaiah 48:17 (NIV)

IN THE PAST, I usually divided my new goals into categories each year: Home, Personal, Marriage and Family, Spiritual Growth, to name a few. But several years ago when my husband retired, something changed. I wanted to accomplish things for Jesus, but I had left my workaholic drive behind. I enjoyed all of life and its activities, but my goals and lists had already shrunk in recent years. Still, the conflict between complex and simple, good and best, battled at times. I wanted to spend more time with my husband during his retirement, yet still fulfill God's personal calling on my life.

So I began asking Jesus more intentionally: What were His plans for me? Did it really matter what I did as long as I tried to honor Him? Was there something I needed to start? Amend? Complete? How could I find the right balance in my life? I needed—wanted—answers. I wanted to hear a personal word from Jesus.

Jesus often answers with principles in His Word, rather than specific instructions, giving us the power of choice and discernment. But within days of my prayer, He directed my eyes toward a Scripture verse that had my name on it—one that promised He would teach me what was best for me...and direct me in the way I should go. And Jesus has been faithful to do that.

An assortment of good things begs for our attention every year. But only Jesus knows what the best ones are. That's why I started exchanging my lists for a blank page. And trust is at the top of that page. —REBECCA BARLOW JORDAN

FAITH STEP: *List some good things you have been involved in during the past year. Then ask Jesus to teach you what is best for you this coming year.*

TUESDAY, JANUARY 3

*[Jesus said] "Whoever finds their life will lose it,
and whoever loses their life for my sake will find it."*
Matthew 10:39 *(NIV)*

A FRIEND TOLD ME about a day she got so wrapped up in her current project that she missed lunch and started dinner late. The more she wrote, the more ideas came to her. By the time she took a break, she noticed the streetlights coming on and heard her stomach growling.

I know the feeling of getting lost in a good movie, an interesting conversation, or a challenging craft project. I'm all too familiar with being so absorbed in a well-written novel that I'm oblivious to everything else, especially the numbers on my bedside clock.

These things are good in and of themselves, but what I need to experience more often is getting lost in Jesus. Meditating on His love and mercy. Seeking to know Him on a deeper level. Focusing on how I can learn to follow more closely in His steps.

Jesus calls on us every single day to live for Him, making decisions that help us replace a self-centered life with a sacrificial one. As we get lost in Him, we'll discover a new richness in our relationship, new opportunities for ministry, and renewed meaning and purpose in our lives...worth exceedingly great value.
—DIANNE NEAL MATTHEWS

FAITH STEP: *Today try to find a quiet moment to lose yourself in Jesus so much that everything around you fades away and His presence fills you to the brim with love, joy, and peace.*

WEDNESDAY, JANUARY 4

"No, do not be afraid of those nations, for the Lord your God is among you, and he is a great and awesome God."
Deuteronomy 7:21 (NLT)

AT THE BEGINNING OF EACH NEW YEAR, I ask Jesus to give me a specific word on which to focus for the next twelve months.

One year He gave me "joy." Apparently He knew I'd need it because less than two weeks later I ruptured an Achilles tendon. Nine days after that, I suffered a knee injury on the opposite leg and thus lost mobility for three months. Shingles hit me two weeks after I started walking again. Later that year, my husband was diagnosed with cancer. Learning to choose joy despite difficulties was a lifesaver for me.

Last year He gave me "deeper." He used a difficult family relationship to peel me like a human onion, but the experience—albeit more painful than I could have imagined—catapulted me into a more intimate walk with Him.

This year's word is "great." I have no idea how Jesus will use it to accomplish His purposes in and through my life, but I anticipate good things—not necessarily easy, but rich in life lessons.

Spiritual writer and pastor Jack Hayford said, "We have a great Savior. Therefore, we are encouraged to expect great victories, knowing that great battles are necessary for conquest, but confident because He is leading us." I posted this quote on my fridge where I'll see it often. It fills me with hope and courage for whatever the next twelve months hold. —GRACE FOX

FAITH STEP: *Write Pastor Hayford's quote on a recipe card and post it on your fridge. Ask Jesus to reveal His greatness to you and to your loved ones.*

THURSDAY, JANUARY 5

"He must increase and I must decrease. The one who comes from above is above all things. . . . " John 3:30–31 (CEB)

RUNNING IN THE BACKGROUND of my thoughts this year has been *more or less?* I've been challenged to ask myself the question with every activity I tackle, every opportunity that crosses my path, even what I put in my mouth or view with my eyes.

Do I need *more* of this or *less* of it in my life?

The question is rooted in a desire to bring everything I do into compliance with what Jesus expects of me and longs to see in me.

It's not an easy challenge, but necessary.

A mildly interesting television show follows the one I really wanted to watch. Do I need more or less television in my life? Less.

A girlfriend asks me to lunch to discuss a concern weighing on her heart. Do I need more or fewer lunches with friends? More. The process of deepening friendships has too often been neglected in recent years.

A coupon for free frozen custard is burning a hole in my pocket. It's free! But I need less frozen custard in my life right now, not more.

More time for prayer; less social media. More handwritten notes; less e-mail. More quiet; less noise. More of Jesus; less of me.

He must increase; I must decrease. But what does it mean, practically speaking? One way I'm working to apply that principle this year is by doing more of what comes naturally to Him and less of what comes naturally to me. As only He can, Jesus makes the math work out beautifully. —CYNTHIA RUCHTI

FAITH STEP: *Remember simple math symbols like 6 >3? Create a bookmark with this abbreviated expression from John 3:30: Jesus >Me. It's a principle not of diminishing returns but of increasing joy.*

FRIDAY, JANUARY 6

"Blessed is she who has believed that the Lord would fulfill his promises to her!" Luke 1:45 (NIV)

THIS YEAR JOHN AND I brought four girls into our home through foster care. After seven months, we celebrated their official adoption. Having them join our family has been both joyful and challenging. These girls are preteens and teens, and they've already faced a lot of heartache. Some of them have struggled to believe we'd keep them. It's easy to understand; they've been told before that they were going to be adopted, and it didn't happen. They worried about getting their hopes up only to be sent away again. They tested us over and over to see if we would keep our word.

Yet, when it came to the youngest of the girls, Florentina, there has been no doubt. Florentina moved in and acted as if our house has always been home. She's never wavered. She still struggles with the pain and heartache of the past, but she's found home…and she believes it.

I asked her why she never questioned this adoption. She told me that one night she was praying and Jesus spoke to her heart. She felt Him saying that He had a family picked out for her, and she just had to believe. Even at the young age of eleven, she clung to that.

At the very same time Jesus was speaking to my husband and me about opening our home to more kids, Jesus was speaking to Florentina, giving her assurance that she would receive a family.

Faith is trusting that Jesus has your good in mind, even when it's hard to see. My hope is that I would learn to believe that Jesus would fulfill His promises to me with equal assurance! —TRICIA GOYER

FAITH STEP: *Pray for children in foster care. Pray for Jesus to stir the hearts of couples to open their homes. Pray for foster children to know Jesus and believe He cares for them.*

SATURDAY, JANUARY 7

Surely goodness and mercy shall follow me all the days of my life:
and I will dwell in the house of the Lord for ever.
Psalm 23:6 (KJV)

JANUARY 7, 1987, IS A DATE I will always remember. It was two days before my thirteenth birthday. It was also the day my grandmother died.

My mother got the urgent call before daybreak. Grandma had taken a sudden turn for the worse. My brother and I awoke hours later to discover our mom sitting in the breakfast nook of the kitchen, her face soaked with tears.

"She's gone." I could almost hear her heart crumbling as she said it. My brother immediately hugged her and cried in her arms, but I froze, unable to imagine what that meant—life without our matriarch. My mother reminded us that the doctor had said just days earlier that my grandmother would fully recover from her heart attack. "If only," my mother cried, "the doctors had done more to save her."

The Bible talks about the only time Jesus wept after arriving to find that His dear friend Lazarus had died. In John 11:32 (NKJV), Mary cried out when she saw Him: "Lord, if You had been here, my brother would not have died."

If only. The promise within that chapter is something I now know is the promise my grandmother received. Jesus restored Lazarus in this life and restored my grandmother in the next.

My grandmother's favorite Scripture was always Psalm 23. Those words have been a comfort to me over the years because I know she will dwell in the house of the Lord forever. —TARICE L. S. GRAY

FAITH STEP: *Are you missing a loved one? Grieving? Read Psalm 23 and take comfort in the promises of God.*

SUNDAY, JANUARY 8

. . . Fixing our eyes on Jesus, the pioneer and perfecter of faith.
For the joy set before him he endured the cross, scorning its shame, and
sat down at the right hand of the throne of God. Hebrews 12:2 (NIV)

AS A YOUNG MINISTER'S WIFE AND A MOM, I visualized a life filled with a sense of adventure, extraordinary surprises, and joyful moments. And Jesus has been faithful to give me many of those blessings. But what I didn't expect was that ordinary, routine tasks would take up so much of my time: planning meals, cleaning house, listening to hurting people, coordinating busy schedules. I've often caught myself complaining about the much more common, necessary, mundane work of my life. I didn't always appreciate its role or its importance.

So in studying the life of Jesus in the Gospels, I was surprised to discover that much of His day was filled with ordinary tasks: teaching stubborn disciples the same lessons again and again; loving angry enemies day after day; walking long, dusty roads to get to the next town, and then to arrive only to greet complaining and hurting people everywhere He turned. It was a life filled with repetition and unexceptional moments. And yet because of one underlying purpose, Jesus's work became extraordinary. Everything He did—all the mundane, difficult, annoying, ordinary tasks—was to bring glory to God (John 12:27–28). That was the "joy set before Him" from the very beginning.

Our routine life was never intended to confine us or define us, but it can refine us, if we let it. When we keep our eyes on Jesus and do everything for the same joy—to bring glory to God—every one of our tasks becomes extraordinary too. —REBECCA BARLOW JORDAN

FAITH STEP: *List your daily, ordinary tasks. Then draw a smiley face or an exclamation point beside each one to remind you of the extraordinary "joy" set before you.*

MONDAY, JANUARY 9

A voice came from the cloud, saying, "This is my Son, whom I have chosen; listen to him." Luke 9:35 (NIV)

I'D PHONED IN A PRESCRIPTION RENEWAL, but the pharmacy called back to say it had expired, so they'd talk to the doctor. The next day my caller ID showed a missed call from the doctor's office. *What if insurance won't cover the medicine? What if the clinic is calling to tell me I need to make another appointment?* I was having a rough day and didn't want one more complication, so I didn't play the recording.

The next morning my husband noticed the blinking light and played the message: "Hi. This is the doctor's office letting you know we sent the prescription you requested to the pharmacy."

Simple. Solved. No big deal. I shook my head at my earlier anxieties.

It made me wonder what other helpful news I postpone hearing. How often do I slap my hands over my ears, afraid to hear the message Jesus has for me in case it complicates my life? Sometimes I beg Him for direction but then quickly say "Amen" and turn away, not willing to listen to His guidance. Other times I read His Word, come upon a Scripture that challenges or convicts me, and stick my bookmark there to think about the passage another day.

When God spoke from the cloud on the mountain where Jesus was transfigured, Peter, James, and John heard a specific instruction: "Listen to Him."

I can study the life of Jesus. I can wear a cross as a symbol of being His follower. I can talk about Him with others. But if I'm not willing to listen to Him, I'll miss many blessings. His words are light and truth and good news. —SHARON HINCK

FAITH STEP: *Next time you listen to a voice-mail message, use that as a reminder to pause. Take that moment to ask Jesus to help you listen to Him.*

TUESDAY, JANUARY 10

This is the day the Lord has made. We will rejoice and be glad in it.
Psalm 118:24 (NLT)

OUR FAMILY HAS A NEW PUPPY, a three-pound bundle of fluff! Tawny-haired with black tips along her back and tail, she's a Poochon, a mix between a miniature poodle and a Bichon Frise. Jasmine Beatrice—aka Jazzy Bea, Bea-Bop, Jazz, or simply Bea—stole our hearts.

As I'm writing this, Bea is thirteen weeks old, so we're in the throes of puppy love and she's slowly catching on to housebreaking and obedience training. She's a smart little thing with an infectious greeting every time we wake up or come home or invite her to play or curl up on a lap. She knows the word *out* better than her name (Who can fault her with that smattering of nicknames?), and just last night she begged at the door to be taken out to do her business like the rock-star pup she's proving to be.

She came to us in the midst of a draining year: a job loss, a new business, a new home, caring for elderly parents, stress, grief, and adjustments galore! Although Bea is part of the redirection that sums up our year, I see Jesus's kind of consuming joy in her every day. Each morning she opens her eyes and then morphs into a mass of wiggles at rediscovering the wonder of living. She reminds me to focus on the life Jesus offers me and its many blessings, including His faithful presence and the peace of knowing He has my days and concerns in hand.

My joy may waver, but it's so like Jesus to place a living reminder of His joyful life in my path in the tiny form of Jasmine Beatrice.
—ERIN KEELEY MARSHALL

FAITH STEP: *Take the joy challenge in Scripture and ask Jesus to help you claim His joy. He wants us to choose daily to thrive in joy's wholeness. We will rejoice!*

WEDNESDAY, JANUARY 11

In all my prayers for all of you, I always pray with joy because of your partnership in the gospel from the first day until now, being confident of this, that he who began a good work in you will carry it on to completion until the day of Christ Jesus.
Philippians 1:4–6 (NIV)

THESE DAYS I FIND I am easily distracted. I can set out to work on a project and ten minutes later find I have completely gone off task due to a text from my kids or the realization that I haven't done laundry in the past three days. It doesn't take much to get me going on a completely different tangent. And then two hours later I realize, *I still have to write that chapter.*

So I have been working on my focus lately. It takes discipline to stay on task. But keeping my mind focused on the work in front of me is really my heart's desire because I love knowing that I have accomplished what I set out to do.

Jesus has set out to accomplish something too. He is set on shaping you into the person He created you to be, if you will let Him. If you will keep your eyes focused on Him. If you will yield your life and your mind and your desires to Him.

It is easy to get distracted in this life. So many things are pulling at us and competing for our attention. But if we keep our eyes on Jesus, the author and perfecter of our faith, He will do exactly what He set out to do—He will carry out the good work He began in us and He will complete it. He never gets distracted.
—SUSANNA FOTH AUGHTMON

FAITH STEP: *Write down the distractions that are pulling at you and then refocus your attention on Jesus. Offer Him your plans, expectations, and desires and then say, "Jesus, I want You to complete Your work in me."*

THURSDAY, JANUARY 12

"First wash the inside of the cup and the dish, and then the outside will become clean, too." Matthew 23:26 (NLT)

LAST WEEK MY HUSBAND AND I did our first ever coconut oil pull. It isn't the best taste, but it's hardly disgusting, and we've heard the potential benefits are awesome: powerful detox, healthier body, whiter teeth. Reportedly, coconut oil pulls have even healed dying, decayed teeth.

We melted a tablespoon or so of quality, unrefined coconut oil and swished it in our mouths for fifteen to twenty minutes. We didn't swallow it because it was pulling toxins from our bodies, and we didn't want to send them back down to our stomachs. When time was up, we spit into the trash can, not the drain, so all that junk didn't end up in our plumbing.

Body detox is trending as people try to get healthier quickly. But even more important than cleaning out physically is making sure we're pure spiritually.

Jesus purifies us from the toxins we can't see and may not even know are messing us up. Toxins such as dissatisfaction, ungratefulness, messed-up priorities, dishonesty, envy, and irritability can slowly build while we don't even realize their filth-causing trouble.

But Jesus knows precisely the methods that will be most effective for each of us. He promises to make everything new, including us. Sometimes His processes take longer than we'd like because He isn't into a quick fix. He's into the eternal.

What better way to begin the year than by asking Jesus for a spiritual detox? —ERIN KEELEY MARSHALL

FAITH STEP: *Do a coconut oil pull sometime this week. While you're swishing the oil, ask Jesus to do the necessary work in you to help you be filled with Him.*

FRIDAY, JANUARY 13

God said, "Let there be light." And so light appeared.
God saw how good the light was. . . . Genesis 1:3–4 (CEB)

I'VE NEVER LIKED THE DARK. As a little girl, I often lay in bed at night with my imagination running wild. I visualized all sorts of scary things lurking around me. Maybe that explains why I love that God's first command during the creation of the world called for light. He commanded light to shine and then separated it from the darkness. On day four God fashioned the sun, moon, and stars to light up the sky and divide day and night.

Later, Jesus arrived on the scene and lit up the world in a new way. He proclaimed, "I am the light of the world. Whoever follows me will have a life filled with light and will never live in the dark" (John 8:12, GW). Jesus offered love, grace, and truth to people living in the darkness of sin and fear of death.

Jesus also said that those who follow Him are to let their light shine for others to see. If I claim to know Him, people should see something distinctive in my behavior, my conversation, and my life. My character should demonstrate the difference between living for Jesus and living apart from Him—a difference as big as day and night.

These days I typically wake up way too early, sometimes two hours or more before dawn. As I wait for the sun's rays to chase away the darkness of night, I feel thankful that God created the lights in the heavens. And during troubled times in my life, I'm grateful for the Light of the World Who lives in me. I know that His light is great enough to help me find my way through any darkness. —DIANNE NEAL MATTHEWS

FAITH STEP: *Be sure to catch a sunrise one day this week. As you watch the sun's light gradually dispel the darkness, ask the Light of the World to shine through you in a special way to everyone you meet that day.*

SATURDAY, JANUARY 14

But encourage one another daily, as long as it is called "Today," so that none of you may be hardened by sin's deceitfulness. Hebrews 3:13 (NIV)

I JUST GOT BACK INSIDE from tending the outdoor wood boiler that keeps our cabin and bunkhouse wonderfully warm all winter. It isn't difficult, but it has to be done every day.

When I wake up, I go outside and check the temperature and water level while I wait fifteen seconds until it's safe to open the door. Before I clear ashes from the vents, I use a tool called a Wonder Bar to remove any gunk or creosote off the edges of the door opening. Jet-black and gooey, the residue sticks to the end of the tool as I scrape, eventually falling like crinkled ribbons into the firebox.

I lost my Wonder Bar last year and couldn't get the edges clean for a couple of days while I looked frantically through the snow. Nothing else worked, and if I didn't scrape it down to the bare metal every day, the door wouldn't seal and the system would break down. In the time it took to order another Wonder Bar, that sticky black stuff baked hard—almost to a point where I couldn't get it off at all.

Dealing with unhealthy areas of our lives is similar.

Following Jesus isn't weekly; it's daily. Dailiness is a theme in the Bible, from manna being given and gathered daily; to prayers, sacrifices, and worship being offered; to Jesus teaching the disciples to pray for daily bread.

Coming to Jesus daily is the remedy for anything gunky and black in our lives. And the tool He uses? A community of like-minded people who can encourage us to walk in step with Him.
—SUZANNE DAVENPORT TIETJEN

FAITH STEP: *Pray to find a like-minded friend who is open to sharing struggles, prayer, and encouragement.*

SUNDAY, JANUARY 15

He was despised and rejected—a man of sorrows, acquainted with deepest grief. . . . Yet it was our weaknesses he carried; it was our sorrows that weighed him down. Isaiah 53:3–4 (NLT)

SOMETIMES LIFE PACKS A PUNCH. And then another. And then maybe another. Life's been like that for several months among my close network of friends. Multiple health hits, some losses of life, financial setbacks, depression—struggles that reverberate like unsettled rings of a stone dropped into water. As faith people, we encourage each other to take our heartaches to Jesus, to lay them at His feet, to surrender and let go, to leave it at the Cross. It can almost sound clichéd to a broken heart.

Letting go sounds good and light and freeing and godly and the way we're supposed to do things as followers of Jesus. But if we're not careful, we can turn letting go into one more legalistic have-to. Or we can mistake letting go for stuffing our emotions that need to be acknowledged and given room to ebb and flow and run their course.

So when I'm faced with a loss, guilt can set in if I feel that I'm not getting over it quickly enough. But I've been reminded of one hiccup—a question, really—in the concept of letting go. When tears keep coming in waves, one word troubles me: *How?*

Appearing to move on from pain or disappointment in record time doesn't equate with heroism. We're not better people by refusing to be honest with ourselves regarding what truly hurts.

Jesus is not hurried, ever. He is patient. He's caring. He offers new grace and mercy daily. He gets that sometimes we hurt for a long time. And through that time He wants us to hang on to Him and lean into Him for healing. He is with us for the long haul.
—ERIN KEELEY MARSHALL

FAITH STEP: *Simply thank Jesus for knowing your heart.*

MONDAY, JANUARY 16

"Everyone who hears these words of mine and does not put them into practice is like a foolish man who built his house on sand. The rain came down, the streams rose, and the winds blew and beat against that house, and it fell with a great crash."
Matthew 7:26–27 *(NIV)*

AT WORK I HAVE A QUOTE by William Wilberforce stuck to my computer. He led the movement in the British Parliament to abolish slavery. It says, "You may choose to look the other way, but you can never say again that you did not know." He said this when confronting people who considered themselves moral, even Christians, while they were actively or passively condoning the slave trade. I use the quote to inspire me in my quest to stamp out ignorance on our college campus by making my students read and discuss controversial issues, instead of burying their heads in the sand.

It occurs to me that the same principle applies to the teachings of Jesus. When we read His Word, listen to it taught, study it— then we are exposed. As Wilberforce admonished, we may choose to look the other way, but only some of us can say we didn't know. We know. There's just a disconnect between knowing and doing sometimes. But that disconnect is the way of foolishness. The way of wisdom is to internalize the message and then act on it.
—GWEN FORD FAULKENBERRY

FAITH STEP: *What words of Jesus do you need to act on today? Perhaps they are words you've heard all of your life—you can't say you don't know what to do. It's just a hard thing to do it. But step out in obedience. Rather than shifting sand, you'll find solid rock beneath you.*

TUESDAY, JANUARY 17

Be completely humble and gentle; be patient, bearing with one another in love. Make every effort to keep the unity of the Spirit through the bond of peace. Ephesians 4:2–3 (NIV)

JOHN AND I RECENTLY CELEBRATED our twenty-fifth wedding anniversary with a cruise because we knew that around the time of our actual anniversary we'd be bringing four new girls into our home through adoption, making us the parents of ten children. It's not how most people celebrate their silver anniversary, but we are thankful.

Adding children to our home has made us weary and frustrated at times, but it has also brought us together. During times when I've been overwhelmed, I've pulled my husband aside and asked, "Can you pray for me?" He's done the same. We've stayed up late and talked through issues to find solutions. There is nothing that makes John more handsome to me than to see him talking patiently with an unreasonable teen or cuddling with an unruly preschooler. Seeing my husband being humble and patient makes him all the more lovable.

Marriage is hard, raising kids is hard, and conflicts in life can pull us apart. They can also pull us together if we turn to each other for help and support. Even when we disagree, we come together before Jesus and pray for His Spirit to unify us. We need Jesus because we need humility, gentleness, patience, love, and unity. If marriage and parenting were easy, then we wouldn't need to turn to Jesus as often. Marriage isn't about having a perfect life or relationship but about turning to Jesus and discovering that He never disappoints.
—TRICIA GOYER

FAITH STEP: *Are you facing conflict in your marriage, or do you know of someone who is? Pray and ask Jesus to bring humility, gentleness, patience, love, and unity into that marriage today.*

WEDNESDAY, JANUARY 18

Then Moses said to them, "No one is to keep any of it until morning."
However, some of them paid no attention to Moses; they kept part of it
until morning, but it was full of maggots and began to smell.
So Moses was angry with them. Exodus 16:19–20 (NIV)

I'VE WATCHED TV SHOWS about people who believe society is nearing destruction, so they prepare supplies of food. They build huge stockpiles—sometimes at remote, hidden properties or just under their beds and in their garages. It helps them to feel secure.

Security isn't a bad thing. I like having a bit of a cushion in our budget, shelves of canned goods in the pantry, a lock on my front door. But it's easy to find security in my own plans and efforts and forget to trust Jesus.

When the Israelites needed food, God provided it daily, with instructions to use it up each day. No security blanket. No savings account. Just daily trust that the One Who led them out of captivity would also care for them as they traveled through the desert. I wonder if I would have squirreled away a little extra, thinking I'd get a head start on the next day. Maybe my intentions would even have been noble. I'd have more to share if someone else needed it.

Those who relied on their own efforts for security and provision soon ended up with maggots. When you hear the whisper of Jesus saying, "Trust Me. I am the Bread of Life," how do you respond?

I'm afraid my answer is often, "Yes, but." Yes, I trust You to meet my needs, but I will push past the point of exhaustion to get more work done in case the projects dry up later. Soon I'm picking maggots out of the mess of my striving. Instead, I can work joyfully, and also rest joyfully, knowing that Jesus is my constant provider. —SHARON HINCK

FAITH STEP: *Choose some items from your kitchen cupboards to donate to a food bank, and thank Jesus that you can trust Him to provide.*

Thursday, January 19

"I know that my Redeemer lives. . . ." Job 19:25 (NAS)

"Daddy, what is *redeemed*?"

My three-year-old Stella, lying between us in bed, posed the question. She'd been eyeing her father's tattoo, a broken shackle around his ankle with the word in bold letters: *Redeemed*.

I looked up from the book I was reading.

Stone cradled her face. "It means that even though we make mistakes, we are worth a lot to Jesus, enough that He would die to save us."

"Why, Daddy?"

"Because He loves us so much."

This answer seemed to satisfy our little theologian, who snuggled down and went to sleep. I lay there awake, though, unpacking Stone's definition and thinking over what it means to be redeemed.

There's a story behind that tattoo—a story of redemption so important to Stone that he wanted it inked onto his body. A trophy of grace, in a way. And a memorial. Lest he ever forget the price that was paid. How valuable he is. How loved. That he has been set free.

Redeemed, in a sense, means giving something value. Understanding that Jesus values us is the beginning of faith. The work of redemption in our daily lives, though, means that He gives value to our sufferings, and even our mistakes, by bringing good out of them. Beauty from ashes. Hope from despair. Life from death. —Gwen Ford Faulkenberry

Faith Step: *Is there a choice you made that causes you grief? Or are you suffering over something that wasn't your choice? Write this on your heart today:* **My Redeemer lives.** *There is no place so dark that His light can't shine there. Jesus lives to redeem you. Trust Him.*

FRIDAY, JANUARY 20

Your life is hidden with Christ in God. When Christ, who is your life,
is revealed, then you also will be revealed with him in glory.
Colossians 3:3–4 (CEB)

UNABLE TO RESIST the lure of creating art with fabric, I took up quilting for a season. I purchased a few tools and then visited the fabric shop. As a beginner, I gathered my materials for that first project, spreading the fat quarters as one might fan a deck of cards.

Even before I laid out the pattern for my first block, the project held beauty. Colors of fabrics make art, even preassembly.

A friend of mine is a landscape and still-life artist. He squeezes dollops of pigment onto his palette. He notes the unexpected artfulness of the colors before they ever reach the canvas.

My grandson separates Legos by color before building. The piles of pieces are impressive before he snaps two together.

Our lives—in both preassembly and disassembled stages—hold undeniable beauty. We can't always see it ourselves; we're too close. But Jesus has a clear view of who we are and what we will become.

"I don't even have two puzzle pieces connected right now!" But the pieces are beautiful.

"I see nothing but scraps and bits." Look at how colorful they are. It'll come together soon.

"I feel as if I'm starting from scratch. Everything's been ripped out." Jesus is an expert at rebuilding lives torn apart, disassembled.

You are on your way to a beautiful end product.

—CYNTHIA RUCHTI

FAITH STEP: *If your life isn't in tiny scraps right now, someone with whom you cross paths feels that way. Watch for an opportunity to let that person know you see beauty in his or her life, even at this preassembled stage.*

SATURDAY, JANUARY 21

Rejoice always, pray continually, give thanks in all circumstances;
for this is God's will for you in Christ Jesus.
1 Thessalonians 5:16–18 (NIV)

IT'S TAKEN ME A WHILE to feel that I understand prayer and to consider myself a praying person. Maybe it's because of a misconception that I had since childhood that prayer was an event. I felt it was something I needed to remember to tack on at the end of my day, just like brushing my teeth before bed. It was a time when I needed to be still and come before Jesus. There are times when I do that. I love quiet mornings on my couch. Sometimes I even get on my knees before Him, but I've grown to discover prayer is not an event; it's a continual conversation.

In the last week I prayed when I started homeschooling seven children at one time. (I prayed we'd all learn and get along!) This morning I prayed as I watched my son drive away in the rain. (I prayed for his protection and for a bubble to surround his car from crazy drivers.) Last night I prayed for a friend when she shared a need on Facebook. I didn't wait until the next morning's quiet time to pray. As I sat in front of my computer, I closed my eyes for a moment and I asked Jesus to be with her and to give her peace.

We don't need to wait for a certain time of day to pray; instead we can go to Jesus anytime. Longer prayer times are important—to listen as well as to make requests—but Jesus's ear is always attuned to even our smallest request. Each of us can be a praying person, and today is a wonderful day to start. —TRICIA GOYER

FAITH STEP: *Whenever you hear of prayer needs during the day, pause and lift your requests to Jesus. Then set a time to pray for a longer period, taking care to listen for Jesus's whispers to your heart.*

SUNDAY, JANUARY 22

Return to your rest, my soul, for the Lord has been good to you.
Psalm 116:7 (NIV)

WHILE GOING THROUGH A KEEPSAKE BOX, I found a notebook that my younger son had used during third grade. His teacher had asked the students to describe a family member. At the top of the page, Kevin wrote "My Mom." Underneath were six words: *Curly hair. Big smile. Always working.*

When I first read those words almost thirty years ago, I felt glad Kevin noticed how hard I worked to care for our home and family, along with helping out at church, school, and in the community. But now, from this vantage point, that word *always* tugs at my heart. Looking back, I wish I'd done a little less scrubbing and more playing with my children.

I grew up on a small family farm and got used to physical work at an early age. But that work ethic can tempt me to live an unbalanced life. I tend to evaluate my day solely by how much I get accomplished. When I go on vacation, I start a new chore list before I get home. This narrow focus can make me miss opportunities to grow spiritually and affect others.

The Bible promotes the value of hard work but also makes it clear that we need physical rest (Genesis 2:3). Later, Jesus explained a different kind of rest we desperately need—soul rest. In Matthew 11:28–29, He invites us to become yoked together with Him and learn from Him. Once we accept Christ's unconditional love and become His, our approach to life changes. Our past is forgiven, our future is secure, and His loving presence guides us each day. And then we can finally enjoy the deep, refreshing soul rest He offers. —DIANNE NEAL MATTHEWS

FAITH STEP: *Examine your soul for any signs of turbulence, unrest, or striving. Ask Jesus to show you what keeps you from experiencing restorative rest in Him.*

Monday, January 23

All things were made through him, and without him was not any thing made that was made. John 1:3 (ESV)

I'm still waiting to use my passport, but my husband and I have done without other things in order to be able to travel over the years to some breathtaking spots. The Grand Canyon. The Rocky Mountains. California. Cannon Beach in Oregon. The Atlantic Ocean. Florida's Gulf Shore. Texas Hill Country. The waterfalls of Wisconsin. (Yes, there are waterfalls in Wisconsin. One county boasts forty of them!)

In regard to terrain and vistas, it's a tough call. The vastness of the Grand Canyon or the vastness of the ocean? The power of immobile mountains or the power of waves crashing onshore?

Imagine the most beautiful scenery you've been privileged to observe. Picture being there, in that location, breathing that air, feeling those inescapable sensations of wonder. And now consider this: Wherever we stand on the earth, however high we soar above it by plane or hot-air balloon or space station, we have to acknowledge that as glorious as this is, we have yet to see all Jesus can do!

Our appreciation of those breathtaking places leads to another thought: *Everything we've already seen pales in comparison to what is yet to come.* Jesus hasn't—and won't ever—exhaust His creativity, His imagination, His joy at delighting us. Envision Him watching tourists on the edge of the Grand Canyon enraptured by what they see and saying to Himself, *You think that's something? Just wait!*
—Cynthia Ruchti

Faith Step: *Revisit photos of your favorite vacation or getaway spot. Use those images as a praise prompt—a reason to celebrate what Jesus is planning for those who love Him. "No eye has seen, nor ear heard" (1 Corinthians 2:9, ESV).*

TUESDAY, JANUARY 24

I will remember the deeds of the Lord; yes, I will remember your miracles of long ago. . . . Your path led through the sea, your way through the mighty waters, though your footprints were not seen. Psalm 77:11, 19 (NIV)

WE HAD A FRESH SNOWFALL YESTERDAY. This morning the world is blanketed and still. A casual glance would reveal a frozen emptiness. Nothing stirs.

But as I study the snow, I notice evidence of a busy world. Tracks weave around the backyard. Squirrels, rabbits, deer, perhaps even a coyote. If I understood them, the marks would tell a story of fascinating nighttime wanderings and interactions.

At times my life feels like a barren snowscape. When my husband and I talk over our day, I sigh and tell him, "I didn't get much done." I'm tempted to doubt I've been of any use to Jesus. I'm also tempted to doubt that He is working out His purposes in my day-to-day life.

When you look at your current circumstances, do you feel frustrated by prayers that seem unanswered? Take heart! Jesus is always present and active in the lives of the believer. If you can't see His work at the moment, look further back as the Psalmist did and remember the many times He was at work in your life—even if you couldn't see it at the time. Those memories make it easier to stand in faith. Even when we can't see the proof today, behind the scenes Jesus is leading us, protecting us, and using our lives to share His love with others. One day we'll look back on today and see His grace-filled footprints all over our lives. —SHARON HINCK

FAITH STEP: *Pull out a diary or a photo album and remember the deeds of Jesus in your life in the past. Ask Him to give you faith to trust Him, even when you can't see His footprints today.*

WEDNESDAY, JANUARY 25

You are altogether beautiful, my darling; there is no flaw in you.
Song of Solomon 4:7 (NIV)

THE THOUGHT CAME TO ME this week as I was trying on dresses for my niece's wedding that I could sure do with some of the muscle tone I had almost twenty years ago when I got married. It came to me with some other thoughts like, *If I am holding in my stomach, why doesn't it look like I am holding in my stomach?* and *Why is the skin on the top of my knee trying to fold over on itself?*

I know beauty is fleeting. My knee skin seems to be confirming that. But the truth is we all want to feel beautiful. Here's the thing: regardless of age, thigh circumference, and nose size, beautiful is what we are. Whether we believe it or not. With our various ages, unique faces, and different shapes, we are beautiful. Truly. When we are brought low by the thickness of our ankles or our overly large ears, the deep truth that needs to wedge itself into our hearts is that the One who created us made us in His image, His glorious, unfathomable image. We need to let our feelings about ourselves reflect what He actually thinks of us.

Jesus took great delight in the details of shaping our high foreheads and sturdy legs and strong hands. He loves us. He considers us lovely. He loves us completely—wholly—with His entire being, no matter what. Jesus likes what He made; He likes whom He made: you. —SUSANNA FOTH AUGHTMON

FAITH STEP: *Look in the mirror and say, "Jesus loves me. I am made in His image. I am lovely. In Him, I am truly loved."*

THURSDAY, JANUARY 26

So letting your sinful nature control your mind leads to death. But letting the Spirit control your mind leads to life and peace. Romans 8:6 (NLT)

RECENTLY WE DISCOVERED that a very close friend had been living a secret life. He was caught in an act of sin and, once discovered, confessed to years of struggles and hiding. His deeds put him in jail, hurting his family and friends. The ripple continued, affecting his church and work environment too. Numerous people were hurt by this man's actions. Yet this path all started with one bad decision that he hid, and after that another, until he'd dug a pit of sin so deep he didn't know how to escape.

The truth is often hard to confess, but secret lies are used to build a stronghold of deception. Hearing stories like this reminds us to confess our small sins to Jesus and others before they build an impenetrable wall of shame around our hearts. Only truth, filling each part of us, will cause every brick of deceit to crumble.

If there is truth, Jesus is there. John 14:6 says, "Jesus told him, 'I am the way, the truth, and the life. No one can come to the Father except through me.'"

When we allow more of Jesus into our lives, we let truth in. When we hold on to lies, we are blocking out Jesus—and hurting ourselves and others. Confession is hard, but the result of not confessing is worse. And when we confess, we have accountability, which protects us even more. Admitting our secrets may be hard to face for a time, but it helps us walk closer to Jesus and brings truth into every part of our lives. —TRICIA GOYER

FAITH STEP: *Do you have any secret sins, big or small, that you need to confess? Confess to someone you trust who will help lead you to Jesus. Ask Jesus to fill you with truth.*

FRIDAY, JANUARY 27

And looking at them Jesus said to them, "With people this is impossible, but with God all things are possible." Matthew 19:26 (NAS)

FOR YEARS I'VE ENCOURAGED PEOPLE to focus on the *I wills* of Scripture. David, the Psalmist, offers countless, positive resolutions for the future: "I will give thanks to the Lord" (Psalm 7:17, NIV); "I will praise you, Lord" (Psalm 57:9, NIV); "I will put my trust in you" (Psalm 56:3, NAS); "I will tell of all your deeds" (Psalm 73:28, NIV).

But along the way it occurred to me that my encouragement to others should include more. Although the psalmist never intended those verses to become self-driven statements, I can do that easily if I leave out one component: Jesus. Without His help and power, all my intentions will fall short and I'll fail every time.

So I began researching the Bible for the *I wills* or *I ams* of Jesus: "I will give you rest" (Matthew 11:28, NIV); "I am with you always" (Matthew 28:20, NIV); "I will counsel you" (Psalm 32:8, NIV); "I am the resurrection and the life" (John 11:25, NIV).

Researching His names and character, I learned that with Jesus I can succeed. He not only has the answers, but He *is* the answer. He makes a way, but He's also the Way. In my weak attempts to love and to serve Him, He gives me both strength and motivation.

Living for Jesus requires more than positive affirmations and good intentions. Jesus puts the initial "want to" in my heart. Only when I rest in His power, His strength, and His character do I find the way to accomplish anything. With Him, all things really are possible.

—REBECCA BARLOW JORDAN

FAITH STEP: *Scan through a few chapters in the New Testament and make your own list of encouragements that Jesus offers. Then pass on that encouragement to someone else.*

SATURDAY, JANUARY 28

The minute I said, "I'm slipping, I'm falling," your love, God, took hold and held me fast. When I was upset and beside myself, you calmed me down and cheered me up.
Psalm 94:18–19 (MSG)

MY HUSBAND WAS DRIVING US to the airport amid heavy traffic. A car ahead of us slowed suddenly. I hissed in my breath and slammed my foot onto a nonexistent brake on the floor in front of me. My husband, an excellent driver who was completely alert to the traffic, sighed.

"Sorry." I forced my fingers to relax their grip on the armrest.

When I ride the shotgun seat in a car, I can be a bit annoying. Even though I don't need to make decisions to direct the car, my instincts won't turn off. If a car enters traffic from the side, I flinch. If I spot a pothole, my body tightens up. When a light ahead turns red, I've even been known to yell helpfully, "It's red!"

Like I said, I can be an irritating passenger.

So I've learned to close my eyes, stop my alert scanning, and remind myself I'm not in the driver's seat.

I want to let Jesus steer my life. Yet when possible threats arise, I often act in alarm. I tense. I flinch. I slam imaginary brakes. My reflexes demand that I take over the speed, direction, and movement of my life.

Instead, when life throws us a challenge, we can close our eyes, take a deep breath, and remember that we are not in the driver's seat. Jesus bought us. We are His. We can invite Him to direct our lives and ask for His help to relinquish our craving for control.
—SHARON HINCK

FAITH STEP: *Next time you're a passenger in a car, close your eyes and think about the gift of allowing Jesus to safely guide your life.*

SUNDAY, JANUARY 29

We also pray that you will be strengthened with all his glorious power so you will have all the endurance and patience you need. May you be filled with joy.
Colossians 1:11 (NLT)

MY FRIEND CINDY skis every single day. I do not.

When the snow comes, Cindy puts on her skis and glides into the forest. I join her once in a while. She's kind, waiting for me, huffing and puffing behind her. She probably goes back out after I leave to get a proper workout, but she still invites me. I want to improve, but I let other things keep me from getting out on my skis. I feel bad for slowing her down, but I haven't made the changes needed to build the endurance that comes easily to her.

But that's just it—Cindy's endurance developed not by wishing or hoping but by skiing. In one sense, it did come easily—a natural result of the activity. Her muscles and lung capacity changed from the exertion. Skiing daily made her strong in a way good intentions couldn't.

In the same way, Jesus calls me to follow Him. He expects daily action, saying, "Everyone who hears these words of mine and puts them into practice is like a wise man who built his house on the rock" (Matthew 7:24, NIV). He told stories about faithful servants who worked when no one was watching. He wants me not just to credit His teachings but to abide in them, saying, "If you stick with this, living out what I tell you, you are my disciples" (John 8:31, MSG).

I'm learning to stick with His teachings daily, making them a way of life. And I'm finding strength and endurance for the journey ahead. —SUZANNE DAVENPORT TIETJEN

FAITH STEP: *Are you in something for the long haul? A difficult job or marriage, caring for a loved one? Parenting? Pray, and then with Jesus's help, show up and show love. Today. Then again tomorrow.*

MONDAY, JANUARY 30

Cast all your anxiety on him because he cares for you.
1 Peter 5:7 (NIV)

MY MOTHER-IN-LAW, SANDY, is one of my favorite people. She loves our family wholly and completely. She is always stopping by with treats for the boys. She looks in on us regularly. Lately, she has been reminding us to check our blind spots when we drive. So we check our blind spots because we know that "check your blind spots" really means "I love you and I don't want anything bad to happen to you." She thinks of us constantly and prays for us. Whenever things get tough, I call her. "I am praying heavy," she says. We're thankful for the prayers because we know she's praying God's will for us. Sandy shows us in a million ways that she is thinking about us. Her presence brings me momentary peace.

Jesus also shows me in a million ways that He is thinking about me. He loves me wholly and completely. And He cares about every single thing that is going on in my life—my family, my work, my dreams, my problems, and all of my anxious thoughts. He cares about my body, mind, soul, and spirit. He knows that life can be too big and overwhelming for me and so He stands, arms wide open, and whispers, *Why don't you let Me hold on to all those cares, all that worry, all those fears? I would love to do that for you.*

It is a fantastic thing to throw off that heavy weight, cast my anxieties on Him, and know that the One Who loves me most of all has got it all under control. His presence brings me lasting peace.
—SUSANNA FOTH AUGHTMON

FAITH STEP: *Picture yourself throwing each of your worries, one by one, into the capable arms of Jesus. Leave them there and rest in the knowledge that He cares for you.*

TUESDAY, JANUARY 31

Then [the criminal] said, "Jesus, remember me when You come into Your kingdom!" And He said to him, "I assure you: Today you will be with Me in paradise." Luke 23:42–43 (HCS)

WHEN I THINK ABOUT FORGIVENESS, I tend to think big, like in the situation with the criminal on the cross. I think about people who have wronged me greatly and how hard it is to forgive—but how necessary for my own peace. Or I may think, cringingly, of things I've done to hurt people on a large scale and how I hope they've forgiven me. It seems like most sermons I hear about forgiveness are like this too. Aimed at helping listeners forgive the big things. But what about the little things?

Henri Nouwen writes that "forgiveness is the name of love practiced among people who love poorly. The hard truth is that all people love poorly. We need to forgive and be forgiven every day.... That is the great work of love among the fellowship of the weak that is the human family." Forgiveness is the great work of love every single day. So true, isn't it?

How many times per day am I called on to forgive little offenses? My son forgets to take out the trash, my daughter loses her phone. My husband doesn't call and comes home late. The cashier gets my order wrong. A student falls asleep during my carefully prepared lesson. These seem like big deals until I go over the list of my own little offenses. I forgot to get milk. Answered a text in the middle of dinner. Snapped at a colleague. Came unprepared to music practice.

The example of Jesus is forgiveness. All day, every day, offenses big or small, of ourselves and others. —GWEN FORD FAULKENBERRY

FAITH STEP: *Is there something big you need to forgive? Get it over with! Then go about practicing the great work of forgiveness with everyone you encounter today, including yourself.*

WEDNESDAY, FEBRUARY 1

I focus on this one thing: Forgetting the past and looking forward to what lies ahead. Philippians 3:13 (NLT)

IN *MY UTMOST FOR HIS HIGHEST*, his classic book of devotions, Oswald Chambers says, "Never let the sense of past failure defeat your next step." I encounter opportunities to make wise choices. But when I ignore these opportunities, I can't recapture those moments. All I can do is ask forgiveness and move forward. One of those opportunities occurred during the early years of my marriage. My husband and I must have "slept" through those years, ignoring the need—and the choice—to work on our relationship. The result was a painful communication breakdown that led to our having to do some major rebuilding later on. We couldn't recapture those lost years; we could only move forward (which, thankfully, we did).

When the disciples fell asleep on the night Jesus prayed before His arrest, Jesus woke them and warned them to stay alert. They not only fell asleep again but within hours they had all scattered, leaving Jesus alone to face His captors (Matthew 26). Yet what they did in the coming months after His Resurrection was what mattered.

I'm not sure I really want to know how much more I could have done for Jesus in the past—if only. That knowledge could be disheartening. I want to know what I can still do for Him. Because I think Jesus is more concerned with where I am now and where I'm headed with Him tomorrow than where I was yesterday. Jesus knows that I'll fail at times, just as His disciples did. But He gives me the motivation and the strength to press in to what's ahead.

—REBECCA BARLOW JORDAN

FAITH STEP: *Write down three positive things you'd like to focus on in the coming year that will help you move forward in your life, looking to Jesus to clear the way.*

Thursday, February 2

Therefore confess your sins to each other and pray for each other so that you may be healed. The prayer of a righteous person is powerful and effective. James 5:16 (NIV)

My husband and I pray for our kids. We make a practice of it in the car on the way to school and at bedtime. We hug them, hold them close, and speak peace and life over them. But the other morning, I needed some prayer myself. Scott was gone on a retreat, and I was in charge of getting us all up and out the door by 7:00 a.m. I was yelling like a drill sergeant: "Where are your lunches?" "Have you brushed your teeth?" "We are going to BE LATE!"

My twelve-year-old, Will, came and put a hand on my back. "Mom, can I pray for you?"

I blinked a couple of times. "Yes. Please."

He rested his hands on my shoulders and said, "Dear Jesus, please help my mom not to be cranky. Amen." He squeezed my shoulders and went into the kitchen.

And I...I just stood there. And felt the stress ease between my shoulder blades. And then echoed Will's prayer with another: "Yes. Please." I took a deep breath and let that prayer settle into my soul.

Sometimes life makes me cranky. I need Jesus's help to do a mighty work in the cranky places of my heart. And He uses the people who are close to me to give a shoulder squeeze and say, "Hey, can I pray for you? And maybe your crankiness?" The best thing is that Jesus always answers that prayer, pulling me close, reminding me of His peace and letting His love wash over me. I'm soaking it in.
—Susanna Foth Aughtmon

Faith Step: *Pray for each of your family members for Jesus's peace and love to flood their hearts and surround them today.*

FRIDAY, FEBRUARY 3

We must focus on Jesus, the source and goal of our faith. He saw the joy ahead of him, so he endured death on the cross and ignored the disgrace it brought him.... Hebrews 12:2 (GW)

I SMILED AND POLITELY DECLINED my doctor's offer of a prescription to calm me during an MRI. I've never liked drugs with a sedative effect, and besides, it seemed silly to need one just to slide through a big metal tube. The next week, I lay inside what felt like a tomb, silently screaming and wishing I could change my mind. The tube turned out to be much smaller than the pictures I'd seen. Plus, I learned that I would be inside for forty-five minutes as the machine took images of different areas of my spine.

The tube was clear but too close to my face. Just knowing that I couldn't stretch out my arms or raise myself up made me panic. I prayed and recited Bible verses, but twice the attendant had to pull me out in between sessions to sit up. The second time, she told me that the tube's opening was only inches from the top of my head. "If you roll your head backward, you'll be able to see that," she said.

Thankfully, her tip worked. I finished the last session with my head in an unnatural position, gazing at the open space beyond the narrow tube.

Being confined to a small space isn't the only thing that fills me with anxiety. Sometimes I get claustrophobic when circumstances beyond my control press in on me and no escape is in sight. During those times I need to focus on Jesus and draw from His power, wisdom, and peace. I need to remember that whether I'm stuck in a crisis, a bad relationship, or an MRI tube, He will see me through to the other side. —DIANNE NEAL MATTHEWS

FAITH STEP: *What is making you feel anxious and panicky right now? Imagine Jesus holding your hand and asking you to trust Him to guide you through it.*

SATURDAY, FEBRUARY 4

"Anyone who listens to my teaching and follows it is wise, like a person who builds a house on solid rock. . . . But anyone who hears my teaching and doesn't obey it is foolish, like a person who builds a house on sand."
Matthew 7:24, 26 (NLT)

ONE OF MY FAVORITE GETAWAYS is Yellow Point Lodge in British Columbia. The main building is an impressive multistory log structure. But the best part is it sits on a huge weathered rock that juts into a saltwater passage alongside Vancouver Island.

My husband and I used to spend our anniversary at Yellow Point. Because it's in February, we often witnessed winter storms. Talk about exciting! Wind and rain pounded the lodge, and whitecaps pummeled the rock beneath it. But the lodge stood firm because the property owner was a wise man and had built it upon an immovable stone base.

Jesus says that those who hear His words and apply them are wise, like the property owner who builds his house on solid rock. Temptation might hammer them, but they withstand the blows because they've built their lives on divine truth, which is an unshakable foundation.

Imagine Yellow Point Lodge's fate if its owner had constructed it on a sandy beach. The waves' ceaseless motion would have eroded the foundation until the building collapsed. "Foolish man," Jesus would have said. "You're just like the person who hears My teaching and walks away without putting it into practice. He's building his life on a foundation guaranteed to fail."

I know that I want to build wisely, like our friend did when he constructed the lodge on the rock—to last. —GRACE FOX

FAITH STEP: *Either collect a handful of little rocks or buy some decorative stones at a craft store. Put them in a clear vase, and use them as a visual reminder to put Jesus's teachings into practice.*

SUNDAY, FEBRUARY 5

They recognized that they had been with Jesus.
Acts 4:13 (ESV)

LATELY I'VE BEEN CHALLENGED BY the idea of abiding in Christ. It's an intriguing concept. Abiding implies constancy. It doesn't just show up for visits. It hangs around and studies. It pursues at the same time it rests.

How does abiding in Christ happen? By realizing first that I need Jesus as Savior. And then by realizing that it's through abiding in Him that He speaks to my spirit and shows me the answers I need.

When I acknowledge my need for Him, I move toward Him, I ask for His help, I give Him the worship due Him for His majesty and holiness, I thank Him for His grace and mercy, and I stay near Him to learn His ways and develop a character like His. I move toward Jesus, understanding all the time that He moves toward me first and more perfectly and faithfully.

When I'm truly abiding in Jesus, I'm soaking Him up, and then He overflows from me. As I take Him in, He pours Himself out. It's through this input and output of abiding in Jesus that people can recognize I've been with Him.

I want to be recognized as having been with Jesus, to have His spirit show in my countenance. There is no other relationship more important. When I abide in Him, my love for my husband is deeper and truer, my patience with my kids comes more readily, my sacrifices for others is more joyful.

When I abide in Christ, I am changed, molded into a person like Himself. And I am able to have an eternal impact on countless others.
—ERIN KEELEY MARSHALL

FAITH STEP: *Read and meditate on John 15:1—17.*

MONDAY, FEBRUARY 6

*That's why we can be so sure that every detail in our lives of love
for God is worked into something good.*
Romans 8:28 (MSG)

THE ABOVE SCRIPTURE may be the best loved—and most disliked—
verse in the Bible. Often offered as a pat answer, there it stands,
promising that God works everything together for good.

Sometimes that's hard to believe. When I was a young mom with
three preschoolers, I fell in love with Jesus and wanted to please
Him. I'd finish my prayers by listening, and at times in the silence
I'd think of something I should do.

Once I was moved to write an encouraging letter to a friend, so I
did. I stamped it and set it by the door. The next morning I tucked
the letter safely in the car's glove box…where it stayed, forgotten for
weeks until I opened the box again. I cried when I saw the letter. I'd
been so sure I needed to write to my friend.

I did my best and failed. I came close to throwing the letter out,
but I mailed it anyway. We don't always know the ends of our stories, but this time I heard back from my friend within two weeks.
She'd hit a rough patch in her life a day or two before receiving it.
She had prayed, "Lord, I need to know You care," on her way to
the mailbox, where she found the letter from me, delayed just long
enough to have arrived at the perfect time.

Romans 8:31–32 explains that God knew us in advance, and He
wants to make us like Jesus. He's doing it too, making even our fail-
ings part of the story. —SUZANNE DAVENPORT TIETJEN

FAITH STEP: *Today when you pray, take time to listen. You don't need to hear
an audible voice. Does anyone come to mind? Any loving action? If so, consider
doing it, in Jesus's name.*

TUESDAY, FEBRUARY 7

"For in him we live and move and have our being." Acts 17:28 *(NIV)*

WE MOVED FIVE TIMES in the first five years we were married. That was a long time ago. Someday we may have to move out of our current home that is, surprisingly, aging faster than we are. (It had a head start.) I'm not sentimental about the idea because I love to move. That's right. I love fresh starts and purging, reorganizing and redecorating.

No matter how smooth the process is, questions are inescapable. "Is this even ours?" "Didn't this table have legs in the old house?" And the king of all questions—"Hey, lady, where do you want this?"

Whether moving from home to dorm, apartment to house, or condo to retirement community, most of us intend to move only the items we want in our new place. If there's time, we hold a rummage sale before packing. We make multiple trips to Goodwill before loading boxes. An efficient move hinges on careful planning, careful organizing, and not moving things destined for the trash.

Can you picture the moving man asking, "Hey, lady. Where do you want this box of uncertainty?" "Where do you want this storage bin of bad habits?"

Hard to imagine? We move through life hauling baggage. We drag them with us or balance them on our shoulders when we should leave them behind before we take another step of our journey. It's in Jesus that we live and move and have our being. When He asks where we intend to put regrets and uncertainty, let's point to the trash can. He's standing beside it with the lid in His hands. —CYNTHIA RUCHTI

FAITH STEP: *Consider adding this to today's prayers: Jesus, help me move through my day free of regrets, hurts, disappointments, grudges. I want to move freely.*

WEDNESDAY, FEBRUARY 8

"I am the true vine, and my Father is the gardener. He cuts off every branch in me that bears no fruit, while every branch that does bear fruit he prunes so that it will be even more fruitful."
John 15:1–2 (NIV)

PRUNING THE ROSES in my backyard is one of my least favorite things to do. The rose bush that leans up against our gardening shed is about seven years old. Some of the stalks are as thick as tree branches. I almost always prick my fingers on a few of the thorns when I'm trimming the bushes. Even with gloves on. And then when I go to prune the climbing rose that is against the fence, I tend to lop off the uppermost branches awkwardly and they fall on my head. So I usually end up with a few scratches on my forehead.

But every year, I put on my thick gloves and go after it. Because I love how the climbing rose blooms and cascades across the back fence. And I love how my rose bush begins to fill out with huge, old-fashioned, yellow roses at the first hint of spring warmth. I know that if I don't trim them back when it gets cold, they won't grow to their full potential when it gets warm.

That is what Jesus does when He disciplines us. He is trimming off all of the deadweight. He wants us to flourish in every area of our life. The process of pruning is painful. We don't like it when Jesus begins to trim and prune and shape our lives using trials and daily circumstances. But we do want to become all that Jesus created us to be. So let's let Jesus do His best work in us so that we can do ours for Him. —SUSANNA FOTH AUGHTMON

FAITH STEP: *Place a flower in the center of your table. Let it remind you that Jesus is shaping you into who He wants you to become.*

THURSDAY, FEBRUARY 9

The high priests, conspiring with the Jewish Council, tried to cook up charges against Jesus in order to sentence him to death. But even though many stepped up, making up one false accusation after another, nothing was believable. Matthew 26:59–60 (MSG)

SOON AFTER JESUS BEGAN His public ministry, His reputation spread (Luke 4:37). Miracles of healing, casting out demons, and befriending society's outcasts all captured people's attention for miles. Why? No one had ever done what Jesus did. He was different: gentle and doing good wherever He went, yet confident and loving.

But not everyone agreed with Jesus. As His good reputation spread, so did false reports, personal attacks, and ultimately threats on His life. But His defense was speaking the truth, giving glory to God, and continuing on the obedient path His heavenly Father assigned Him, like the time He healed a man on the Sabbath (John 5:17). "Faithful" characterized Jesus, even to His death.

We, too, earn our own reputations. Through our lives, people often tag us for our actions and character. How do we respond when someone criticizes us? I can remember so many times when I've fallen into the trap of defending myself.

Criticism isn't easy to take. But seeing how Jesus responded to His critics has made me more sensitive to my own responses. Do I really need to defend myself? Or do I simply speak the truth and give it to Jesus? If the assessment is true, I will ask Jesus and others for forgiveness. But if not, I can state the truth and choose faithfulness instead of rebuttal.

More and more, I'm striving to mirror Jesus's response—and His good character. —REBECCA BARLOW JORDAN

FAITH STEP: *Think about how you've responded to criticism in the past. Ask Jesus today to help you respond with truth and love the next time that happens.*

FRIDAY, FEBRUARY 10

I may know Him and the power of His resurrection and the fellowship of His sufferings, being conformed to His death.
Philippians 3:10 (NAS)

THIS WEEK I WAS GRAPPLING with discouragement. Ongoing setbacks in health and work were beating me down. Even so, I had work to do. A friend had asked me to write a guest blog about it for her site. After I submitted the article, we exchanged a few more e-mails and gradually discovered we both were battling the same chronic illness.

Through e-mails and then a phone conversation, we rejoiced in the precious gift of someone who could understand so many details of the struggle. We had a thousand shared experiences. And we marveled at the way Jesus had connected us during the particular week that we both needed the "fellowship in suffering" so deeply.

We all have times when we feel alone on a painful path. Illness, death of a loved one, job loss, a move to a new city, parenting challenges, or a fractured relationship can send us reeling. It can be a tremendous comfort to find someone who can relate and who is walking a similar road. It's a different level of encouragement from that of friends who have never experienced our specific struggle.

Jesus often sends us the gift of those sorts of connections. He also offers another source of fellowship—Himself. He has experienced every human struggle and knows us inside and out. He invites us to unite with Him both in our moments of suffering and in the resurrection power that He provides. That is the most blessed connection of all. —SHARON HINCK

FAITH STEP: *Think of a specific struggle in your life. Reach out to someone else in a similar battle and offer the gift of empathy.*

SATURDAY, FEBRUARY 11

One day soon afterward Jesus went up on a mountain to pray, and he prayed to God all night. At daybreak he called together all of his disciples and chose twelve of them to be apostles.... Luke 6:12–13 (NLT)

I CONFESS I'VE MADE a few impulsive decisions in my life. I once brought home a free puppy without stopping to consider whether owning an energetic, untrained dog was doable while parenting three preschoolers and operating a daycare in my home. Bad, sad choice. We had to give Blackie away only three weeks later.

On several occasions I've experienced unnecessary stress, all because I said yes in haste. Teach a Bible study? Sure. Host an annual Sunday school party for two dozen people? Of course. Deliver meals to a shut-in? You bet! Never mind that I had four deadlines fast approaching and would be leading a three-week missions trip to Nepal the next month. Never mind that I hadn't asked God whether or not He wanted me to invest my time and energy in those opportunities, as legitimate as they were.

Age and experience are good teachers, and I finally understand a very important lesson—it pays to pray before making decisions. Even Jesus—the all-wise, all-knowing Son of God—did so. What does that say about *my* need to seek divine guidance before plunging ahead with my plans or best intentions?

Thanks to Jesus's example, I understand that I can make decisions with confidence after praying for direction. Jesus sought the heavenly Father's guidance, trusted Him to answer His prayers, and then He acted accordingly. He never wrestled with indecision or fear. He never second-guessed Himself. Neither will I if I follow His example. —GRACE FOX

FAITH STEP: *When people ask you to do various tasks, say, "I'll pray about it for a few days before giving my answer."*

SUNDAY, FEBRUARY 12

"I tell you," he replied, "if they keep quiet, the stones will cry out." Luke 19:40 (NIV)

RECENTLY, I DECIDED TO LOOK for a new church home. My daughter and I were both in need of spiritual refreshment. So we visited a nearby Baptist church that looked good online.

They started the service with the greeting of "Namaste" and invited those who had congregated to do deep-breathing exercises to get rid of any anxiety that might have followed us into the pew. *Great!* I thought, believing I might have found a new home.

I listened as the choir began to sing in perfect harmony, a distinct difference from my old church. I was sold.

Then it happened.

The deacon announced that they would be taking up the offering, and someone blew a whistle, a loud whistle like the kind used to referee a game. It was startling. I assumed they really wanted that money!

But when the sermon started, the whistling continued. Every time the pastor said something that the woman with the whistle liked, she blew. And she *really* liked his sermon.

I left with a headache and fond memories of *Namaste*.

Curious, I contacted the church the next day to ask about the "whistle-blower" and if that was normal. They responded by saying the whistle-blowing was the way she worshipped. They quoted Jesus in Luke 19:40: "I tell you," he replied, "if they keep quiet, the stones will cry out."

They'd accepted her form of praise, and if I returned I should keep an open mind. It was a less than subtle reminder that God appreciates and desires our praise. And even ringing in our ears can be music to His.
—TARICE L. S. GRAY

FAITH STEP: *Find a new and unique way today to praise God during your alone time together.*

MONDAY, FEBRUARY 13

"It is finished," and he bowed his head and gave up his spirit.
John 19:30 (ESV)

BESIDES *I LOVE YOU*, are there any three words more awesome than the final three Jesus spoke on the Cross? "It is finished" marked the shift creation had been waiting for since that awful day in the Garden of Eden when our sin broke our connection with the Lord. Three small words held the weight of salvation, the turning point from death to life.

But I've been thinking about how those words may have sounded to Jesus's enemies watching that day. They thought that by killing Him, His influence would be finished, so it may have seemed logical for them to assume He was accepting His loss.

Others might have been curious about what He meant. What was finished? If anyone had been on the fence about whether to follow Him or not, those cryptic words might have been the catalyst to help understand He was who He claimed to be.

And then to His followers, family, and friends, "It is finished" held intense grief because Jesus had died. The words also likely gave some relief that the brutal dying hours were over. But His words also might have signaled hope as they considered all He had told them would happen and why He came to die. Some might have believed those three words meant exactly what He intended them to mean: "Sin is conquered. The age of separation from God is over for all who believe that Jesus finished it."

He did it. And we get all the benefits. In Him, our death is finished. In Him, our hopelessness has ended. In Him, we have all the spiritual blessings. Because He finished it, we are not finished. —ERIN KEELEY MARSHALL

FAITH STEP: *Simply be still sometime today, even if only for five minutes, to dwell on the enormity of how we benefit because Jesus finished what He came to do.*

TUESDAY, FEBRUARY 14

Watch what God does, and then you do it, like children who learn proper behavior from their parents. Mostly what God does is love you. Keep company with him and learn a life of love. Observe how Christ loved us. His love was not cautious but extravagant. He didn't love in order to get something from us but to give everything of himself to us. Love like that. Ephesians 5:1–2 (MSG)

I LOVE THIS PARAPHRASE OF EPHESIANS. The idea that we watch what God does and then do it. That's our assignment. And when we watch, we find that mostly what God does is love us. Through Jesus, we see His extravagant love giving us everything of Himself, all of the time. Our job is to *love like that*. How different would my life be if I made loving my job? And yet that's what the Bible tells us to do.

Mother Teresa said, "Many people mistake our work for our vocation. Our vocation is the love of Jesus." That's interesting to me, coming from someone who spent her life serving the poorest of the poor. But what she's saying is that the work, no matter what it is, is secondary. Our vocation—what we do—our fundamental focus and calling—is the love of Jesus.

This applies to me as I teach at the university. My work may be reading and writing. But my vocation is love. My doctor friend cares for the sick; my cosmetologist friend styles hair. My auto-tech friend changes oil and tires, and my brother administrates the school. But our vocations are all the same: love. Jesus's love informs whatever daily tasks there are to perform and infuses them with purpose and meaning. —GWEN FORD FAULKENBERRY

FAITH STEP: *What is your work? And how does it serve the purpose of your vocation, which is the love of Jesus? Evaluate your daily tasks in light of your true vocation, looking for ways to share the love of Jesus through the work He has given you to do.*

WEDNESDAY, FEBRUARY 15

"If you love me, keep my commands." John 14:15 *(NIV)*

MY BOYS HAVE A HARD TIME listening to me. Especially when it comes to doing things they don't like to do. When I say things like, "Please go clean your room" or "Come set the table" or "Pick up your towel off of the bathroom floor," I am often met with blank stares, as if the children don't speak English. And I know they do since both their father and I have taught them English.

When I ask them, "Did you hear what I asked you to do?" they will often substitute another command that I have given them as their response. Just last night I told Will, "Please clear your plate from the table." He came into the kitchen with a confused look on his face. "Mom, I know you asked me to do something, but I can't remember what you said...did you ask me to make my lunch for school tomorrow?" It is amazing that we get anything accomplished around here.

I bet Jesus feels the same way. He gives us clear commands like "Love the Lord your God with all your heart, soul, mind, and strength" and "Love your neighbor as yourself" and "Forgive those who trespass against you." We give Him blank stares and say, "What did you say again? About loving and forgiving? That can't be right. I think what You wanted to say was take care of myself. Is that what You wanted to say?"

The best way I can love Jesus is to obey Him. Plain and simple. The bonus is that the more I obey Him and follow His commands, the more my heart begins to look like His.
—SUSANNA FOTH AUGHTMON

FAITH STEP: *What is a command of Jesus's that He has put on your heart to do? Find a way to obey that command and love Him today.*

THURSDAY, FEBRUARY 16

*My brothers and sisters, when you have many kinds of troubles, you should
be full of joy, because you know that these troubles test your faith, and this
will give you patience. Let your patience show itself perfectly in what you do.
Then you will be perfect and complete and will have everything you need.*
James 1:2–4 (NCV)

I LOVE STUDYING THE BIBLE, but I have to admit that there are a few
passages I don't always enjoy reading, like the verses about the necessity of trials and troubles. I used to tell people I believed I could grow
more Christlike if I didn't have any trials, if everything in life went
smoothly and I never had to suffer. I said this half-jokingly, but deep
down I knew that a trouble-free life is not only impossible, it would
probably make me shallow rather than spiritually mature. I might
enjoy myself, but I would not be growing in godliness day by day.

As I study Jesus's life, He is gradually adjusting my attitude toward
suffering and trials. Insults, false accusations, persecution, physical
assault—Jesus faced them with a quiet strength, trusting that each one
had a higher purpose behind it. The night before His Crucifixion, He
prayed, "Father, if you are willing, please take this cup of suffering away
from me. Yet I want your will to be done, not mine" (Luke 22:42, NLT).

Christ's example encourages me to learn to embrace trials as part
of my growing process so that His purposes can be worked out in
my life. Part of that plan is for me to become mature and complete,
lacking nothing. For that to happen, I must develop perseverance,
which requires trials. So I'm trying to change my goal from avoid-
ing suffering to accepting whatever trials Jesus deems necessary and
then trusting Him to see me through. —DIANNE NEAL MATTHEWS

FAITH STEP: *Anytime you think about a trial you are facing in your life, ask
Jesus to use it to help you develop patience.*

FRIDAY, FEBRUARY 17

The servants and the guards had made a fire because it was cold.
They were standing around it, warming themselves. Peter joined them there,
standing by the fire and warming himself. John 18:18 (CEB)

THE BIBLE TELLS US THAT Peter warmed himself by a fire the night he denied knowing Jesus. Don't pass over that detail too quickly or you'll miss the layers of meaning. It wasn't just any fire. It was started by servants and guards. He didn't try to blend in with the crowd. He joined the enemy camp.

Peter was getting warm while Jesus was being stripped, flogged, beaten, humiliated, and falsely accused. It was cold. All the more so for Jesus. But Peter stayed warm.

His words—"I don't know the man"—formed only part of Peter's betrayal. He stood by, watching and denying any affiliation with Jesus, and warming himself at the fire.

We know Peter was forgiven because Jesus is faithful, even when we are not. But I can't imagine Peter ever looked at fire in the same way again.

Some families celebrate an annual tradition of a regret bonfire. This event marks a time for reflecting on and setting ablaze the past year's regrets. Each stick thrown into the fire represents their "Peter moments"—decisions they wish they could reverse, words they wish they could retract. Gone. Burned to ashes.

Can you see Peter sitting before a similar fire? "Jesus, forgive me for not speaking up for You when I should have said, 'Know Him? I love Him. He's the Messiah!' Forgive me, Jesus, for betraying You. For noticing… I…was…cold." —CYNTHIA RUCHTI

FAITH STEP: *What regrets do you harbor that need to be burned in a real or virtual bonfire so you can move forward unhindered? Peter not only found forgiveness but also became a world-changer. It's time to make a pile of regret ashes.*

SATURDAY, FEBRUARY 18

Create in me a new, clean heart, O God, filled with clean thoughts and right desires. Psalm 51:10 (TLB)

MY DAUGHTER RECENTLY GOT INSPIRED by the "40 Bags in 40 Days Decluttering Challenge," which encourages people to inspect one area of their home at a time, removing at least one bag of unnecessary stuff from each space. One blogger has completed the challenge annually since 2011 and claims that it has "changed my life forever," as well as the lives of thousands of other people.

I've only seen the TV show *Hoarders* twice because I find it hard to watch. In both episodes, forty bags would have barely made a dent. It's hard to understand how anyone can let his or her home get so crammed with junk that it's difficult to even walk through a room. But once these people get help clearing out their houses, their demeanor and attitude toward life seem transformed.

Clutter can be a problem in an emotional and spiritual sense too. I may allow my life to be filled with harmful habits or destructive relationships. My heart and mind can get crammed with worries, doubts, fear, or immoral thoughts and desires.

Wouldn't it be great if we could lug bags of jealousy, greed, anger, and the like to the curb to be picked up? Obviously it's not that simple, but Jesus wants to help us clear the undesirables out of our hearts and minds. We just need to invite Him to show us what has to go and then depend on His power day by day to keep from allowing it back in. Jesus challenges us to a decluttering that is truly life-changing. —DIANNE NEAL MATTHEWS

FAITH STEP: *This week make decluttering a part of your daily prayer time. Ask Jesus to show you what "junk" needs to be removed from your heart, mind, and day-to-day living. Visualize Him helping you drag those discarded emotions and habits to a Dumpster.*

SUNDAY, FEBRUARY 19

"Give us this day our daily bread." Matthew 6:11 (AMP)

TODAY'S VERSE, from the Amplified Version, is remarkably unamplified. Without subtle shades of meaning in parentheses or brackets, it stands in its simplicity. This is how Jesus taught us to pray. It looks simple, but it's not easy.

God made us to eat daily. We can't consume a month's food at one sitting and then live that month on the strength of it. When Moses said to gather enough manna for one day, some smart aleck had to try taking twice as much to save having to work the next morning. He got maggots for his trouble. I might have done the same.

C. S. Lewis said, "Relying on God has to begin all over again every day as if nothing had yet been done." That doesn't make sense to me. It's hard to admit my neediness. I want to be strong on my own. I don't realize how much I need His strength, but God wants me to acknowledge my dependence on Him. Daily.

You know the gift-shopping quandary: "What do you give someone who has everything?" We really do have a Father who has everything. He doesn't need whatever puny "strength" we can muster up. All we can offer Him that He doesn't already have is our weakness. Oddly enough, our weakness is the medium He uses to accomplish His will.

When I've prayed about a need and God meets it, sadly I find that, along with no longer praying for that need, I often end up not praying very much at all. Jesus knew what we are like, so when the disciples asked, He told them to pray for their *daily* bread.

We need dailiness. It keeps us coming back.

—SUZANNE DAVENPORT TIETJEN

FAITH STEP: *When Jesus asked His Father for enough bread to feed thousands, He was sure of God's provision. What do you need today? Have you asked for it? Ask Jesus to help you believe.*

MONDAY, FEBRUARY 20

*As he walked along, he saw Levi son of Alphaeus sitting at
the tax collector's booth. "Follow me," Jesus told him, and
Levi got up and followed him. Mark 2:14 (NIV)*

I HAVE FIVE DIFFERENT PROJECTS I'm working on due in the next six months. And the craziest part is that three of these projects are writing devotions: short essays, prayers, and Scriptures that point the reader Christ-ward. I told my husband the other day, "I may be slow on the uptake...but I think Jesus thinks I need to do my devotions."

"I think you're right," Scott said. He knows. Personal devotions have never been my strong suit.

But I want in on knowing Jesus. This morning I was reading in Matthew when Jesus calls the disciples. Jesus went out of His way to find each of these men. Then He said, essentially, "Come on! Let's go! And I am going to amaze you with all we are going to do together."

Jesus couldn't change the disciples until they chose Him. He couldn't do a thing until they decided to chase after Him. Jesus loved them. He knew them. He called them. But the amazing, mind-blowing shift in their lives would come only if they took that first step toward Him.

Jesus comes to me...and then I get to go to Him. Jesus is inviting me to hang out with Him. What He makes of my life comes only after I let go of my fear and follow Him. He is saying, "Let's go! I can do more than you could ever hope or imagine, if you chase after Me." He is three steps ahead of me, looking over His shoulder, with laughter in His voice, saying, "Are you ready for this? It's about to get good! Come on!"

I definitely want to follow Him. —SUSANNA FOTH AUGHTMON

FAITH STEP: *Go on a prayer walk, and with every step, tell Jesus, "I am following You!"*

TUESDAY, FEBRUARY 21

"Come, follow me," Jesus said, "and I will send you out to fish for people."
At once they left their nets and followed him.
Matthew 4:19–20 (NIV)

THERE ARE TIMES WHEN following Jesus is inconvenient, especially for those around me. It was inconvenient when Jesus called me to help start a crisis pregnancy center. It was inconvenient to homeschool my children. It was inconvenient to adopt more. In each of these cases, following Jesus meant that someone close to me "suffered." I had less time for my children because I was serving women in crisis. I had less time for my husband because I was creating lesson plans. And, after we adopted more children, I had less time for everyone!

Oswald Chambers said, "When we think seriously about what it will cost others if we obey the call of Jesus, we tell God He doesn't know what our obedience will mean. Keep to the point—He does know. Shut out every other thought and keep yourself before God in this one thing only—my utmost for His highest."

Jesus knows what His call requires. Yet He also knows that when we follow His directives, we will receive blessings we never imagined. One of the young women I mentored is now one of my best friends. Through homeschooling, my children are building a strong foundation of faith. And even though it's been hard, my biological children have solid relationships with my adopted children.

The truth is that what is inconvenient now will often turn out to be a huge blessing in the long run. We simply have to be willing to follow Jesus, even when it seems easier not to. —TRICIA GOYER

FAITH STEP: *What is one thing you feel that Jesus is asking you to do that is inconvenient? Make a list of reasons why it's easier to not follow Jesus. Then cross out each one of those reasons and write, "Still, Lord, I will follow."*

WEDNESDAY, FEBRUARY 22

The men of Israel looked them over and accepted the evidence.
But they didn't ask God about it. Joshua 9:14 (MSG)

JOSHUA IS ONE OF MY FAVORITE Old Testament biblical characters. He was obedient, almost to a fault. But one day as a leader, he made a costly mistake. Following their victory at Jericho, the Israelites learned that the disobedience of one man, Achan, greedy for gain, had lost them a battle. They dealt with it, and once again God granted victory. A huge altar signified the entire group's obedience to a holy God.

Soon after that, travelers visited Joshua's camp. Dressed in tattered clothes, carrying moldy bread, mended wineskins, and patched sacks on their donkeys, they claimed they'd traveled from a far-off country, when in reality they lived next door in Gibeon. They feared the God of the Israelites and wanted the Israelites to make a covenant with them. Believing the evidence, the men of Israel agreed.

But one of God's conditions for His people was to drive out the enemies from the land He had given them. How could Joshua and his men have made such a huge mistake? The same way all of us do: they failed to ask for divine guidance.

We, too, don't always learn our lessons well. Any temptation can sneak up on us, dressed in different clothes, slyly tempting us. It may sound right and good, but in our haste, if we forget to ask for Jesus's advice, the result can be disastrous. The bad news is that, like the Israelites, we may have to live with the consequences of our hasty decisions.

But the good news is that Jesus promises to forgive and restore (1 John 1:9). And His covenant with us can never be broken.
—REBECCA BARLOW JORDAN

FAITH STEP: *Thank Jesus for His forgiveness and restoration. Ask Him daily for wisdom to make the right decisions in every area of your life.*

THURSDAY, FEBRUARY 23

Enter his gates with thanksgiving; go into his courts with praise.
Give thanks to him and praise his name. Psalm 100:4 (NLT)

MY CHILDREN WERE OF elementary-school age when I began praying weekly with several other moms. We interceded for our kids' behavioral issues, academic struggles, and friendship problems. How easy it would have been to spend our entire hour only on requests! But we chose a different path.

Rather than immediately launching into requests, we dedicated the first few minutes to praising the Lord. We applied Psalm 100:4—we entered His presence with thanksgiving for the answers He'd already given and with praise for Who He is.

When the disciples asked Jesus to teach them to pray, He instructed them to begin with praise. "Pray like this: Our Father in heaven, may your name be kept holy. May your Kingdom come soon. May your will be done on earth, as it is in heaven." Then He moved into requests beginning with "Give us today the food we need and forgive us our sins" (Matthew 6:9–12, NLT).

Why did Jesus use this prayer model? Because it focuses our minds on Almighty God rather than on our individual concerns. Our circumstances seem less intimidating when we see them through God's power and presence. As we remember to whom we pray, we find courage to pray for and expect big things.

If Jesus began His prayers with praise to His Father, then I ought to do the same. It's not a magic formula to get the answers I want. Instead, it focuses my thoughts in precisely the right place. —GRACE FOX

FAITH STEP: *Focusing on praise rather than requests is more difficult than it sounds. Try it. Set a timer for two minutes and refrain from telling Jesus your needs. Spend those minutes only in thanksgiving and praise.*

FRIDAY, FEBRUARY 24

*Now, like infants at the breast, drink deep of God's pure kindness.
Then you'll grow up mature and whole in God. 1 Peter 2:3 (MSG)*

THE LAST TIME I hugged my son, Zachary, I was amazed by what a big man he'd become. "How'd you get so big?" I asked.

He answered, "I just kept eating, Mom."

That he did. As a newborn, he was hungry every two or three hours. His weight was off the charts at his well-baby checkups. The doctor asked what I'd been feeding him and looked doubtful when I said he was exclusively nursing. The doctor laughed and said he guessed he couldn't cut his calories then. And Zachary kept growing.

The apostle Peter may have seen some babies like my son because he used the image of an eagerly nursing baby to illustrate what's required to grow in Christ. We, like hungry babies, should "(thirst for, earnestly desire) the pure (unadulterated) spiritual milk, that by it you may be nurtured *and* grow unto [completed] salvation" (1 Peter 2:2, AMP).

In my twenties, I asked God to help me love Him more. He did—I fell in love with Jesus. I felt as if I were seeing Him for the first time. Jesus said, "Blessed are those who hunger and thirst for righteousness, for they shall be satisfied" (Matthew 5:6, NAS). I couldn't get enough of the Bible. I was drawn to read and study God's Word, losing all track of time. Like a baby, I didn't analyze this desire; I simply pursued it.

The hunger and thirst haven't faded. And although there are no scales or measurements, like at Zachary's well-baby checks, I'm still growing as the Word works in me. —SUZANNE DAVENPORT TIETJEN

FAITH STEP: *Do you sometimes feel like you're going through the motions in your faith walk? Ask Jesus to help you love Him more. See what happens.*

SATURDAY, FEBRUARY 25

"Repent and be baptized, every one of you,
in the name of Jesus Christ for the forgiveness of your sins.
And you will receive the gift of the Holy Spirit."
Acts 2:38 (NIV)

A WHILE BACK MY SISTER AND I were talking about some uncertainties in our lives that impacted our families. Our confusion was broad-reaching, involving job insecurities, decisions for our kids, and wondering how best to hang on to Jesus as our source of peace.

I heard myself ask, "When you hear the name *Jesus*, don't you feel like taking a deep breath of comfort?"

She agreed.

On any given day, I could name a circumstance or three that doesn't feel comforting. Even if my circumstances are fairly steady, just watching the news about what other people are dealing with can trigger anxiety and fear that similar suffering could happen to me. I may look for comfort in other places: time on the couch with a good book, hot tea, a big piece of lasagna, a warm bath, a day at the beach, a heart-to-heart talk with a good friend. *Yes, please, all of them, now,* I think.

But Jesus is the truest comfort. I have His spirit within me, the Holy Spirit, who is called Comforter (John 14:26). His comfort is like no other, just as His peace is not of this world (John 14:27). And the above verse sums up why His very name is a comfort to those who believe in Him. Jesus's comfort can go deeper than any possible trouble on earth. It cannot be replicated by anything the world might offer because there is only one name that saves (Acts 4:12), the name of Jesus, now and forever. Jesus's name is living and active; it seals with an eternal comfort those who are His. —ERIN KEELEY MARSHALL

FAITH STEP: *Look up the references in today's reading, and pick one to memorize.*

SUNDAY, FEBRUARY 26

He chose David, his servant, handpicked him from his work in the sheep pens. One day he was caring for the ewes and their lambs, the next day God had him shepherding Jacob, his people Israel, his prize possession. His good heart made him a good shepherd; he guided the people wisely and well. Psalm 78:70–72 (MSG)

I SEARCHED "LEADERSHIP EDUCATION" and found millions of resources, but shepherding was absent. Apparently, shepherding may have been part of leadership education in biblical times. Shepherding was often delegated to the youngest child, who had to lead the sheep to food and water, name and count them, separate them, find them when they strayed, help them with difficult deliveries, and protect them from predators. Much is said about servant leadership. Shepherding is living it out.

Moses had been schooled in all of the best Egyptian wisdom, but then while trying to help a kinsman, he killed a man and fled for his life. He spent the next forty years in the desert, keeping sheep. He learned leadership, selflessness, and patience as a result. He was a different man when God called him, "more humble than anyone else on the face of the earth" (Numbers 12:3, NIV). Now he was someone God could use.

Abel, Abraham, Isaac, Jacob, Rachel, Amos, and David were all shepherds. David's experience as a child shepherd even equipped him to lead the nation of Israel for forty years.

But there is one Shepherd greater than all of these: Jesus, the Good Shepherd, Who laid down His life for His sheep (John 10:11). He leads us still today. —SUZANNE DAVENPORT TIETJEN

FAITH STEP: *If you've never been a shepherd, maybe you've mothered a newborn. Do you remember any time that required extreme selflessness? Were you willing to serve? How did it change you? Thank Jesus that He leads you selflessly today.*

MONDAY, FEBRUARY 27

And the life that I now live in my body, I live by faith, indeed,
by the faithfulness of God's Son, who loved me and gave himself for me.
Galatians 2:20 (CEB)

SOMETIMES THE RESEARCH I conduct for writing projects takes me into new worlds—like the realm of deep brain trauma and terms like *perpetual vegetative state* versus *permanent vegetative state*.

My empathy for patients and families who know details of those conditions grew as I studied what they meant, what the illness looked like, the challenges for medical teams and family members. Love in spite of the lack of response from the one loved.

I watched videos documenting daily life for family members of those who couldn't move, communicate, or even breathe on their own. Brief movements sent hope soaring. Was it a sign that their loved one was emerging from the comatose state?

Hope sank when it was obvious that the movement was an involuntary spasm. "It looks like life, but it's only activity," a nurse would explain.

What happens to the heart of Jesus when our flailing reveals itself to be mere activity? When we read our Bibles solely to mark off another day of devotion on our calendars or say the wrong words while stifling the right words?

Looks like life, on the surface. But it's mere activity, as heartbreaking for the One hovering over us, longing to see us come alive in Him, as it is for a family waiting for a sign.

Jesus loves, despite a lack of response sometimes from the ones He loves. Is that who you want to be—an unresponsive follower, twitching with activity but no real life? —CYNTHIA RUCHTI

FAITH STEP: *Observe your activities over the next twenty-four hours. Are they pure-hearted signs of the life of Christ within you? If so, then press on!*

TUESDAY, FEBRUARY 28

*"You will not have to fight this battle. Take up your positions; stand firm and
see the deliverance the Lord will give you, Judah and Jerusalem.
Do not be afraid; do not be discouraged. Go out to face them tomorrow,
and the Lord will be with you." 2 Chronicles 20:17 (NIV)*

WHEN I WAS A DANCER, I studied many ways for stretching and
strengthening muscles. One effective technique looked easy but constantly challenged me. A long, sustained hold with gentle tension on
the muscle can do a great job of increasing flexibility over time. The
problem was that it felt so static. Energetic movement, huffing and
puffing—that all felt useful. Holding still was maddening.

I wonder if King Jehoshaphat had that same problem. A vast army
of Moabites and Ammonites was on its way to attack. People gathered at the temple from all over Judah, while he wisely turned to God.
In his prayer he said, "For we have no power to face this vast army
that is attacking us. We do not know what to do, but our eyes are on
you" (2 Chronicles 20:12). The next day, the king discovered God
had caused the enemy armies to attack and destroy each other.

There are times when Jesus calls on us to bravely fight a battle—to
speak up for someone treated unjustly, to intervene when a family member is self-destructing, to actively engage in a new ministry. But at other
times, He calls on us to stand firm, to wait, and to give Him room to
work. I wish it was easier to discern in every circumstance whether to
wait or to act. I tend to launch into battles I wouldn't need to face if I'd
first pray like King Jehoshaphat: "Lord, what do you want me to do?
Move forward? Stand still? My eyes are on You." —SHARON HINCK

FAITH STEP: *Next time you feel the adrenaline rush and heightened emotions
of impending battle, take a deep breath and ask Jesus whether this is a time He's
calling you to stand and watch Him work.*

ASH WEDNESDAY, MARCH 1

"You are dust, and to dust you shall return." Genesis 3:19 (NRSV)

ONE COOL EVENING I sat by a campfire as flames flickered and died. Embers glowed a while longer, then logs turned to charcoal and collapsed into gray dust. The warmth and life inside the fire ring was gone. The fire was temporary, and when its time ended, it left behind only ashes.

Ash Wednesday is a day to repent "in dust and ashes." But why are ashes a symbol of penitent prayer? Ashes remind us that we all face death. Like the campfire, we may shine brightly for a time, but one day our bodies will return to dust.

Even while we confront our mortality, we also think about another kind of death. Our old natures have been crucified with Christ. Jesus calls us to die to ourselves and to live in Him. That's a joyful sort of death. We relinquish our unhealthy ways and the destruction they cause, we surrender our selfish desires, and we watch the embers of that old life crumble into ash. Then we respond anew to Jesus's offer to live in us. He breathes into us the immortal flame of eternal life, redeemed natures, and the promise of a new body. When we attend services on Ash Wednesday and receive ashes on our forehead, we celebrate with the tangible reminder that we are forever marked by the Cross.

In *The Cost of Discipleship*, Dietrich Bonhoeffer wrote, "When Christ calls a man, he bids him come and die." And in the beautiful, upside-down world of the Gospel, that is where we find life. The fragile and temporary nature of our mortal lives no longer causes us fear because Jesus has promised us life everlasting with Him.
—SHARON HINCK

FAITH STEP: *If you can, attend an Ash Wednesday service today. If not, prayerfully use your fingertip to mark your forehead with the Cross.*

THURSDAY, MARCH 2

Everything that goes into a life of pleasing God has been miraculously given to us by getting to know, personally and intimately, the One who invited us to God. 2 Peter 1:3 (MSG)

MY MAILBOX OFTEN FILLS UP with unsolicited invitations and catalogs, all touting must-have products with instant promises: save time and energy; make life more comfortable, simple, successful, and secure. Advertisements use words like *refreshing, perfection, guaranteed,* and *gorgeous.* In many cases the products seem destined for those whose homes, closets, and offices are already stuffed to capacity—yet lacking that unique item: automatic dog-treat launchers, magnetic hourglasses for desktop amusement, scented-juice markers. I read through one catalog recently and thought, *Seriously?*

Those advertisements sometimes make me wish for a kind of "product" for the Christian life—something that promises to refresh, simplify, glamorize, and guarantee a great life of perfection. After all, searching through the Bible we can find derivatives or synonyms of those advertising words, like *simple, refreshing, perfect,* and *blessing.*

But unfortunately, Jesus offers no unique inventions to assure success. He suggests no quick-fix products to make life easier. Jesus even uses words like *death, tribulations,* and *sacrifice* repeatedly through Scripture. And He experienced all those things Himself.

Yes, this life involves dying to self, overcoming harmful habits, and enduring difficulties and heartbreak—none of which we could manage apart from Jesus. But what He offers is far better than any mail-order catalog full of overblown promises. Jesus promises peace, joy, love, hope, freedom, and security—and so much more. —REBECCA BARLOW JORDAN

FAITH STEP: *Take time to do a Bible word search. List a few promises that Jesus offers through a relationship with Him. Then give thanks for that relationship.*

FRIDAY, MARCH 3

Your ears will hear a word behind you, "This is the way, walk in it,"
whenever you turn to the right or to the left. Isaiah 30:21 (NAS)

I LIVE IN A CABIN in a clearing in the woods. If you walk from the southeast corner of our property and go a few hundred yards, you'll come to a tree with a blue blaze marking the intersection with Bruno's Run. It was named for the bear that chased a long-ago resident in the nine-mile circle that today is a year-round hiking, biking, and snowshoeing trail.

I don't imagine the frightened man had a destination in mind (once he startled the bear, anyway). He fled for his life. Each time I hike Bruno's Run, I have to figure out the way on the trail—a problem because I am, shall we say, navigationally challenged. Just when I start thinking I might be lost, I spot another blue blaze on a tree up ahead. I've done it often enough now that I can be confident I'll get where I need to go.

When Jesus told His disciples He was going to prepare a place for them and that they knew the way to where He was going, Thomas objected. Without knowing the destination, how could they know the way to get there? Jesus answered, "I am the way" (John 14:3–6, paraphrased). The disciples didn't get it. They hadn't recognized the trail markers.

How did these poorly educated, fearful, doubting people find their way? The same way all of us do. We follow our Shepherd. When He went to heaven, Jesus asked His Father to send the Helper, the Holy Spirit, to work in us and through us. We can be confident that we will hear His voice saying, "This is the way. Walk in it." He'll get us home.
—SUZANNE DAVENPORT TIETJEN

FAITH STEP: *Remember a time when you felt lost. What would you have given for a guide who knew the territory? Thank Jesus today for anticipating how much you will need help—and a Helper.*

SATURDAY, MARCH 4

Whatever you do, work at it with all your heart, as working for the Lord, not for human masters, since you know that you will receive an inheritance from the Lord as a reward. It is the Lord Christ you are serving.
Colossians 3:23–24 (NIV)

THERE ARE ELEVEN PEOPLE living in the Goyer home, and six of them are girls, ages five to fifteen. That's a lot of noise, a lot of drama, and a lot of laundry. If I wash and dry three loads a day, I can keep on top of it. That's a big *if*. On catch-up days, I can spend hours in my laundry room, washing, drying, and folding. Thankfully, it's everyone else's job to put their clothes away!

Growing up I wanted to be a teacher. Instead, I became a writer and speaker. I thought that the words I offered were my most meaningful work, but I don't think that anymore. The core of all my work is *serving others*. Sometimes that serving is writing a chapter of a book, and sometimes it's folding a pile of towels. That's serving in another way.

Brother Lawrence, a lay brother in a seventeenth-century Carmelite monastery in Paris, learned this lesson centuries before me. The message of his life declared that it's in the most humble places that we find the most peace with Jesus. In his book *The Practice of the Presence of God* he writes, "We ought not to be weary of doing little things for the love of God, who regards not the greatness of the work, but the love with which it is performed."

Being truly loving means being truly loving *in all we do*—even laundry. It's there we find Jesus, our very great Reward. —TRICIA GOYER

FAITH STEP: *Today as you complete a humble task such as washing dishes or doing laundry, turn your mind to Jesus. Ask Him to strengthen you for your tasks and pray with a joyful heart for those you are serving.*

SUNDAY, MARCH 5

Let him lead me to the banquet hall, and let his banner over me be love.
Song of Songs 2:4 (NIV)

I ENJOY BIBLE STUDIES that dig deep into the Scriptures, looking at the context and cultural setting of a passage. Studying the historical background and checking cross-references. Looking up Hebrew and Greek words to gain additional insights on the meaning of a verse.

Lately, I've also been digging deep into the meaning of a basic truth I learned as a child: Jesus loves me. Sounds simplistic, but I've discovered that although I had those words planted in my brain, I didn't always live out the reality of them day to day. The fact that God took on human form so He could suffer and die to pay for our sins is proof enough of His unconditional love. But He gives more. So much more.

As I move through my day, Jesus is with me every step of the way. Each breath I take is a gift from Him. The azaleas in my front yard, the food in my fridge, and this sweater in my favorite shade of blue all come from Him. The singing birds outside, my granddaughter's voice on the phone, the gorgeous sunset. These are all expressions of His love.

A faith-filled life is about loving God and others. But it's also about being loved. Because of Christ's great love for me, serving others becomes joy, not drudgery. Sacrifices and suffering don't seem as significant. And I find courage to face trials and troubles.

Jesus loves me. When I move this concept from my brain to the context of my life, it changes everything. —DIANNE NEAL MATTHEWS

FAITH STEP: *As you go throughout your day, watch for ways that Jesus says, "I love you." Thank Him each time you notice an expression of His tender care. Before going to sleep, review your list!*

MONDAY, MARCH 6

Don't fool yourself into thinking that you are a listener when you are anything but, letting the Word go in one ear and out the other. Act on what you hear! Those who hear and don't act are like those who glance in the mirror, walk away, and two minutes later have no idea who they are, what they look like. James 1:22–24 (MSG)

HAVE YOU EVER ARRIVED AT WORK only to realize you were wearing two different shoes? Or maybe you've forgotten to put both earrings in. Been there, done that. I've also gotten somewhere only to see that my outfit doesn't coordinate as well as I'd thought in the different lighting at home. Those stories are fun to joke about with friends, who inevitably have their own tales of times they didn't pay attention to their appearance like they'd thought.

I remember once in college, a sleepy-looking girl trudged into the classroom with a roller still in her hair. I'm not sure anyone told her or if we all figured she'd get a good laugh later.

Speaking of not paying attention, I can't tell you how many times over the years I've thought I was listening well in church or comprehending a Scripture passage, only to be utterly lost later trying to recall *anything* about it. I know it meant a lot to me at the time, but…did it really?

One habit I've adopted to help develop my memory so I can retain what Jesus is teaching me is to read through one book of the Bible at a time and focus on each chapter. The next day I'll skim the previous day's chapters again before starting on the new ones. That way I get a double dose of all of it and a reminder to apply what I read.

By training myself to retain Jesus's Word, I help myself apply it. If I can't recall it, reading it didn't help much. Gaining knowledge is good but only as far as it changes my life, my character, and my faith in Christ day to day. —ERIN KEELEY MARSHALL

FAITH STEP: *Read Matthew 7:24, another verse about applying Jesus's teaching.*

TUESDAY, MARCH 7

"He who is faithful in a very little thing is faithful also in much." Luke 16:10 (NAS)

THE TINY HOUSE CRAZE. Have you read about it? A growing percentage of the population is seeking an intentional, dramatic downsizing of living space for a variety of reasons. To save money otherwise spent on high mortgage payments, to leave a smaller carbon footprint, to simplify their lives, to conduct a social experiment about Americans' ability to live on—and with—far less than we currently think possible.

We lived in a tiny house once. At 720 square feet, it probably wouldn't qualify as tiny *enough*, but I'm reminded of the days when the only way to get into bed was to crawl in from my husband's side, since a standard double bed filled the entire room except for a narrow walkway to the only closet in the home, which doubled as a bathroom—half bath, no tub or shower until we added one.

I know a family on its fifth downsize. As in cooking, each reduction in space intensifies the *flavor* of their relationships as they reduce their possessions to the most essential and meaningful. Hard to go small? Yes. But they're making it work because of their commitment to the One Who converts small into enough.

The Bible says, "Better a little with righteousness than great profits without justice" (Proverbs 16:8, CEB), echoed by the words of Jesus in Luke 16:10 regarding our faithfulness with little expressing evidence of our faithfulness with much.

Whether a twenty-thousand-square-foot mansion or a tiny house on wheels, letting Jesus inhabit the space makes it enough. —CYNTHIA RUCHTI

FAITH STEP: *No matter its size, is your home feeling cramped these days? Maybe it doesn't need more square footage but more of the imprint of Jesus.*

WEDNESDAY, MARCH 8

"Father, if you are willing, take this cup from me;
yet not my will, but yours be done."
Luke 22:42 (NIV)

LAST YEAR MY LIFE took a turn for the worse when a close friend misunderstood something I said and took offense. She withdrew, refusing to discuss her feelings or engage with me.

My heart broke. I blamed myself. I cried. I lost sleep. I lost the ability to focus on my work. I prayed, and then I prayed some more. I also spent time with a Christian counselor to gain insight about what had happened and how I should respond.

The counselor shared many words of wisdom, but one thing she said especially resonated with me: "This woman is on a spiritual journey of her own. Perhaps God has allowed this experience to bring about growth in her life. Be patient. Love her. And continue praying."

Her advice altered both my perspective and my prayers. I stopped focusing on my heartache and began looking at the bigger picture. I stopped begging for relief from the pain and began asking God to accomplish His eternal purposes through this hurtful situation. Basically, I began praying as Jesus did in the Garden of Gethsemane: "Your will, not mine, be done."

I followed Jesus's example and surrendered my wishes in exchange for God's higher purposes. I was able to focus once again on my work. Peace replaced the angst I'd felt. And my ability to sleep was restored.
—GRACE FOX

FAITH STEP: *Are you wrestling amid a painful situation and telling Jesus how and when to fix it? Surrender your wishes to the One Who knows best and invite Him to do His will. Thank Jesus for modeling true surrender.*

THURSDAY, MARCH 9

Commit your work to the Lord, and your plans will be established.
Proverbs 16:3 (ESV)

I CURRENTLY HAVE OVER fifty books in print, and I get e-mails all the time asking me what my secret is. It's this: you have to put in a lot of hard work. Many people don't realize that an overnight success means a lifetime of costly sacrifices. Of course people don't want to hear that. They want a quick and easy path.

There are few things in life that come easily. Behind every breakout singer are thousands of hours of voice lessons and practicing. Behind every famous artist are hundreds of canvases that never see the light of day. And every popular musician has played their fair share of scales. The most important thing, though, isn't succeeding. It's working hard and committing our work to the Lord. We wish for quick success, but if that happened we'd miss many lessons along the way. It's in the hard work and striving where we discover how much we can really turn to Jesus.

As Pastor Charles Stanley says, "Our heavenly Father understands our disappointment, suffering, pain, fear, and doubt. He is always there to encourage our hearts and help us understand that He's sufficient for all of our needs. When I accepted this as an absolute truth in my life, I found that my worrying stopped."

No one should worry about whether hard work will lead to success. Instead they simply need to work for Jesus and do their best for Him. And Jesus will see that our plans are established. I'm thankful for every book I've been able to write, but I'm even more thankful that Jesus has been with me every step of the way. —TRICIA GOYER

FAITH STEP: *Write down a definition of success in the world's eyes. Then write down a definition of success in Jesus's eyes. How do they differ? Pray and commit your way to the Lord and ask that your plans will be established.*

FRIDAY, MARCH 10

"I go to prepare a place for you. . . . "
John 14:3 (CEB)

THESE WORDS OF JESUS have always comforted me and shown the depth of love Jesus has for us. He wants us with Him, even in eternity. And He isn't just making a way, He's *preparing* that place.

That's what gives me pause. Does Jesus need *time* to prepare a place for us? Not in the traditional sense. He can create something out of nothing in an instant, the Bible tells us.

Why did He choose to use a word that implies it would take time for those preparations? He doesn't say, "I go to speak into existence a place for you" or "I go to unlock the door for you."

Is it possible that the preparations in this place for us mean He adjusts things during our time on earth?

When we walk through difficulties, does He add something to the blueprint that provides the *opposite* of that pain? Does He watch people who should care for us ignoring our heart's needs or neglecting our heart's longings and then adjust the blueprint to accommodate what we didn't receive on earth? Adding even more attention to provision for our heart's needs and longings? Is that the reason for the supposed delay?

That may not be what Jesus meant by His choice of the word we understand as "prepare." He knows the end from the beginning, so nothing surprises Him. He knows what we wouldn't receive on earth and has prepared in eternity past for our every need to be met in Him.

But seeing His promised preparations as a personally tailored act of love on His part warms my heart. Yours too? —CYNTHIA RUCHTI

FAITH STEP: *Use a paint chip sample card in your Bible as a bookmark to remind you to thank Jesus for His ongoing preparations for your eternal home.*

SATURDAY, MARCH 11

---

*Let perseverance finish its work so that you may be mature and complete,
not lacking anything. If any of you lacks wisdom, you should ask God,
who gives generously to all without finding fault, and it will be
given to you. James 1:4–5 (NIV)*

OUR DRYER BROKE while I was gone on a trip. I saw the laundry
pile when I got home (picture Mount Vesuvius made out of dirty
socks). "When was the last time you did laundry?" I asked Scott.

"When did I have time to do laundry?" my husband said.

I called Sears the next morning to come fix our dryer. They said
they would be happy to come out… in ten days. Sweet mercy.

I had the boys bring all of their dirty clothes out of their rooms
(picture Mount Everest made out of smelly towels). Too. Much.
Laundry. So I told the boys, "Starting next week, I am teaching
you all how to do your own laundry." It was at this point that the
weeping and gnashing of teeth commenced. The nine-year-old
announced, "But I am just a baby."

"It's time to be a big boy," I said, unblinking.

I used to have a Laundry Fairy (my mom), then I became the
Laundry Fairy (not as much fun as it sounds). And now it is time to
pass on the legacy (welcome to the world, sweet sons of mine). Soon
they'll be as expert at it as I am. Maturing is never easy. But it is the goal.

When we first came to know Jesus, there were so many things we
didn't understand. But His plan is to grow us up in His truth, power,
wisdom, and grace. In every difficult situation, He wants to move us
forward in our faith. And the best part is, when we grow, we begin to
look and act more like Him. —SUSANNA FOTH AUGHTMON

FAITH STEP: *Is there an area of your life in which you feel like saying, "But I am
just a baby!"? Ask Jesus to grow you in His wisdom.*

SUNDAY, MARCH 12

The Lord is close to those who are of a broken heart and saves such as are crushed with sorrow for sin. . . . Psalm 34:18 (AMP)

I'VE GONE TO CHURCH since I was a baby. Most of my childhood memories of church are good, but as an adult—like everything else—it's more complicated. I've come to believe church is a lot like any relationship. It takes a lot of work for it to be good. But the biggest lesson I've ever learned about church came from my daughter Stella.

We were in the nursery together during Sunday school. There was a bracelet on my wrist that kept falling off. I'd pick it up and try to fix the clasp, and it would fall off again. Finally, I laid it to the side.

"What's wrong, Momma?"

"Oh, I guess it's broken. I can't get it to work right."

Stella picked up the bracelet. "It's okay, Momma. It's okay to be broken. I will help you."

When I left the nursery, I saw church with new eyes. There were people in bad health, people with eating disorders, gossips. In another row sat an adulterer. Teenagers. Loud people. Lonely people. And me.

I sat down at the piano. All of my troubles spread out before me like sheets of music. I thought about what Stella said: *It's okay to be broken. I will help you.* It dawned on me that this is exactly what church is for.

We find Jesus together in the midst of our brokenness.

—GWEN FORD FAULKENBERRY

FAITH STEP: *Is your church a place where it's safe to admit you are broken? If not, you may need to leave, but first consider ways you might effect change. Start by being honest about your brokenness, which invites others to do the same.*

MONDAY, MARCH 13

"You have your heads in your Bibles constantly because you think you'll find eternal life there. But you miss the forest for the trees. These Scriptures are all about me! And here I am, standing right before you, and you aren't willing to receive from me the life you say you want." John 5:39–40 (MSG)

ONE OF MY FAVORITE PHOTOS shows my three-year-old granddaughter lying on her back, eyes closed, pitching a full-out tantrum. My daughter said the child was upset because she wanted a flower—the very flower the photo shows her holding in her tiny clenched fist. Her desire, belief, and temper made it impossible for her to hear the truth. She couldn't see the flower for the tantrum.

Just like the Jewish leaders Jesus was talking to, she was angry. They, too, knew what they knew. Jesus acknowledged that His powerful critics knew the letter of the law. They would have known that when Jesus called Himself the Son of Man a moment earlier, He was taking a messianic title as His own. This made them even angrier. They were experts on God's Word, but they didn't *believe* it deeply and personally. Their knowledge gave them status and respect, so they chose tradition and rules over truth. They didn't see the Word or themselves rightly and therefore saw no need to humbly repent or apply hard truths. God's Word was in their hands and heads, but not in their hearts.

I can act this way too. I may value tradition or see myself as having a certain standing in the congregation. When something threatens what I want, I may decide to take a stand, thinking, *It's about the principle!* when it may really be about having my own way.

The truth can be so hard to see. Jesus, open my eyes to see You.
—SUZANNE DAVENPORT TIETJEN

FAITH STEP: *Pray today to slow down and take a measured approach. Things may not be what they seem. Ask Jesus to help you make room in your heart for His truth.*

TUESDAY, MARCH 14

A second time they summoned the man who had been blind. "Give glory to God by telling the truth," they said. "We know this man is a sinner." He replied, "Whether he is a sinner or not, I don't know. One thing I do know. I was blind but now I see!" John 9:24–25 (NIV)

MY SON WAS DESCRIBING a theological debate he'd been having with a friend in his small group at church. His eyes lit with enthusiasm as he talked about their ongoing discussions and disagreements. For him, a good argument is fun.

I'm the opposite. I run from conflict of any sort. I want everyone to hold hands around the campfire and sing "Kumbaya."

That fear of conflict can influence my willingness to share Jesus with others. I worry that if someone disagrees with me, I won't have intelligent answers to their questions.

The story of the man who was born blind and healed by Jesus gives me great comfort. The Pharisees were in a dither about the miracle and kept drilling the man for an explanation. He truly didn't yet know much about Jesus, had no great theological background, but he was still able to share the truth: "I was blind but now I see!"

If we're not ones to enjoy debate, we can still talk about our faith in Jesus—even to those who don't agree. Our job isn't to convince, to prove, to shame, to demand, or to defend Jesus. Jesus just asks us to tell. We can invite people to examine the Scriptures for themselves. We can let them know they are loved by their Creator and Redeemer. And we can do what the blind man did and share our experiences with Jesus. "I don't know all the answers, but I know that He changed me." —SHARON HINCK

FAITH STEP: *Today, think of a way that Jesus has brought change into your life. Then, like the blind man who was healed, simply tell someone what He has done.*

WEDNESDAY, MARCH 15

Your love has given me much joy and comfort . . . for your kindness has often refreshed the hearts of God's people. Philemon 1:7 (NLT)

I HAVE A FRIEND whose greatest talent is looking out for the hearts of others. She's the first to call if she senses someone is down, the first to take a meal to someone in need, and she's quick to offer to watch someone's kids so a tired mother can have a break.

Another friend of mine is a pursuer of hearts as well. She's a mentor to me in the ways she offers encouragement to stick close to the Lord and to keep trusting Jesus more deeply through the seasons of life. I've sat with her at roundtable discussions among women and listened to her share her experiences with Jesus, and I've watched the faces of other women like me glean from her wisdom.

Both friends leave me thinking, *I want to be like her when I grow up!* Little by little, I believe I'm learning to love like Jesus, to see others through His power in me. I still can be short on patience at times, but maybe not so short as I used to be. I still can be too hardwired to my to-do list, but more and more I'm led to put it aside when someone I know needs care.

Who might be refreshed by watching you refresh others? And who is learning to share the love of Jesus with words and attitudes and acts of kindness because he or she has observed your life?

Each act of kindness we extend to someone not only nourishes that person, but it also nourishes anyone else within range. Let's never underestimate the reach of Jesus's arms through us; it's probably further than we can imagine. —ERIN KEELEY MARSHALL

FAITH STEP: *Jot down a list of people who have shown you by example how to refresh others. Now list others in your circle of influence who may be refreshed from watching you live out Jesus's love.*

THURSDAY, MARCH 16

He then asked, "And you—what are you saying about me? Who am I?"
Peter gave the answer: "You are the Christ, the Messiah." Mark 8:29 (MSG)

A FRIEND OF MINE recently accompanied her husband to the doctor. He was a new patient, so the nurse had to fill out his medical history. When she asked about past surgeries, Anthony mentioned having his wisdom teeth removed and a couple of other minor procedures. The nurse's next question was, "How many kids do you have?" He looked up toward the ceiling and said, "How many? Oh...about twenty."

His wife's jaw dropped; then she repeated the nurse's question to her husband. "Oh—kids," Anthony responded. "I thought she said 'How many teeth do you have?'" His slight hearing loss combined with a nurse who talked while turned away from him gave them all a laugh. It also demonstrated that in order to give the right answer, we have to understand the question.

Jesus asked His disciples an all-important question that each of us must answer as well: "Who am I?" Do we believe that Jesus was a good man? A powerful teacher and prophet? Or do we accept what Jesus proclaimed about Himself? "Whoever has seen me has seen the Father" (John 14:9, ESV) and "I and the Father are one" (John 10:30, ESV). Every day our actions, if not our words, reveal what we believe about His identity.

The only true foundation for a life that brings meaning, peace, and joy is a relationship with Jesus. That only happens once I get the right answer—after I understand the real question.

—DIANNE NEAL MATTHEWS

FAITH STEP: *Tell Jesus your answer to the question He asked Peter. Now think about the biggest need, problem, or challenge in your life right now. How does the way you handle this concern show what you believe about Jesus?*

FRIDAY, MARCH 17

And so we know and rely on the love God has for us. God is love.
Whoever lives in love lives in God, and God in them.
1 *John 4:16 (NIV)*

MY MOM WARNED ME: the years fly by. Before you know it the preschooler who clung to your knees is shrugging off hugs as they run to make it to class before the elementary school bell. And then they fly away. Literally. To Washington, DC, for their eighth-grade trip. My son Jack is becoming a young man. When did this happen? When did he become the one big enough to give piggyback rides . . . to his mother? When did his voice take on that hint of bass?

When I dropped off Jack at the airport at 5:00 a.m. this past Sunday to board the plane for his DC trip, he gave me a quick hug. I grabbed him and buried my face in his shoulder and kissed his neck. I am pretty sure I horrified him. But he smiled anyway, slung his backpack over his shoulder, and said, "Bye, Mom." I felt hopeful and terrified and proud, all at the same time.

Is that what parenting becomes? I'm watching this boy come into his own life—his own purpose, pain, and joy—and thinking, *Man, I love this kid.* I blinked back a couple of tears.

I think Jesus feels this same huge love for us when He looks at us coming into our own. Each time we lean into His wisdom and grace, when we let Him change our hearts and overcome our fears and become more of the person He created us to be. He is shouting down from the heavens saying, "Man, I love this kid!" He might even be grabbing some of the angels and giving them a hug . . . until He can get His hands on us. —SUSANNA FOTH AUGHTMON

FAITH STEP: *Imagine Jesus grabbing you up in a giant hug and know beyond a shadow of a doubt that He is holding you close in a place of love.*

SATURDAY, MARCH 18

And behold, one of those who were with Jesus stretched out his hand and drew his sword and struck the servant of the high priest and cut off his ear. Then Jesus said to him, "Put your sword back into its place. For all who take the sword will perish by the sword." Matthew 26:51–52 (ESV)

THERE IS DEEP SADNESS in this part of the Gospel narrative, beyond the obvious fact that Jesus was being arrested. He's been in the garden praying, struggling with His mission and the pain it will cost Him. You would think the least His companions could do is stay awake. But they didn't. And we see in that the likelihood that they didn't understand what He was facing. However, it's in this moment, when the ear is cut off, that their utter cluelessness is revealed. In Jesus's admonishment we hear a sigh of sorrow: *Guys. Stop it. This is not what I'm about.* And He heals the ear of His enemy.

I think there's a lesson in this for us today. Do we understand what Jesus is about? Do we know Him well enough to represent Him? We have to be careful as we answer those questions because I'm not sure anyone could ever know Him better than the disciples. And if they could misunderstand His mission, isn't it possible we could today?

The question should give us pause. I wonder how many times we encounter an issue, and in our haste to defend our faith and this Jesus we love so much, we break out our swords. It doesn't have to mean we use violence. Sometimes our damage is more subtle. The Bible says reckless words pierce like a sword, but the tongue of the wise brings healing. And as in the case of the ear, Jesus was about healing. —GWEN FORD FAULKENBERRY

FAITH STEP: *Is there a cause you feel strongly about? Perhaps a political or social issue? Before drawing your sword, ask Jesus to show you His perspective. Make sure your stance is one that fosters healing.*

Sunday, March 19

---

*And so, dear brothers and sisters, I plead with you to give your bodies to
God because of all he has done for you. Let them be a living and holy
sacrifice—the kind he will find acceptable. This is truly the way to worship him.*
Romans 12:1 (NLT)

I became a Christian at seventeen. After making horrible decisions in my teen years, I prayed, "Jesus, I give my life to You. If You can do anything with it, please do." I was tired of the pain of my decisions. I wanted life to be different.

The truth is that my motives were mostly for myself. I wanted to become a Christian so I could have an easier life. I wanted to do good things for Jesus to make up for my bad choices and to prove to others that I wasn't a complete failure. Jesus soon showed me that my desire to live for Him was mostly about making myself look good. It was a heartbreaking lesson to learn.

"Our motive for surrender should not be for any personal gain at all," says Oswald Chambers. "We have become so self-centered that we go to God only for something from Him, and not for God Himself. It is like saying, 'No, Lord, I don't want You; I want myself. But I do want You to clean me and fill me with Your Holy Spirit. I want to be on display in Your showcase so I can say, 'This is what God has done for me.'"

When we accept Christ and live for Him, He often does beautiful things in our lives, but that shouldn't be our goal. That is an added benefit of living for Jesus. Our ultimate goal of surrendering to Jesus is Jesus. He deserves our dedication and our worship. He deserves everything that we have to offer. —Tricia Goyer

---

Faith Step: *Is there anything in your life or in your heart that you've been holding back from surrendering to Jesus? Is there any part of you that serves Him for your sake rather than His? Take a moment and truly surrender to Jesus.*

MONDAY, MARCH 20

"For in him we live and move and have our being."
As some of your own poets have said, "We are his offspring."
Acts 17:28 (NIV)

I HAVE FIGURED OUT that I am a one-person-at-a-time kind of gal. I love my people in small doses. I love a cup of coffee with a friend, one-on-one time with my sons, or a date night with Scott. But if I walk into a room with twenty of my favorite people, I think, *Sweet mercy! Take me now! There is no way I can talk to everyone!*

But I do need that one-on-one connection with people desperately. It is life-giving. I need to sit down and laugh and learn with the ones who know me inside and out, who have seen me at my most neurotic, and who still hang around and love me anyway. I need their wisdom, encouragement, and truth-telling to help shape who I am becoming. When I come away from time spent with a dear friend, I feel richer, built up...more alive.

There is one friend with whom I need to connect more than anyone: Jesus, the Lover of my soul. I need to spend time in His presence, soaking up Who He is. I need His wisdom, encouragement, and truth-telling to shape who I am becoming. I need to learn all the truth He has for me. I need His forgiveness and mercy to color my life. I need His passion and His love to change how I love the people around me. When I spend time with Jesus, I truly become more alive. —SUSANNA FOTH AUGHTMON

FAITH STEP: *Spend a moment thinking about how you feel when you are in the presence of Jesus. Then write down some moments when you've felt most alive. Compare the lists. Are they the same?*

TUESDAY, MARCH 21

And David said, "Is there still anyone left of the house (family) of Saul to whom I may show kindness for Jonathan's sake?"
2 Samuel 9:1 (AMP)

MY MOTHER HAD AN UNUSUAL FRIENDSHIP with an older woman named Spencella who was close to ninety years old and just over four feet tall. Her wrinkled deep-sepia-brown skin told the story of her life. Spencella was an orphan raised by a family member who said she wouldn't amount to much. She married a man who was rarely kind, and they didn't have children. Never having the benefit of higher education, Spencella mostly worked in domestic jobs for lower pay than she deserved.

She'd met my mother as a spry eighty-seven-year-old who had been taken in by her cousins and last-known living relatives in Cleveland, Ohio, the Edwards family. The explanation for how Spencella ended up there was simple: the family took care of their own. The matriarch, Mrs. Edwards, was a giving spirit and took primary care of Spencella. When Mrs. Edwards—who earlier had nurtured my mother after my grandmother died—passed away, Mom stepped in to help Spencella.

Mom took Spencella shopping, to her doctor's appointments, and to church each Sunday. Spencella also became a fixture at our family gatherings. It was almost as if, once Mrs. Edwards died, my mother had asked, *Is there anyone left in the family of the Edwards I may show kindness to?*

Jesus provided the best example of "family" inclusion and kindness. He is the reason we get to see God's goodness and grace. He adopted us into His family through the ultimate selfless act so that we could always belong. —TARICE L. S. GRAY

FAITH STEP: *Reach out to an elderly family member or an acquaintance and remind them of why they are special to you.*

WEDNESDAY, MARCH 22

God loves (He takes pleasure in, prizes above other things, and is unwilling to abandon or to do without) a cheerful (joyous, "prompt to do it") giver [whose heart is in his giving]. 2 Corinthians 9:7 (AMP)

WHEN I WAS A YOUNG MILITARY WIFE, my husband, Mike, was a cheerful giver. Me? I was the cautious one. Money was tight. Since I kept the checkbook, I was more aware that we often had more month than money. I wanted to be sure we had enough before giving, while Mike wanted to write the tithe check first thing every payday. He said, "God comes first." I didn't understand at the time why that was so important.

I understood it better when I became a shepherd. I learned that the most valuable and precious fleece a sheep would ever produce was its very first. These fleeces sell high, if they sell at all. These are the fleeces the Israelites had to give back to God to clothe the Levitical priests. These were the fleeces they would most want to keep for themselves.

The concept of firstfruits runs through the Bible, from Abel's sacrifice to Jesus, who gave Himself for us. Every firstborn, human or animal, belonged to God and had to be redeemed in order to stay in the family or their fields. God was serious about this—the firstborn could not be held back. If an animal wasn't redeemed or sacrificed, it had to be killed.

I'd been wrong to want to hold back our meager funds. Through the years when I've honored Jesus with my best, He has always provided for my needs. —SUZANNE DAVENPORT TIETJEN

FAITH STEP: *Jesus, sure of His source, said give and it will be given to you (Luke 6:38). What will you offer up today of your time, talents, or treasure? Ask Him to provide the joy.*

THURSDAY, MARCH 23

He cuts off every branch of mine that doesn't produce fruit, and he prunes the branches that do bear fruit so they will produce even more. John 15:2 (NLT)

FOR NEARLY A DECADE our family lived on a yard bordered by a fence on which grapevines grew. The yard also held a peach tree, a plum tree, two apple trees, and about two dozen raspberry bushes. I'm no horticulturalist, so I asked the former residents to teach me how to care for these plants so they'd produce fruit.

Following their instructions, my husband and I brought out the pruning shears every spring and set to work. We snipped and cut vines and branches until it seemed unlikely they'd ever grow back.

The art of pruning seemed a bit harsh to us, but it was obviously effective because the plants always gifted us with a luscious harvest. I canned fruit, preserved jams and jellies, made juice, and baked pies. And still there was plenty of fresh produce to share with friends.

At times in my life I've felt as though Jesus has pruned *me*, and His use of the shears has seemed a bit harsh. He's lopped off pride, procrastination, greed, and even gluttony by allowing me to experience loneliness, physical pain, prickly interpersonal relationships, and financial uncertainty. His labors have taught me humility, gratitude, and self-discipline. Ultimately my faith journey has deepened, and I'm more in love with Him today than ever before.

Jesus's method of helping us flourish really works. The process is painful at times, and we might be tempted to question His care and wisdom. But let's rest in His work, knowing that His desire is to produce in us a harvest of righteousness. —GRACE FOX

FAITH STEP: *Eat a piece of your favorite fruit. As you do, thank Jesus for loving you enough to prune you so your life will produce a rich harvest.*

FRIDAY, MARCH 24

[Jesus] asked a third time, "Simon, son of John, do you love me?"
Peter was sad that Jesus asked him a third time, "Do you love me?"
He replied, "Lord, you know everything; you know I love you."
Jesus said to him, "Feed my sheep." John 21:17 (CEB)

WHY DID JESUS ASK THREE TIMES? I think it's particularly poignant that the Bible says it made Peter sad. He wanted so much to be faithful, for Jesus to know that his friendship could be counted on. And yet, for all of his passion, Peter was often clueless about what it really meant to love Jesus (reference the sinking-in-the-Sea-of-Galilee scene or the cock-crowing denial scene). His sadness is poignant to me because I can relate to it. Can you?

I believe Jesus asked three times not because He didn't know the answer but because He wanted to make Peter think. This time, instead of allowing Peter to answer and act on impulse, Jesus demanded that he count the cost of what he was saying. *Do you love Me? Well, here's what that really means. Feed My sheep. And if you don't feed My sheep, well, don't say you love Me because it's just words.* That's the implication.

So the question comes down through the ages to us today. *Do you love Me?* I'd like to think I do love Him. I write Christian books, play the piano for church, sing songs like "I Love You, Lord," read the Bible, and teach my kids about Jesus. But what does it look like to feed His sheep? It's a question worth pondering, since without implementation of the answer, all of my good intentions are just words.

—GWEN FORD FAULKENBERRY

FAITH STEP: *Do you love Jesus? What do you think it means to feed His sheep? You may have to get your hands dirty. Find one practical way you can be a sheep-feeder today.*

SATURDAY, MARCH 25

"What do you mean, 'If I can'?" Jesus asked. "Anything is possible if a person believes." The father instantly cried out, "I do believe, but help me overcome my unbelief!" Mark 9:23–24 (NLT)

I ENDED THE CONVERSATION with my friend and looked at the clock. We had talked for more than an hour. Time had flown by since we had so much catching up to do. We live almost a thousand miles apart now and rarely see each other. Sometimes we go a long time between calls, but the conversations we do have are therapeutic. I told her about the crisis situation my husband and I had just survived and our present struggles. She told me about her husband's scheduled brain surgery. We both shared our concerns and anxieties and ended with promises to pray for each other.

Isn't it wonderful to have someone you can be honest with, a friend who knows your heart for the Lord even as you admit your biggest battles? That's why I love the story of the father asking Jesus to heal his son, who suffered from violent seizures. This man trusted Jesus enough to admit that he wrestled with doubts even though he believed in Jesus's healing power. He asked Jesus to strengthen his faith.

As long as we live on this earth, our faith will not be perfect. Jesus understands our weaknesses; He knows us better than anyone. He wants us to share everything with Him.

If our prayer times are short or we don't come away feeling encouraged and strengthened, it might be because we aren't trusting Jesus enough to share our doubts and struggles with Him.
—DIANNE NEAL MATTHEWS

FAITH STEP: *Think about an area of your life where you have trouble believing God's promises. Have a long conversation with Jesus, admitting your doubts and asking His help to overcome them.*

SUNDAY, MARCH 26

Jesus said to his disciples, "All who want to come after me must say no to themselves, take up their cross, and follow me."
Matthew 16:24 (CEB)

WHAT AN INTERESTING CONVERSATION this must have been between Jesus and His disciples. This was the first time Jesus let people know He was going to suffer, be killed, and rise again on the third day. His disciples rebelled against the idea, not understanding that it all had to happen in order for any of us to be redeemed.

After chiding Peter for listening to human instincts instead of the will of God, Jesus told His followers that all who want to come after Him would have to say no to themselves (their human instincts and desires), take up *their* cross, and follow Him.

"Whoa. Slow down there, Jesus. *Our* crosses? This is not what we signed up for." Those words aren't recorded in Scripture, but somebody must have been thinking them.

When life gets tough, are you tempted to say, "This is not what I signed up for!"? But it is. To follow Jesus means walking the rocky, painful paths He walked, if that's what's ahead.

Jesus didn't tell us to *pick* our crosses. He told us to pick *up* our crosses and follow Him. "Walk this way," in other words. Head high, despite the weight of that cross, eyes forward, getting up if we stumble, and faithfully obedient, grateful for His promise never to leave us or forsake us, every step of the way. —CYNTHIA RUCHTI

FAITH STEP: *Memorize this related verse for times when you feel the weight of your cross pulling you downward: "For the Human One is about to come with the majesty of his Father with his angels. And then he will repay each one for what that person has done" (Matthew 16:27, CEB).*

MONDAY, MARCH 27

God... not only knows what he's thinking, but he lets us in on it....
We don't have to rely on the world's guesses and opinions. We didn't learn
this by reading books or going to school; we learned it from God,
who taught us person-to-person through Jesus.
1 Corinthians 2:11–12 (MSG)

MY KIDS RECENTLY STARTED music lessons, Paxton on guitar and Calianne on piano. Their dad jokes that he plays the radio. He loves music probably more than I do, so it seems logical that he'd want to learn secondhand through the kids.

He went with Paxton to his first guitar lesson and came home taking turns practicing. Calianne got in on the action and decided Dad should learn piano too. If he hadn't begged off from her ambitions, he would've had a week's worth of lessons to practice!

"You've got to understand this is like reading Portuguese, Cal," he explained more than once. "I don't speak Portuguese."

Have you ever read a passage of the Bible that left you bewildered, like trying to comprehend a foreign language? I love that Jesus's Spirit in a believer not only helps make sense of the Word but interprets it in a personal, timely way. I like to ask Jesus for help in understanding what I wouldn't normally catch on my own. Sometimes I'll see a new perspective in a verse I've read many times.

He gave us His Spirit to help us know Him, and He doesn't leave us to our intuition to figure out His divine language. Through His Spirit, we gain understanding of His Word. —ERIN KEELEY MARSHALL

FAITH STEP: *Memorize John 14:26 (ESV): "But the Helper, the Holy Spirit, whom the Father will send in my name, he will teach you all things and bring to your remembrance all that I have said to you."*

TUESDAY, MARCH 28

I know what it is to be in need, and I know what it is to have plenty. I have learned the secret of being content in any and every situation, whether well fed or hungry, whether living in plenty or in want. I can do all this through him who gives me strength. Philippians 4:12–13 (NIV)

TWO WEEKS AFTER MY OLDEST DAUGHTER, Leslie, turned twenty-one, she moved to the Czech Republic as a full-time missionary. On the way there she had an idea of what she was going to be doing: staying for one year, growing friendships with the people she'd previously met at English camps, and teaching English as a way to connect with students.

When Leslie got there, however, she discovered her friends already had their own lives, and it was hard to squeeze herself in. She also dealt with the grief of leaving her family and extreme culture shock and loneliness. It was hard being the only American in her church and being the only non–Czech in most settings. Even her work looked different from what she'd expected, and the weather was dark and dreary.

Leslie has been there three years now, and she has experienced both want and now plenty. She met and married a wonderful Christian man. She is seeing the fruit of many relationships. And she feels that in the darkest of times, Jesus was the nearest. When she struggled with loneliness, she discovered Jesus as a true Friend Who would always be there with her.

I've never met a strong person with an easy past. And Leslie's experience—the stripping away of a family and friend network—showed her that Jesus gives her strength for anything she faces. It's a wonderful lesson for us all. —TRICIA GOYER

FAITH STEP: *Think about a foreign missionary whom you know and take time to pray for him or her today. Pray for strong relationships, for fruitful opportunities, and that this missionary will discover how Jesus provides strength.*

WEDNESDAY, MARCH 29

Later, as Jesus left the town, he saw a tax collector named Levi sitting at his tax collector's booth. "Follow me and be my disciple," Jesus said to him. So Levi got up, left everything, and followed him.
Luke 5:27–28 *(NLT)*

JESUS HAD A KNACK for looking at people and seeing something different from what everyone else saw. Take Levi, the tax collector, for example. The entire community viewed Levi as a money-hungry cheat. They looked at him in scorn and judged him as a man who lacked integrity. They considered him to be a person who lived to rip off anyone who crossed his path.

But Jesus looked at Levi and saw a man He could trust. He saw a man who was thirsting for truth and who wanted a real reason to live. Not surprisingly, Jesus's estimation was correct. He called Levi to follow Him, and immediately Levi left everything familiar behind to become a loyal disciple.

I love hearing testimonies from people whose lives Jesus has transformed. In some cases, the general population considered them beyond hope. They may have been prisoners or adulterers or abusers or the abused. Others looked at them and their lives and considered them beyond redemption. But Jesus looked at them and saw something different.

How do I view people? Do I judge them by their outward appearance, their current sorry state, or their miserable history and automatically assume the worst? Or do I see them with their full potential as Christ does? I'm learning to see with His eyes. —GRACE FOX

FAITH STEP: *Sometimes we view ourselves through a skewed lens. We see ourselves as unlovable, shamed, or second-class because of past failures. How do you see yourself? How does Jesus see you? Read Zephaniah 3:17.*

THURSDAY, MARCH 30

"Let me tell you why you are here. You're here to be salt-seasoning that brings out the God-flavors of this earth. If you lose your saltiness, how will people taste godliness? . . ." Matthew 5:13 (MSG)

YOU'VE PROBABLY HEARD THE SAYING, "You can lead a horse to water, but you can't make him drink." Trust me, the same is true for sheep.

Water is the most important nutrient—it's involved in almost every body function. But it might be the most neglected because shepherds may not immediately notice when sheep aren't drinking. A good shepherd watches for lethargy or observes loose skin when he checks the animals. Sheep should take in two to three times as much water as grass, grain, and hay. If they don't drink enough, they can't and won't eat enough; ewes won't make enough milk and lambs won't grow. Health problems ensue, even for the rams. The shepherd fixes this by giving them salt from a block or a container on the ground. Just like popcorn at the movies or peanuts at a party, salt makes sheep, like people, thirsty.

Just like those poor sheep need water but aren't drinking it, people need a Savior and drink Him in. This is where we come in. Jesus said we're here to be the salt of the earth. We season our world with grace and the results of knowing Him. We function like salt to preserve our culture. In our neighbors, we create a thirst for the Savior, whose living water they desperately need, by living out our faith in the midst of them. Paul said, "Let your speech always be with grace, *as though* seasoned with salt, so that you will know how you should respond to each person" (Colossians 4:6, NAS).

Give them salt—it will lead them to drink!

—SUZANNE DAVENPORT TIETJEN

FAITH STEP: *Wherever you go today, really look at people. Offer them a smile and be full of grace and salt.*

FRIDAY, MARCH 31

Many are the plans in a person's heart, but it is the Lord's purpose that prevails. Proverbs 19:21 (NIV)

ON A RECENT VISIT to our three-year-old granddaughter, we read the Bible story of Jesus's arrest in Gethsemane. She had many questions about why people wanted to hurt Jesus. Her father did a beautiful job sharing the Gospel with her. He also explained that the religious leaders wanted to keep control and were worried because people were following Jesus. He told her that Jesus allowed Himself to be hurt because He loves us so much. She listened with rapt attention. When he finished, she had one question: "Daddy, how do I get control?"

We laughed, but after she was tucked in bed, we discussed how her question epitomized the human condition. From the Garden of Eden until today, we are presented with the wonderful truth of Jesus's love, grace, and sacrifice on our behalf. Yet often our response is "I want to be the boss."

I'd like to think I'm more spiritually mature now that I'm no longer three, but the truth is I still often miss the point. I dictate to Jesus exactly how He should answer my prayers, but if He doesn't do things my way, doubt twists my thoughts into knots. I set a course for myself, but when I don't get what I want, selfish ambition coils in my heart. I grow impatient with Jesus's timing, frustrated with where He's placed me. Grasping for control causes me to lash out at the One Who offers me peace.

In His tenderness, Jesus reminds me I'm not in control. When I trust His purposes, peace floods me. Then He amazes me as I catch glimpses of those purposes—far richer, deeper, and better than any of my plans. —SHARON HINCK

FAITH STEP: *Memorize today's verse, and ask Jesus to place your plans in His hands.*

SATURDAY, APRIL 1

*He makes me lie down in green pastures. He leads me
beside quiet waters, he refreshes my soul.*
Psalm 23:2–3 *(NIV)*

I FLEW ACROSS THE COUNTRY, from San Francisco to Chicago and from Chicago to White Plains. I woke up at my friend Camilla's house in Connecticut after sleeping for twelve hours. Twelve hours. I think the last time I slept for twelve hours was when I was an infant.

Isn't it funny that in Psalms it says, "He MAKES me lie down in green pastures"? Shouldn't I just do that on my own? Apparently I don't. Sometimes Jesus has to MAKE me lie down.

I am so wound up with work deadlines, the boys' school schedule, the kids' program at church, and life in general that I have forgotten how to rest. I want Jesus to restore my soul. I just don't want to lie down in green pastures or follow Him beside the quiet waters. But, apparently, those are nonnegotiables.

So today, I am recognizing I am tired. Really, super, crazy tired. And really, what I am missing out on when I don't take a nap is restoring my soul. And that's not good.

Maybe you are right there with me, exhausted and bone weary. I have a thought that maybe, just maybe, we should let Jesus *make* us lie down. It could be a start to a new way of living. So let's take a deep breath…and then bring on the nap. —SUSANNA FOTH AUGHTMON

FAITH STEP: *Say, "Jesus, thank You so much for knowing me better than I know myself. Please make me lie down. I am ready for those green pastures and still waters. Show me how to rest in You."*

SUNDAY, APRIL 2

*Let all that I am praise the Lord; with my whole heart
I will praise his holy name.
Psalm 103:1 (NLT)*

MY HUSBAND AND I WILL CELEBRATE our thirty-fifth wedding anniversary this year. Our three grown kids and their spouses are doing well. We enjoy six beautiful grandchildren, a growing ministry, and great health. To the casual observer, my life looks pretty good. But wait—things aren't always what they seem.

A sensitive family matter breaks my heart. How can this be resolved and the relationship restored? I watch my youngest daughter and her husband pursue his desire to attend medical school. Where will this dream lead them, and what will the financial cost be?

And what about my future? Will I land another book proposal, or has that chapter closed? How long should my husband and I continue ministry before handing the leadership to someone else?

Fear of the unknown tugs at one corner of my heart. Grief over the family situation tears at another. These concerns could consume me if I let them, but I choose not to give them such power. Instead, I do what today's key verse says: I praise Jesus with all that I am, including the hidden, broken places of my heart. Doing so reminds me that He's present and powerful. He's sovereign, wise, and aware of every detail. He's faithful and filled with unfailing love.

I worship Jesus with everything I am. I praise Him with my whole heart. And Jesus does what only He can do—He calms my heart and assures me that all will be well. —GRACE FOX

FAITH STEP: *Draw a heart. In it, write the fears and worries you feel today. Ask Jesus to help you praise Him with your whole heart, even those parts that feel anxious or afraid.*

MONDAY, APRIL 3

And God is able to bless you abundantly, so that in all things at all times, having all that you need, you will abound in every good work. 2 *Corinthians* 9:8 *(NIV)*

OUR TV DIED RECENTLY. Or as our children would say... their only reason for living is gone. One of the boys came into my room last night with a distressed look on his face. I thought something horrible had happened. "What's wrong, buddy?" I asked.

A hint of tears glittered in his eyes. I thought maybe one of his brothers had hauled off and punched him... because that happens around here. Instead he whispered, "No TV."

Being the loving and caring mom that I am, I said something like, "We are all disappointed, but you don't get to pout endlessly about not having a TV." I was even getting a little angry. Because we have every single thing we need: food, clothes, shelter, and each other. And doesn't he know his dad and I do EVERY SINGLE THING we can to provide him and his brothers with everything they need?

I was starting to feel justifiably outraged. Then I felt a nudge in my spirit. Almost like Jesus was saying, *He sure sounds like you when you tell Me what you want. By the way, don't you know I do EVERY SINGLE THING I can to provide you with everything you need?*

Sometimes Jesus uses our kids to teach us grown-up lessons. He knows we need to be reminded to be thankful for all He has done for us. He has given us more than we could ever hope for. Jesus is so good. He is so loving, faithful, kind. He never fails us. Not ever. So that we can abound in every good work and praise Him for all His abundant blessings—blessings far greater than any TV.

—SUSANNA FOTH AUGHTMON

FAITH STEP: *Make a gratitude list of ten things you are thankful to Jesus for and meditate on them.*

TUESDAY, APRIL 4

Call out for insight, and cry aloud for understanding. Proverbs 2:3 (CEB)

YEARS AGO, I TOOK MY TWO-YEAR-OLD to a children's museum near our home. Inside, there was an ambulance built for exploration. My little one climbed aboard, excited to see the flashing buttons and pulleys.

A little boy with blond hair was inside the ambulance with his father. He stared at my daughter, then at me. "Is your skin real?" he asked.

Shocked, I took a minute to absorb his question. I looked at the boy and then at my daughter, knowing his curiosity about our brown skin should not be dismissed. At the same time, I value the skin God put us in and I wanted the boy to know that. I searched for the right words as my daughter gleefully turned the steering wheel. "It's as real as your skin," I finally replied.

The boy blinked and turned to his father, who took his hand and led him away.

I don't know if my answer satisfied the boy's curiosity, but I hoped it gave him a morsel of understanding.

Jesus is known as the greatest teacher, and His lessons weren't always clear when they were given. When He said to Nicodemus he must be "born again" to see God's kingdom, the Pharisee was confused, yet Jesus left him with that and it had to be enough.

I hope what I said resonates with the little boy and in time he will become more interested in the character of others than in the package they come in. So maybe one day, if he ever sees my beautiful brown daughter again, whether in a kindergarten classroom or a work cubicle, he will appreciate her for who, not what, she is. —TARICE L. S. GRAY

FAITH STEP: *Reach out to someone with whom you've had a disagreement or quarrel. See if you can find a morsel of understanding.*

WEDNESDAY, APRIL 5

When we were utterly helpless, Christ came at just the right time and died for us sinners. Romans 5:6 (NLT)

I WAS A PRESCHOOLER when my parents hired a contractor to build a house for our family in our small Alberta town. At least a dozen other houses went up in the neighborhood over the course of a few months.

Winter slowed the building projects to a near halt. Finally spring arrived, and the snow and ice melted. That's when the construction vehicles returned to our street, which was yet unpaved. Their constant rumbling to and fro on the road churned the dirt and slush into a mucky mess.

One afternoon I went outside to play. The roadway resembled chocolate pudding. I couldn't resist. Proudly sporting my new lime-green rubber boots, I walked into the center of the street and promptly became stuck. I tried to move, but both feet were mired. That's when I heard it—the roar of an approaching truck. I panicked and began to cry.

Within moments a neighbor appeared. "You're okay," he said as he plucked me from the goo and carried me to safety.

When I was eight years old, I needed a rescuer of another sort. Even as a child, I knew sin carried consequences and understood that I couldn't save myself from them. I was helpless, and Jesus was my only hope. I cried to Him, and He saved me by bringing me into His family.

Decades later, Jesus continues to rescue me. Sometimes I get stuck in fear or uncertainty or insecurity. When that happens, I call to Him for help. He's my faithful friend and Savior. He's the One who never fails to lift me up and set my feet on solid ground. —GRACE FOX

FAITH STEP: *Thank Jesus that He willingly comes to our rescue when we need help. Imagine how different our lives would look if He told us to save ourselves.*

THURSDAY, APRIL 6

By day the Lord commands his steadfast love, and at night his song is with me, a prayer to the God of my life. Psalm 42:8 (ESV)

SOMETIMES I AM AFRAID OF THE DARK. I have reason to be. During spring here in the Northwoods, I have been getting home from the hospital in the wee hours of the morning and park at the bottom of the hill that leads to the cabin. April is mud season when snowmelt and frost heave make the driveway impassable.

It's also the time bears emerge from hibernation, feeling more than a little peckish and very protective of their cubs. They aren't looking for a fight, but anyone who inadvertently steps between Mama Bear and her babies is in big trouble.

So I sing loudly and shake my keys while I trudge uphill through the mire that, in a month or two, will be my driveway again.

This long-ago psalmist's emotional state fluctuated from despair to hope like April's thermometer. He longed for God's presence when people jeered, "Where is your God?" He once led worshippers to the house of God with songs and shouts of joy, but now he was cast down and in turmoil. He poured out his heart in prayer as he faced difficulties and dark feelings. He finally counseled himself to hope in the Lord and believe in His love—a love so real that it felt like a presence—the Lord's song with him in the dark.

Jesus still does that. We are not alone. Jesus is with me—with you—whatever we're going through. He said, "Lo, I am with you always" (Matthew 28:20, NAS).

He meant it. —SUZANNE DAVENPORT TIETJEN

FAITH STEP: *Are you truly alone? Sing a psalm or favorite hymn. Are you feeling alone in a crowd? Try writing a psalm. Whichever you choose, imagine Jesus right there with you in the song.*

FRIDAY, APRIL 7

Create in me a new, clean heart, O God, filled with clean thoughts and right desires. Psalm 51:10 (TLB)

AS A BEAUTY CONSULTANT through the years, I've often encouraged my customers to take care of their skin. Some buy the full package of products, giving attention to foundation, eyes, lips, and cheeks. But others prefer only the basic items for skin care.

Regardless of their preference, when they were in my home, I used a simple illustration to make a point. "What would happen if I neglected to dust my coffee table or furniture very often?" I swiped a finger across the surface of a nearby table to prove my point. And of course, a clean trail always appeared, parting the dust like the Red Sea.

Then I presented the beauty principle: "That's the way impurities collect on our faces. It's why daily cleansing and basic skin care are so important."

Jesus added a different perspective—and beauty principle—when He was dining in the home of a Pharisee one day. Jesus's omission of the Jewish hand-washing custom upset the host. Unfortunately, the host's emphasis on cleanliness was symptomatic of his neglect of inner-heart issues. Jesus's rebuke to the Pharisee went deeper than soap could ever cleanse: "You Pharisees wash the outside, but inside you are still dirty" (Luke 11:39, TLB). He wanted them to know the necessity of soul-cleansing.

Outer cleansing is important for our faces and our bodies. But if we focus on the outside alone, we'll miss the real meaning of beauty. That's why I love to add an additional word of encouragement to my customers and friends concerning beauty: true beauty is reflected from the inside out. —REBECCA BARLOW JORDAN

FAITH STEP: *The next time you wash your face, ask Jesus to keep your heart clean too.*

SATURDAY, APRIL 8

When Jesus saw his mother there, and the disciple whom he loved standing nearby, he said to her, "Woman, here is your son," and to the disciple, "Here is your mother." From that time on, this disciple took her into his home. John 19:26–27 (NIV)

LATE ONE AFTERNOON, my daughter prepared dinner in the kitchen while also monitoring sounds from the living room. Instead of entertaining their baby sister, the two older siblings were bickering. As Holly pulled out a pan of cornbread from the oven, she decided she needed to intervene. During the next few seconds, two things happened simultaneously. Holly walked to the doorway to tell her kids to settle down, and my five-year-old grandson ran to the doorway to complain to his mother. His face collided with the hot pan.

I cringed when I saw the bright red burn on Roman's cheek and lips a couple of days later. "You poor boy," I said. "That must have really hurt when your face bumped that pan."

"Yeah, Nana," he agreed, "it felt just like fire on my skin!" I commented that the pain must have made him cry. But Holly explained that instead of crying, he tried to console *her* since she was so distraught over the accident.

This evidence that Roman's love for his mom overshadowed his immediate pain reminded me of someone else. Even while dying on the Cross, Jesus arranged for John to care for His mother. Jesus made sure she would be protected.

During painful episodes in life, it's easy to get self-absorbed. With Christ's help, I can learn to follow His example of reaching out to others even when I'm hurting or distressed. —DIANNE NEAL MATTHEWS

FAITH STEP: *Ask Jesus to give you an opportunity to set aside your personal problems, struggles, and concerns today and to minister to someone who needs a kind word or loving touch.*

PALM SUNDAY, APRIL 9

They took palm branches and went out to meet [Jesus], shouting,
"Hosanna!" "Blessed is he who comes in the name of the Lord!"
"Blessed is the king of Israel!" John 12:13 (NIV)

IN MY CHURCH on Palm Sunday or Passion Sunday, as it is sometimes called, the children march into the sanctuary singing "Hosanna to the King of Kings" and waving palm branches. It's always a cute spectacle and celebratory in nature. But I find it ironic that it has a much darker meaning.

Passion comes from the word that means "suffer." That we mark Jesus's triumphal entry into Jerusalem as the beginning of His suffering tells us something about the meaning of Palm Sunday. Because while the crowds cheered to welcome Him, they had no idea what He was about. They hoped He was the Messiah, which to their minds meant a political leader Who would overthrow the Romans. This was symbolized by the palms. The focus of the people was the material world—which vastly underestimated Him. Jesus's mission was something far greater.

The crowds also showed the fickleness of the human heart. It only took a few days for the cheers to turn to shouts of anger and insult. The same voices crying "Hosanna!" on this day soon would be calling for Pilate to "Crucify Him!"

As Jesus did, we know where the story is going and we cling to that hope. But even as our eyes are fixed on Easter morning, let us not forget the rough and rocky road He took to get us there.
—GWEN FORD FAULKENBERRY

FAITH STEP: *Holy Week is a time for reflection. In what ways can you identify with Jesus's experience of being celebrated by the crowd, only to soon be maligned? Is there a time you've praised Him, only to discard Him when He didn't perform what you expected? If you haven't already, ask Him to forgive you for that.*

MONDAY OF HOLY WEEK, APRIL 10

*Jesus entered the temple courts and drove out all who were buying and
selling there. He overturned the tables of the money changers and
the benches of those selling doves. "It is written," he said to them, "'My house
will be called a house of prayer,' but you are making it 'a den of robbers.'"*
Matthew 21:12–13 (NIV)

JESUS IS A SOURCE of endless fascination for me, and one of the reasons is that He is so impossible to contain. While writers, teachers, and preachers may try to understand Who He is and then explain that to others, there is no putting Jesus in a box. Just when you think you know what He's up to, He does something that seems totally different. He's always one step ahead, always being about His Father's business (Luke 2:49).

Consider this. On Palm Sunday He rides into town on a donkey to the sound of cheering crowds. Then the next day the very first thing He does is to go to the temple and start turning over tables, driving out corruption as He clarifies what church is for.

One of my favorite memes reads, "When asking what would Jesus do, remember that turning over tables and driving people out is an option." The same humble servant king who rode into town on a donkey rose up the next day and cleaned house with righteous anger.

We'll see other facets of His character as we walk with Him through Holy Week. But the overarching theme of Jesus's life is that He didn't follow any set formula for behavior. He followed the Spirit, wherever God told Him to go. —GWEN FORD FAULKENBERRY

FAITH STEP: *Do you tend to think of Jesus as a one-dimensional figure? A suffering servant? A conquering king? He's so much more than we could ever ask or imagine. Let Jesus enter your mind today and then follow Him—in all of His many aspects—by allowing His spirit to guide your steps.*

TUESDAY OF HOLY WEEK, APRIL 11

The kingdom of God will be . . . given to a people who will produce its fruit.
Matthew 21:43 (NIV)

HOLY TUESDAY IS AN INTERESTING DAY if we look at what Matthew's Gospel says. Jesus seems to start and end the day with a focus on fruit.

Matthew 21 tells us that on the morning of Holy Tuesday, Jesus was walking with His disciples. He was hungry. Verse 19 says that "seeing a fig tree by the road, he went up to it but found nothing on it except leaves. Then he said to it, 'May you never bear fruit again!' Immediately the tree withered."

His disciples were amazed at this, and so am I. It's so human. Almost like opening your fridge to find the last apple or orange has been eaten by your teenager. But Jesus takes it extraordinarily hard. And the fruitless tree pays.

What's going on here? Was He craving figs that badly? I think we find a clue to the deeper theme later in the day, when Jesus tells the parable of the tenants. In this parable He compares the current religious establishment to those who tend a vineyard for their own personal gain. When the landowner learns what they have done, he takes his vineyard and gives it to others he trusts to care for it properly, to produce the fruit.

I think Jesus was discouraged by the lack of fruit He saw being produced in people's lives. After all, it was the religious leaders of the day who sought to kill Him—the very ones who were supposed to be the caretakers of God's kingdom. —GWEN FORD FAULKENBERRY

FAITH STEP: *Jesus promises that the kingdom of God is ours if we produce fruit. In fact, that's how His followers are known—by our fruits. What is one tangible way you can care for a need in your community today?*

WEDNESDAY OF HOLY WEEK, APRIL 12

Then one of the Twelve—the one called Judas Iscariot—went to the chief priests and asked, "What are you willing to give me if I deliver him over to you?" So they counted out for him thirty pieces of silver. From then on Judas watched for an opportunity to hand him over.
Matthew 26:14–16 (NIV)

IT'S WEDNESDAY OF HOLY WEEK—midweek—and what happened on this day truly was the turning point in the drama of the Passion. This was the day, the Bible tells us, that Judas Iscariot, one of Jesus's inner circle, sought out the chief priests and offered to become a spy within Jesus's camp. A betrayer.

Outside of the physical and spiritual pain Jesus suffered, the betrayals by Judas and later by Peter had to be the most emotionally painful things that happened to Him that week. Anyone who has ever been betrayed knows what I'm talking about. When you trust someone to be your friend, to look out for your good, and he or she betrays that trust, it's huge. It's a cancer that devours your soul, leaves you gutted and raw. And even if you are able to heal from the pain of betrayal over time, it's something that changes you forever.

Enter Jesus. Not on this day as a conqueror or a king, but as a comforter. We get the chance to know Him in His own vulnerability—and to see that He knows how it feels, even this. He understands. He could have chosen a different path, but He chose this one. He chose to suffer betrayal so that we could know we are not alone when we are betrayed. —GWEN FORD FAULKENBERRY

FAITH STEP: *Is there someone you need to forgive for letting you down, even for a shattering betrayal? Ask Jesus to help you go there, since He knows the way. In His power, choose to forgive, letting go of the pain, and walk on toward the newness of life.*

MAUNDY THURSDAY, APRIL 13

"A new command I give you: Love one another. As I have loved you, so you must love one another. By this everyone will know that you are my disciples, if you love one another." John 13:34–35 (NIV)

THE WORD *MAUNDY* comes from the Latin word *mandatum*, which is usually translated as "commandment." We call the Thursday before Easter "Maundy Thursday" because it is the day when Jesus ate a meal with His disciples, washed their feet, and gave them this new commandment. The meal was essentially a Passover meal, a time to remember how God had delivered His people so long ago. I wonder if the disciples had any idea what was going on—the significance of the meal, the feet washing and, of course, the commandment.

I don't believe they really did. Jesus says as much when He tells Peter, "You do not realize now what I am doing, but later you will understand" (verse 7). He said this before He washed their feet, but later, when they fall asleep in the garden while He is praying, we see evidence again that they must be clueless.

What a lonely night this must have been for Jesus. For me the loneliest times are not necessarily when I'm by myself. It's worse when I'm surrounded by people—even people who love me—but they have no idea what I'm going through. Here Jesus is facing betrayal, beating, and an agonizing death, and His closest friends don't get it. They love Him, sure. But the burden is His to bear largely alone.

Maundy Thursday is about remembering what Jesus did for you.
—GWEN FORD FAULKENBERRY

FAITH STEP: *If you take communion, see His body broken for you in the bread, His spilled blood in the wine. Remember that He faced it all alone—so you would never have to face anything without Him.*

GOOD FRIDAY, APRIL 14

Jesus said, "It is finished." With that, he bowed his head and gave up his spirit. John 19:30 (NIV)

IMAGINE A WORLD WITHOUT JESUS. You know Him; you love Him; you rely on His presence, His guidance, His faithful love. But, suddenly, He is taken from you—gone. That person Who comforts you in times of trial has vanished. Your security in times of doubt—like a rug pulled from under your feet. The One you turn to when you need someone to listen, to care, to help. He is no more. You are utterly alone.

This must have been how the disciples felt on that Friday—hardly a good Friday—when Jesus was killed. We've seen how limited their understanding was in the events leading up to His death. But now reality has hit them hard. Jesus is gone. Dead. About to be buried in a tomb. His last words: *It is finished.*

I wonder if those standing nearby understood what His words meant. For those people who loved Jesus in His flesh and blood, I wonder how badly those words hurt, if they cut like a sword. *It's over. It's finished. The dream is dead.*

The Bible says that darkness covered the earth. Take a moment to soak that in. The Light of the World literally went out. Beyond sad, it must have been terrifying. Can you imagine a world without Jesus in it?

We don't want to imagine our lives without Jesus. But if we are to enter into His sufferings and fully appreciate what He has done, we must go there. —GWEN FORD FAULKENBERRY

FAITH STEP: *Sit in a dark room with a lighted candle that symbolizes Jesus and the Life that He offers us all. Now snuff it out. This is Good Friday, but Sunday's coming.*

HOLY SATURDAY, APRIL 15

Weeping may endure for a night, but joy cometh in the morning.
Psalm 30:5 (KJV)

WAITING. THAT'S WHAT Holy Saturday's about. As Jesus remained in the tomb, I imagine the disciples beaten and with bloodshot eyes, anxious and afraid. Surely they were asking each other, "What do we do now?"

Like the wife who waits for news of her deployed husband. Like a family in the waiting room during surgery. Like the one waiting on a fertility test. The farmer waiting for rain. Or a child waiting for his parents to come home.

We don't like to wait, especially when we're fearful of the outcome. Waiting can be maddening. Especially when God is silent, we may feel abandoned. At the mercy of our circumstances. It's stressful. Fear-inducing. But Holy Saturday is also the seventh day of the week. I'm sure that was no accident. It's the Sabbath—a day of rest.

There's a message here, I believe, for those of us who wait, a message of rest. Even in the grieving, even in the unknown. Even in the questions and the heartache and the pain. Or maybe especially then. Jesus seems to be calling from the tomb: *Find your rest. And hope in Me.* —GWEN FORD FAULKENBERRY

FAITH STEP: *As you observe Holy Saturday, hold fast to this promise: "They that wait upon the Lord shall renew their strength; they shall mount up with wings as eagles; they shall run, and not be weary; and they shall walk, and not faint" (Isaiah 40:31, KJV).*

EASTER SUNDAY, APRIL 16

Jesus said unto her, I am the resurrection, and the life: he that believeth in me, though he were dead, yet shall he live: and whosoever liveth and believeth in me shall never die. Believest thou this?
John 11:25–26 (KJV)

WE HAVE A BIBLE STORYBOOK from which we read to our kids every night. Usually Harper stretches out on the couch, and Grace and Adelaide take turns sitting on the floor in front of my chair while I comb out their hair. Stone sits in his chair with his reading glasses on, and Stella perches on his lap so she can see the pictures.

The other night we were reading the story of Jesus's Crucifixion, which the writer handled delicately. It seemed to me to have the right balance of realism along with sensitivity to a child's perspective. So there was the sadness of the death without its being gruesome. We all paused to respect the story and give gravitas to the moment of Jesus's death on the Cross. After a silence, Stella bounced up and down on her daddy's lap. "I love the next page! Turn it, Daddy!"

We all looked at her, questioning.

"It's when Jesus comes alive!"

I want to carry that with me every day for the rest of my life. The simple truth, the excitement, the childlike acceptance of the miracle. The anticipation. The redemption. Most of all, the hope I saw in my daughter's eyes.

The story of Jesus is the greatest story ever told. Because He died and rose again, there is hope for the world. —GWEN FORD FAULKENBERRY

FAITH STEP: *This Easter Sunday, turn the page in your own life. Let Jesus take you from death into the promise of His Resurrection. Join with Him and commit to living His abundant life today!*

MONDAY, APRIL 17

And he took bread, gave thanks and broke it, and gave it to them, saying, "This is my body given for you; do this in remembrance of me." Luke 22:19 (NIV)

MY FRIEND VICKI and her family traveled out of state for Easter. Even though they were taking their holiday on the road and her children were high school and college age, she made the effort to bring supplies so that on Easter morning she could surprise them with their traditional basket of treats.

Easter morning, her daughter saw the baskets and complained, "Why didn't you hide them? I liked when we had to hunt for them."

Vicki was crushed. Instead of thanks, she received a complaint. Is it any wonder that moms sometimes feel unappreciated for their efforts?

Her account made me think of how often I react to Jesus's gifts in that way. He guides me toward an area of service, yet I look at someone else's ministry and tell Him, "Thanks, but I'd like that better." He places me in a family of people I love, yet certain actions or attitudes rub me wrong. "Jesus, can't you change them for me?" He provides a work project, but in the middle of it, all I can do is whine. "I know I begged you for this job, but it's too hard."

After Jesus sends a blessing my way, I imagine Him watching with eager anticipation to see my reaction. I do know that He has set a beautiful example for us. On the night He was betrayed—facing ultimate suffering and death for our sakes—Luke tells us that Jesus "gave thanks." That reminds me to set my heart toward gratitude, no matter what the circumstance. —SHARON HINCK

FAITH STEP: *Make this a day of giving thanks. Notice the gifts that Jesus has placed before you—even if you are in the midst of suffering—and thank Him.*

TUESDAY, APRIL 18

Jesus said to her, "Mary." John 20:16 (ESV)

"JESUS SAID TO HER, 'ERIN.'" Try it with your name. Feel anything? I don't know about you, but when I speak those words out loud, my stomach does a flip, my throat feels thick, and my eyes might well up a little.

Mary Magdalene was heartbroken in this scene. She was weeping outside Jesus's tomb, and she'd probably wept much of the time since He was arrested three days earlier. When the risen Jesus appeared to her, she didn't recognize Him at first.

But then He spoke her name. In that one word that was so personal to Mary, she heard not only His knowledge of and familiarity with her but also His call to her to trust in Him and believe He is Lord.

It's beyond beautiful. It creates a yearning in me to experience that kind of closeness with Him. How about you?

Say "Jesus said" again with your name.

Way back in the Old Testament days, the prophet Isaiah wrote, "But now—this is what the Lord says—he who created you, Jacob, he who formed you, Israel: 'Do not fear, for I have redeemed you; I have summoned you by name; you are mine'" (Isaiah 43:1, NIV).

And then one of the first words Jesus, the Redeemer, spoke to someone after He rose was her name. Into her fears and sorrow, in the very middle of her greatest heartache, He called Mary by name.

Say that powerful, life-giving phrase to yourself as often as it takes today to understand that Jesus is calling you right now by name. You are His. He delights in you. —ERIN KEELEY MARSHALL

FAITH STEP: *Whatever ups and downs your day takes, speak Jesus's words to yourself, several times if you have to: "Jesus says to me, '_____.'"*

WEDNESDAY, APRIL 19

Then he [Jesus] said it a third time: "Simon, son of John, do you love me?"
Peter was upset that he asked for the third time, "Do you love me?"
so he answered, "Master, you know everything there is to know. You've got to
know I love you." Jesus said, "Feed my sheep." John 21:17 (MSG)

I CARED FOR NEARLY three hundred sheep in our years on the farm. Some hold a special place in my heart: Claire, who valiantly fought illness and was left stunted, somehow delivered big, beautiful lambs; Patience, who gorged herself and nearly died, then for the rest of her life willingly took medicine while the rest of the flock ran away; and then there was Farah, who loved me.

Jesus talked about sheep when He conducted a kind of healing of the memories for Peter, who had denied Him three times. By the fire where He'd cooked Peter's breakfast, Jesus asked Peter three times if he loved Him. Every time Peter answered, Jesus gave him an assignment using a different word for sheep.

The first time, Jesus said, "Feed my lambs." The second time, He said, "Shepherd my sheep." Then, the third time, when Jesus said, "Feed my sheep," He used a distinctive word, *probátion*, a diminutive that referred to a more mature sheep who was dear to the Shepherd. The word was a term of endearment.

Afterward, Jesus asked Peter, like He asks each of us, to follow Him. Peter did. Brash and impulsive before, now he was confident but humble. He didn't throw his weight around. Transformed, he was diligent in tending the flock.

In following Jesus, we too can expect to be changed. And very much loved. —SUZANNE DAVENPORT TIETJEN

FAITH STEP: *Do you believe you are dear to Jesus? Ruminate on the idea that you are loved and precious. Turn that thought over in your mind several times throughout the day.*

THURSDAY, APRIL 20

But we had hoped that he was the one to redeem Israel. Luke 24:21 (ESV)

IMAGINE YOUR LIFETIME OF HOPES dashed in a day. No, generations upon generations of hopes, seemingly crushed within hours.

This is the feeling the two men on the road to Emmaus talked about to the mysterious man they'd later realize was Jesus resurrected. In those crushing overnights since Jesus's last breath on the Cross, hope was absent. Maybe you know what disappointed hope feels like.

My sweet mother-in-law passed away a month ago. She'd been in failing health for years, particularly in the ten months preceding her going home. While we weren't surprised by her death, we felt the loss of her life and of some hope. We prayed and longed for our hopes of healing to come true, but we were not to see it on earth.

When hopes are yanked from under us, our hope for the future is stolen too. My kids and their cousins won't grow up with their grandmother in their lives. There are no more memories to be made with her in this life.

"But we had hoped that he was the one to redeem Israel." The men on the road spoke the dreams they'd heard from birth.

But Jesus knew something they didn't, just as He knows joys about a believer's future we can't overestimate. When my mother-in-law finally stood before Jesus Himself on that beautiful April morning with a sky backlit by a glorious Technicolor sunrise, she understood real hope. She was forever changed, even more than the men heading to Emmaus were transformed. And we have the hope of forever with our Savior and spiritual family. —ERIN KEELEY MARSHALL

FAITH STEP: *What are you hoping for most? Are you looking at Jesus first and recognizing Him in your circumstances? Ask Him for eyes and a heart to see and trust and hang on to hope.*

FRIDAY, APRIL 21

The Lord bless you and keep you; the Lord make his face shine on you and be gracious to you. . . . Numbers 6:24–26 (NIV)

DURING MY CHILDHOOD, I loved being around my sweet aunt Mary Nelle. As an adult, I rarely saw her after I moved away. But sometimes she stopped by my parents' house when I visited, and she showed up to support me when I signed books at a local store. Years later, due to dementia, Aunt Mary Nelle moved into a nursing home.

One spring day my mom and I decided to visit her. I hadn't seen my aunt in a few years and wondered if she would recognize me. As soon as I walked in, Aunt Mary Nelle's face lit up. I kissed her cheek, and Mom asked her, "Do you know who that is?"

"Yes," my aunt said. "She's . . . she's . . . your daughter."

I held her hand for the rest of the visit as she smiled and occasionally gazed at me with her sparkling brown eyes.

I visited my aunt Mary Nelle a few more times over the next couple of years, but she never recognized me again. When she died, I drew comfort from reading the many messages left on my cousin's Facebook page. People often commented on my aunt's friendliness and how she treated everyone she met with kindness and respect. My tears started when I read how someone enjoyed "seeing her face light up when people she loved walked into a room."

I tried to imagine how my aunt's face lit up when she saw the Savior she loved and served. And how His face glowed as He welcomed her home. I hope to follow my aunt's example of loving and respecting others. And I look forward to seeing my Savior's face light up one day for me too. —DIANNE NEAL MATTHEWS

FAITH STEP: *The next time you pray, imagine Jesus's face lighting up as you approach Him and then gazing at you lovingly as you talk with Him.*

SATURDAY, APRIL 22

The angel of the Lord encamps around those who fear him, and he delivers them. Psalm 34:7 (NIV)

THIS PAST WEEK we found ourselves hunkered down on the floor in my son's bedroom because a manhunt was taking place in our neighborhood. A suspected murderer who was considered armed and dangerous was on the loose. We had been advised to barricade ourselves in our homes. Scott began gathering weapons: a huge candlestick and our industrial-strength blender blade to wield as a sword. He placed wedges under the doors and secured the windows. My job was to be calm and call 911 if someone tried to break down our carefully constructed defenses while Scott took down the perpetrator.

We were an hour and a half into lockdown when we heard a stun grenade go off. Scott and I peeked through our front windows to see the police standing in front of our house and blocking off our street with yellow tape. Helicopters were circling overhead. Knowing they were there gave us a sense of safety.

We prayed heavy, as my mother-in-law would say. For Jesus to keep us safe and that no one would be hurt, especially the officers who were standing guard in front of our house. A half hour later, the police announced that the suspect had been apprehended. Our prayers had been answered.

The truth is that Jesus is always with us, protecting us, in the middle of our fear or when we are in crisis. Life can be scary at times, but Jesus promised to never leave us or forsake us. He is guarding us, surrounding us with His love, keeping us in the circle of His peace.
—SUSANNA FOTH AUGHTMON

FAITH STEP: *Walk around your house and thank Jesus for His daily protection and care.*

SUNDAY, APRIL 23

Do you think anyone is going to be able to drive a wedge between us and Christ's love for us? There is no way! Not trouble, not hard times . . . not homelessness. . . . None of this fazes us because Jesus loves us.
Romans 8:38–39 (MSG)

THE STORY OF RUTH has always inspired me. Having lost her husband and two sons in a foreign land, Naomi, Ruth's mother-in-law, decides to move back home to Bethlehem. She urges her two daughters-in-law to remain in the land of Moab. Orpah stays, but Ruth wants to follow Naomi, accepting her mother-in-law's God and home as her own.

Yet the picture Naomi paints of her God is not accurate. Reflecting beliefs that God's blessing equaled prosperity and His displeasure meant disaster, Naomi's bitter spirit bubbles to the surface as soon as her feet touch home: "Don't call me Naomi; call me Bitter. The Strong One has dealt me a bitter blow. . . . The Strong One ruined me" (Ruth 1:20, MSG).

Her attitude changes, however, when Boaz, a distant relative, walks into their lives as kinsman-redeemer, a groom for Ruth, and producer of Naomi's first grandchild: "Why, God bless that man! God hasn't quite walked out on us after all! He still loves us, in bad times as well as good!" (Ruth 2:20, MSG). That grandchild fit into King David's lineage, a direct line to Jesus.

Even today, we form the same opinion about Jesus, God's Son. We blame bad circumstances on Him, allowing bitterness to rule. We may even waver in our faith—until good times return.

Jesus loves us—in bad times and in good. Once invited, He walks into each life, not only as the Kinsman-Redeemer but as our Bridegroom, Savior, and King. —REBECCA BARLOW JORDAN

FAITH STEP: *Today, thank Jesus that He loves you—in both the good times and the bad.*

MONDAY, APRIL 24

Abraham planted a tamarisk tree in Beersheba, and there he called on the name of the Lord, the Eternal God.
Genesis 21:33 (NIV)

LIFE HAS BROUGHT a lot of changes in the last six years. My husband changed jobs. We moved to the South, when I'd always pictured myself in the North. We added more kids to our family and welcomed two beautiful grandchildren. And we bought a twelve-passenger van to fit everyone inside!

Six years ago John and I had no idea how our life was about to change. And I have no idea what the next six years will hold. Change happens to everyone, and that's why we need an unchanging Savior.

"Jesus Christ is the same yesterday and today and forever," we read in Hebrews 13:8 (NIV). The Lord Whom you read about in the Old Testament and New Testament is the same Lord involved in your life today. Jesus-in-you is still all-sufficient, merciful, and powerful. He still longs to feed the hungry, comfort the hurting, provide rest to the weary and peace to the restless.

Sometimes it's easier to love and trust the Jesus in the Bible than to love and trust the Jesus Who is in us and Who actively wants to be involved in our lives. After all, we can read the outcomes of Bible stories. We can be observers, rather than part of the cast. Yet in all the ways Jesus wanted to work *then*, He desires to work *now*. God's Word isn't just a book about learning about Jesus. It's a book about learning how Jesus can also work in your life if you allow Him.
—TRICIA GOYER

FAITH STEP: *Take time today to read through some of your favorite Bible stories. What attributes of our Lord do you see in those stories? Make a list; then think of your life. What attributes of Jesus do you need to cling to today?*

Tuesday, April 25

Even though you are bad, you know how to give good gifts to your children. How much more your heavenly Father will give good things to those who ask him! Matthew 7:11 (NCV)

EVERY NOW AND THEN when I'm praying for something and doing my best to trust Jesus to provide, I end up battling the temptation to doubt the goodness He has for me. It's crazy, really. I have a long history of experiencing His faithfulness. I've felt His blessings and presence for years. But obviously I still have more abiding in Him to do. When I doubt Him, I'm only revealing that I'm not entering His presence consistently enough or remaining there.

As adults, we know the mixed bag that makes up life. We've felt the thrill of success and the pain of loss. We never know when Jesus will allow something hard to grow us and help us learn to seek Him more.

Long ago a friend commented on how Jesus had answered some long-awaited dreams for marriage and children. She was beyond grateful, but instead of feeling overwhelmed by peace and joy, she was riddled with misgiving about when the hammer blow would strike to even things out because she had reached some unspoken limit of the Lord's gifts to her. Maybe you can relate. I sure can.

The only solution I've found for this dilemma of faith is to pause my focus on the blessings and turn my gaze fully on Jesus. Like Peter, who started to sink when he took his eyes off the Lord, we're bound to lose joy and hope when we look around us instead of up to Jesus.

His blessings aren't intended primarily to highlight themselves. They are intended to point us to the Giver's heart, which is eternally constant and filled with good toward His own. —ERIN KEELEY MARSHALL

FAITH STEP: *Ask Jesus to fill you with His thoughts of love toward you because perfect love scatters fears of the unknown (1 John 4:18).*

WEDNESDAY, APRIL 26

Examine and test and evaluate your own selves to see whether you are holding to your faith and showing the proper fruits of it. Test and prove yourselves [not Christ]. Do you not yourselves realize and know [thoroughly by an ever-increasing experience] that Jesus Christ is in you...? 2 Corinthians 13:5 (AMP)

IN MY NURSING CAREER, I had to maintain the Neonatal Resuscitation Program (NRP) and Pediatric Advanced Life Support (PALS) certifications. Every two years, I reread textbooks and took written exams and simulations. Research shows that most of the content and skills are quickly forgotten if the skills are not used often.

I can attest to that. I was an NRP instructor, so I read the program updates and resuscitated newborns in my work. Passing that certification was a breeze. Not so, however, with PALS. I took care only of babies and rarely cared for children, whose needs are surprisingly different. I had to study much harder for the pediatric certification and needed this recertification experience.

The apostle Paul encouraged the Corinthian Christians to be sure to be grounded in faith and producing fruit from a vital relationship with Jesus. The Message version of the above verse reads, "Don't drift along taking everything for granted. Give yourselves regular checkups."

Just like I needed to submit to examinations in my career, I also need to examine myself spiritually here and now. It might be daily during my devotions; certainly before confronting a brother or sister about a problem; and, as a matter of course, before taking part in communion.

In the same way that I got better at resuscitating babies over time, I can expect to grow in grace as I hold to my faith by the power of Christ Who is in me. —SUZANNE DAVENPORT TIETJEN

FAITH STEP: *Quiet yourself before the Lord and then ask what you felt good about today. Close with prayer.*

THURSDAY, APRIL 27

The news about Jesus spread even more. Many people came to hear Jesus and to be healed of their sicknesses, but Jesus often slipped away to be alone so he could pray. Luke 5:15–16 (NCV)

IF YOU WERE AROUND in the 1970s and 1980s, you probably remember the Calgon commercials. One featured a woman standing in front of a background showing honking traffic, a crying baby, a barking dog, and an angry boss. The woman shouted, "Calgon, take me away!" The scene instantly shifted to her smiling in a bubble bath as the narrator urged viewers to pamper themselves. Those of us with small children laughed at the notion of enjoying a quiet, leisurely bath when we barely had a few minutes in the bathroom alone. But we did use the phrase "Calgon, take me away!" to signal that we needed a break from the pressures of life.

I see many articles about how to deal with stress and tension. Writers may recommend relaxation techniques, hobbies, minivacations, or retreats. But after thinking about the example Jesus set during His earthly ministry, I've come to understand something: when I think that I need "me time," it's really "knee time" that my soul hungers for.

As word spread about Jesus's healings and miracles, huge crowds sought Him. He often found Himself inundated with people clamoring for Him to meet their needs. How did He cope with such stress and demands? Jesus frequently slipped away by Himself to pray.

During certain seasons of life, it seems impossible for me to be alone for even a few minutes. But with the help of Scripture and prayer, I can draw strength, comfort, and wisdom from the One Who also found knee time important. —DIANNE NEAL MATTHEWS

FAITH STEP: *The next time you feel overwhelmed by the stress and pressures of your day, remember Jesus's example. Ask Him to take you away to that place of prayer.*

FRIDAY, APRIL 28

Let us then approach God's throne of grace with confidence, so that we may receive mercy and find grace to help us in our time of need.
Hebrews 4:16 (NIV)

AFTER BEING DIAGNOSED with a long-term illness, I prayed for healing. Weeks stretched to months and then to years. "Jesus," I asked, "do You want me to stop asking? Or should I pray smaller? For just one better day or relief from one symptom?"

No, He whispered to my heart, *pray bigger*.

Jesus reminded me of the millions of others who are struggling with this illness. He nudged me to pray beyond my own needs. Learning from the inside enabled me to pray fervently for others I'd never met…to pray for every person fighting a chronic illness. I'd also learned about research, medical advances, and political barriers that have caused obstacles to getting care for patients.

Excitement flooded me. Jesus was inviting me to be part of a bigger answer. So I began to intercede for change that could lead toward help and healing—not just for myself but for others.

My strength and abilities haven't improved, but I've witnessed startling answers to the bigger prayer. New possibilities for treatments are emerging, but sometimes Jesus allows His disciples to dwell in painful places "for such a time as this."

Are you fighting a uniquely difficult battle? Have you prayed for a breakthrough in your circumstances and felt discouraged? Jesus invites us to pray boldly for what we long for and need. But our circumstances can remind us to also "pray big" and intercede for others suffering in similar ways. —SHARON HINCK

FAITH STEP: *What is an earnest and long-term prayer you've offered? Today, think about others in a similar battle and pray boldly for them.*

SATURDAY, APRIL 29

"I tell you the truth, you will ask the Father directly, and he will grant your request because you use my name. . . . Ask, using my name, and you will receive, and you will have abundant joy." John 16:23–24 (NLT)

I RECENTLY ATTENDED a three-day business course on marketing. The instructor repeated a specific theme over the weekend. "Always network," he said. "Much of your ability to achieve your goals depends on who you know."

I've experienced this to be true. I recall pitching an idea to an editor at a conference. His interest immediately rose when I used songwriter Brian Doerksen's name.

"Brian wrote 'Come, Now Is the Time to Worship,'" I said. "That song was born in a very difficult season. Your readers would benefit by hearing its story."

The editor gave me the go-ahead to pursue the article.

On another occasion, a magazine asked me to write a drama-in-real-life account about a fishing boat accident. Researching it required contacting the Coast Guard, the police, a coroner, the survivors, and the deceased fishermen's widows. None of these people knew me, but they all recognized and trusted the name of the publication. Everyone granted interviews as a result.

Using influential names can gain us access to places where we'd be otherwise denied entry. But no name on earth is more powerful than that of Jesus. When we've chosen to follow Him, then we have the right to use it because we know Him. Doing so grants us access to the Father, guarantees answered prayer, and promises abundant joy.
—GRACE FOX

FAITH STEP: *God gave Jesus a name that is above every other name. Someday every knee will bow to it (Philippians 2:10). If physically able, spend a few moments on bended knee pondering and reverently repeating His name.*

SUNDAY, APRIL 30

---

*Jesus answered, "It is written: 'Man shall not live on bread alone,
but on every word that comes from the mouth of God.'" Matthew 4:4 (NIV)*

BIBLES WITH WIDE MARGINS on the sides for journaling thoughts and artwork right inside the Bible rather than in a separate book have rapidly gained popularity. Some have blank margins for that purpose. Others have artwork already sketched out for the reader to color in or embellish.

At first, I must admit, I thought of it as an offshoot of the scrapbooking craze. Or as a relaxation technique, which made me wonder if the journaling feature would enhance or detract from the true study of the Word.

As Jesus so often does when I listen to Him more carefully, He fed me another perspective, a different way of looking at the process.

During His ministry on earth, Jesus made it clear that He knew the Word, often quoting from the Old Testament and catching supposed scholars when they misspoke or misrepresented the Word.

My new perspective? What if Bible journaling increases memorization? What if coloring an illustrated verse becomes an exercise in meditating until the verse becomes locked in the reader's memory—and heart? What if lingering on the page isn't for art's sake, but for the sake of getting to know Jesus better as we hover over His words?

The Bible I use most frequently for study has narrow margins filled with artwork—musical notes beside verses that form worship songs, hearts for personally beloved passages, dates for when a verse came alive with new meaning.

How much stronger would our faith be if we *knew* God's Word like Jesus did? —CYNTHIA RUCHTI

FAITH STEP: *No matter how familiar you are with what the Bible says, make an effort to commit a verse, or even a phrase, to memory before the day ends.*

MONDAY, MAY 1

It is of the Lord's mercies that we are not consumed, because his compassions fail not. They are new every morning: great is thy faithfulness.
Lamentations 3:22–23 (KJV)

THE ABOVE PASSAGE is what formally ushered me into the church. I grew up Lutheran, and we were required to select and stitch into our minds and hearts a verse that would guide us on our faith journey. At twelve years old, the verse spoke to me in an innocent way, like a morning lullaby that soothes the uncertainty of the day.

As those uncertainties evolved from anxiety over a pop quiz in algebra to making the next month's mortgage payment after I lost my job, I grew more dependent on that verse and God's mercy.

During the great recession in 2008, my job was eliminated and I discovered I was expecting my first child. The news of my pregnancy was met with joy and anxiety from my husband and me as we wondered how we'd provide for our baby. Our stress was amplified a month after my daughter's delivery when our portion of the maternity bill came due: $90,000. *Mercy!* When we opened the bill, we looked at each other and laughed. There wasn't much else we could do.

But that night I prayed, desperately hoping the words of Jesus in Matthew 7 to "ask, seek, knock" would ring true in our lives. I asked Him for a financial miracle with the expectation that a windfall would sweep away our money woes. Instead, a week later we received a call from the hospital. Because we were able to confirm a substantial income loss, the debt was forgiven, gone, completely wiped out! Mercy. —TARICE L. S. GRAY

FAITH STEP: *Start your day with a thank-you to God for something He has done for you.*

TUESDAY, MAY 2

What the people of Israel sought so earnestly they did not obtain.
The elect among them did, but the others were hardened, as it is written:
"God gave them a spirit of stupor, eyes that could not see and
ears that could not hear, to this very day."
Romans 11:7–8 (NIV)

I GREW UP HEARING that Jesus died for everyone and that He keeps calling us to Himself. And all that is true. But it still surprises me to know that He sometimes hardens a heart (see Exodus 14, for instance). If someone willfully rejects Him, eventually He may close off her heart to Him and let her go her way into destruction.

For generations, the people of Israel, the nation Jesus was born to save, had been looking for a savior from Rome. But Jesus came to save them from their own sin. Although some Israelites saw Him as the Savior He was, as a nation they rejected Him and still do. The Bible is clear that the Lord has and may still harden people's hearts who choose to reject Him.

Jesus will not reject one of His own, but He does allow us to grieve His Holy Spirit. If we harden our own hearts with perpetual sin, Jesus will let us miss out on the richness of His presence, peace, and the other fruits of His Spirit. For instance, He'll let me choose not to forgive someone, and that choice won't negate my salvation. But it's a lose-lose decision for myself, for others in my life, for my relationship with Him, and for glorifying Him with my life.

Jesus is a warrior for my soul, but He also lets me have free will. When I ask Him, He will help keep my heart tender toward His work in me. —ERIN KEELEY MARSHALL

FAITH STEP: *Ask Jesus to give you a heart for Him so that you will know Him as He longs to be known.*

WEDNESDAY, MAY 3

*I reflect at night on who you are, O Lord, and
I obey your law because of this.*
Psalm 119:55 (NLT)

SOME PEOPLE, LIKE MY HUSBAND, Gene, enjoy the gift of sleep. I must have been absent on the day that gift was handed out.

My body lies still in bed, but my brain flits in a gazillion different directions. First my thoughts land on my family members, then on my work projects, and then on our finances and ministry obligations. Thoughts wing from one topic to the next, often dragging worry along with them.

Turning those worrisome thoughts into prayer (at times a difficult process) helps calm my mind and still my soul, especially when I take time to focus on the character of the One to Whom I pray.

"I praise You, Jesus, for loving me and my family," I whisper. "I praise You for being our protector, our provider, our Prince of Peace. I praise You for being faithful, a fortress in whom we can hide, and a refuge from the storms of life."

Reflecting on the character of Christ settles my anxious thoughts and soothes my spirit during the night. When I finally do fall asleep, it also causes me to sleep more restfully and wake with a more positive outlook the next morning.

I may have gone to bed concerned about a particular situation, but meditating on Jesus changes everything. My appreciation and love for Him deepens, and my trust in Him grows to handle every difficult situation I face. —GRACE FOX

FAITH STEP: *Write a couple of favorite Bible verses on a card and keep them by your bedside so you can meditate on truth when you can't sleep.*

THURSDAY, MAY 4

I have set the Lord always before me; because he is at my right hand,
I shall not be shaken.
Psalm 16:8 (ESV)

SUPERHEROES HAVE NOTHING OVER JESUS. That's an unnecessary statement for most of us. Or is it? Do we need an occasional reminder that He is not bound by time or space, by obstacles or hindrances like locked doors or prison walls? He leaps tall universes in a single bound. He walks through walls when necessary (John 20:26) and time travels at will (Luke 24:31).

He can be both before me, behind me, beside me, and within me at the same time (Colossians 1:27, Psalm 16:8, Isaiah 52:12). So what's the significance of verses like this one in the Psalms: "I have set the Lord always before me"?

By acts of will, faith, and invitation, we envision Jesus positioned between us and anything or anyone we might face. To-do list overwhelming? I can't even see it without looking at Jesus. Future uncertain? Jesus stands between me and my future. He stands between me and my reflection in the mirror. He stands between me and the threat of the doctor's prognosis or the award I was tempted to covet.

"Jesus, I'm facing an uncomfortable conversation with my neighbor. Would You please stand right here, in front of me, between us?"

"Jesus, my husband and I are not connecting as well as we should. Please stand between us; serve as the link that bridges the space between."

"Jesus, I disappointed my friend. Standing before me, would You intercede between us, please, and filter my words?" —CYNTHIA RUCHTI

FAITH STEP: *Until it becomes habit, you may need to visualize the moment of invitation when you "set" Jesus always before you. Imagine how safe you can feel with the ultimate Superhero standing between you and any disappointment, any threat!*

FRIDAY, MAY 5

Now I have a word for you who brashly announce, "Today—at the latest, tomorrow—we're off to such and such a city for the year. . . ." You don't know the first thing about tomorrow. You're nothing but a wisp of fog, catching a brief bit of sun before disappearing. Instead, make it a habit to say, "If the Master wills it and we're still alive, we'll do this or that." James 4:13–15 (MSG)

WHENEVER I TOLD HER what I was going to do, my grandma May corrected me, saying, "You don't know what tomorrow will bring. Say 'the Lord willing' instead." I couldn't see the point at the time.

Grandma May's warning hit home for me when I worked as a tech in the emergency room during nursing school. There I saw things that rocked my soul: death and dismemberment, people hurt so badly that their driver's license photos couldn't be used to identify them. More disturbing was the survivors' grief, worse because of the unexpectedness of the accidents or sudden violence.

No one expects to die today. Those who remain behind never imagined this and were left to think of what had gone unsaid, or worse, to remember what they *had* said before the door slammed behind someone they'd never see again in this world.

Working there, I realized the arrogance behind my illusions of invulnerability. Because I didn't appreciate how fragile life is, I treated others less carefully, less lovingly, than I could have.

My time in the ER had a disproportionally large effect on my life outside the hospital. Since then, I don't presume to lay claim to more than this moment. "The Lord willing," I say now, grateful for every new day. —SUZANNE DAVENPORT TIETJEN

FAITH STEP: *Today, secretly weigh your words, speaking to each person as if one of you will be gone tomorrow. Don't be gloomy—emphasize joy and laughter. Make pleasant memories.*

SATURDAY, MAY 6

Yet for us there is but one God, the Father, from whom all things came and for whom we live; and there is but one Lord, Jesus Christ, through whom all things came and through whom we live. 1 Corinthians 8:6 (NIV)

AT MY DESK ONE MORNING, I read Psalms about the majesty, power, and love of God. I thanked Him for life, for a new day.

My eyes strayed to my wooden in-box and a stack of mail that waited for responses. Spring meant graduations, weddings, and several birthdays. I wanted to make cards and send gifts. My computer screen winked, reminding me of a deadline for a project. The streak of dust on my desk warned that I wasn't keeping up on housework.

I forced my gaze back to the Psalms and continued to thank Jesus for being the Lord of the universe, yet pressure built in my neck. My shoulders tightened as I felt the weight of my to-do list. I was grateful for occasions to celebrate, grateful for work, grateful for a home. Yet I felt overwhelmed and exhausted, and my day had barely begun.

"Jesus, I acknowledge You are the Lord of the wind and waves, of life and death."

And . . . the quiet whisper prompted me.

My mind spun with mountains and oceans, with epic movements of the Gospel throughout history, with speculations about the grandeur of heaven. Yet those didn't seem to be the answer Jesus was waiting for.

Then I smiled, the tension easing from my muscles. "And You are the Lord of my to-do list!"

While I joyfully proclaimed His lordship over all the universe, I sometimes forget that He is strong and caring enough to guide the details of my day. —SHARON HINCK

FAITH STEP: *Write a to-do list for the day, then hold it up in prayer, acknowledging that Jesus watches over your goals and responsibilities.*

SUNDAY, MAY 7

*Then people brought little children to Jesus for him to place his hands on
them and pray for them. But the disciples rebuked them. Jesus said,
"Let the little children come to me, and do not hinder them, for the kingdom
of heaven belongs to such as these." Matthew 19:13–14 (NIV)*

I LOVE TO IMAGINE THIS SCENE. I wonder what it really looked like.
I mean, why were people bringing their kids to Jesus? Just to have
Him bless them? I doubt it was only this. I bet there were individual
needs. Even though in the illustrated Bibles I've seen for kids, the
children in this scene are mostly white, round-faced, and healthy
with happy looks on their faces, that's not how I imagine it at all.

First, I bet some of them were kicking and screaming. My three-
year-old certainly would have been. She hates Santa, the Easter
Bunny, and virtually anyone else, suited or not, that we've tried to
present her to, including the pastor of our church.

I'm also fairly certain these kids weren't white. And I bet they weren't
all healthy. Jesus was known as a healer, and surely parents were desperate for Him to touch their kids, pray for them, and make them
whole. All I know is that the message I get from Jesus in these verses
is that He wants them all. They are the owners of His kingdom.

There's a lot we can learn from children. Rather than the serene
picture that is sometimes painted, childhood can be tough. Kids are
honest—sometimes brutally so. They are not in good control of their
emotions, and they question everything. They get dirty and messy.
And they are very needy. They're a diverse group. Kind of like us. But
Jesus wants them all to come to Him. —GWEN FORD FAULKENBERRY

FAITH STEP: *Two things to remember today. First, Jesus loves you and wants
you to come to Him. And second, He also loves and wants everyone else. No
exceptions.*

MONDAY, MAY 8

I have come that they may have life, and have it to the full.
John 10:10 (NIV)

MY LIFE REVOLVES AROUND FOUR BOYS: my husband and our three sons. Every day I am cooking, cleaning, picking up, making grocery lists, buying socks, washing clothes, and running errands on their behalf. Not because I love doing these things, but really because I love these boys of mine.

My husband, Scott, thanks me regularly for all that I do. My boys, on the other hand, tend to forget that I have done anything. They seem to think a magical fairy resides in the house, meeting their every food and clothing need.

But I try not to be too hard on them because I am just like them when it comes to my faith. Sometimes I forget how much Jesus has done for me, like how He has given me everything I need for this life. Sometimes my brain gets so crowded with thoughts and plans and dreams and sorrows that I forget to recognize the One Who brings order out of my chaos. I forget that Jesus gave everything so that I could live out my life in His presence, surrounded by His love, held up with His grace.

There is only one thing we can do when we remember what Jesus has done for us. We get to say "thank you" with our lives. We love Him back because He first loved us. We fling ourselves into His arms and live out the life He gave us with gratitude and hope and abandon.
—SUSANNA FOTH AUGHTMON

FAITH STEP: *Write a thank-you card to Jesus for all that He has done for you.*

TUESDAY, MAY 9

But be doers of the word, and not hearers only, deceiving yourselves.
James 1:22 (ESV)

I HAD THE OPPORTUNITY to join a twelve-week small group focused on healthy, biblically based eating, exercise, and strength training. Great idea!

A week after adding my name to the list, sign-up remorse set in. Wait, *those* twelve weeks?

I'd counseled others that if we wait for perfect conditions to move forward, the conditions will never seem perfect enough, and those good intentions will rust, crumble, or start to stink with regret.

But listing excuses comes so naturally to us. It's the *doing* that is unnatural.

The heart of Jesus cried out for people to understand that a religion of good intentions is worthless and offensive. A relationship that births obedience and follow-through is His desire for us.

We deceive ourselves into thinking we're justified in delaying or resisting forgiveness because of the level of hurt we've experienced. We deceive ourselves into thinking that "just this one time" or "but I've been working so hard" or "I'm tired" are reasons enough to abandon—temporarily—what Jesus expects of us.

Seeing it in print exposes the self-deception for what it is, doesn't it? It certainly did for me. I went from excuses to action. Twelve weeks later, I'm so glad I did. —CYNTHIA RUCHTI

FAITH STEP: *You may already exercise consistently and make healthy eating choices. Is there a different area of your life in which excuses keep you from what you know Jesus is asking you to do? Be a doer. Excuses spoil fast.*

WEDNESDAY, MAY 10

*Those who live in the shelter of the Most High will find rest in
the shadow of the Almighty. . . . For he will order his angels
to protect you wherever you go.*
Psalm 91:1, 11 (NLT)

I STEPPED OUT OF THE SHOWER to find my husband on the couch,
holding an ice pack on his forehead. "A wasp stung me," he
explained. Panic rushed in. My husband's first allergic reaction—
massive swelling—had occurred decades ago in pre-EpiPen days.

What should I do? I quickly checked online for instructions. "Take
an antihistamine," read one source.

"Jesus, touch Him," I cried, handing my husband the pill. As soon
as he swallowed it, his eyes glazed. He was unresponsive to my questions, so I called 911. Then he passed out. Within minutes the para-
medics and ambulance arrived and started an IV, but they insisted he
go to the ER and get checked out. In hours, he was back to normal,
so we returned home.

Reflecting later on the above passage from Psalm 91 convinced
me that angels do, indeed, hover near. My husband, the man I've
loved for almost five decades, was protected and restored to me
without any further complications. It made me wonder, *How many
other times has Jesus ordered His angels to protect us?* I'm sure there
were many.

When we reach heaven one day, maybe Jesus will pull back the
curtains so we can see all the times danger stalked and angels walked
beside us, keeping us safe. Until then, we'll keep an EpiPen nearby
and rest in the shadow of the Almighty. —REBECCA BARLOW JORDAN

FAITH STEP: *Read Psalm 91 today and hold someone you love a little bit
closer.*

THURSDAY, MAY 11

"You wearied yourself by such going about, but you would not say, 'It is hopeless.' You found renewal of your strength, and so you did not faint."
Isaiah 57:10 (NIV)

THE MORNING AFTER an evening showdown with my then three-year-old daughter, Marin, I couldn't wait to get her to school. I was weary from the tantrums and her inability to communicate because of her slowed language development.

As I ushered her into the car, I felt desperate and dismayed. I needed protection from feelings of hopelessness. So I silently recited a familiar hymn: *Jesus, be a fence all around me every day.*

Later that afternoon I trudged toward the school's playground gate as disenchanted with the little girl I loved as when I'd left that morning. Then I spotted Doug, her preschool teacher, racing to greet me.

"You should have seen her today!" His breathy words were peppered with excitement. "See that climber?" He pointed to a wooden piece of playground equipment that resembled a rock wall.

I nodded.

"Well every day since Marin started school, she's tried and failed to make it to the top." He took a breath. "Today she did it!" He rejoiced like he'd witnessed her conquering Mount Everest. "She cheered and celebrated! I wish I'd recorded it!"

His words comforted me. My daughter had an *I-think-I-can* mentality. She spotted me and then ran into my arms as if she wanted to share something with me. I hugged her like I already knew.

Jesus was a fence around us both, and at long last I felt renewed.
—TARICE L. S. GRAY

FAITH STEP: *Are you weary and feeling hopeless? Sing, "Jesus, be a fence all around me every day." Feel His protection and His love surround you today.*

FRIDAY, MAY 12

Love . . . is not irritable. 1 Corinthians 13:4–5 (NLT)

RIGHT NOW AN OBNOXIOUS cartoon jingle is shouting at me from the TV. The dog had two accidents today. My husband's business computer refused to send two important e-mails for hours, throwing a hitch in the workday flow in our shared office. I chronically have to repeat myself before anyone in the house can hear me. And my stomach is upset.

I am irritable.

I think it would be lovely to have wisdom ready at my fingertips because the fruit of the Spirit is in bloom in my heart 24–7. But there's the problem of *me* to consider. Sometimes I'm more accomplished at irritability than I am at having anything else together. And you know what? That frustrates me.

I heard a message about irritability a while back that won't leave me alone, but honestly I appreciate its quiet nudge because I believe Jesus is working on my character in this regard.

The speaker said that irritability is easily overlooked in our busy days. We underestimate and even excuse this character liability because we feel justified feeling it; we deal with a lot of stress.

But irritability has nothing to do with love, which makes it a serious issue to Jesus. When I exhibit irritability, I have a problem that can't be ignored because I'm grieving the Spirit, hurting others, and getting in the way of Jesus's peace, hope, joy, and love shining in and through me.

Conquering irritability will have to be a Jesus-thing in me because it's fairly well entrenched. But with Jesus's help, one day I just may be able to reflect on irritability from the perspective of success!
—ERIN KEELEY MARSHALL

FAITH STEP: *Write today's verse one hundred times. Thank Jesus that He is never irritable toward you.*

SATURDAY, MAY 13

Finally, brothers, whatever is true, whatever is honorable, whatever is just, whatever is pure, whatever is lovely, whatever is commendable, if there is any excellence, if there is anything worthy of praise, think about these things. Philippians 4:8 (ESV)

IT SEEMED LIKE A GOOD IDEA at the time—planting a small patch of mint in the big flower bed by our deck. The idea of adding home-grown mint leaves to water sounded so refreshing for hot summer months.

I soon regretted my decision and regretted it for years. The mint quickly took over the flower bed, spreading and encroaching on the space for the colorful annuals. I dug up the plants and threw them away, thinking, *Good riddance!* Yet, year after year, a few curly green leaves popped up somewhere in that bed, no matter how many times I dug them up. The tag on the mint had read "Perennial"; I thought a more appropriate label would be "Immortal."

I hate to admit it, but I have a few other things that keep popping up even after I think I've gotten rid of them. It might be a bad habit that I assume I've beaten. Or an attitude that's not truly openhearted. Sometimes it's a thought that I know is not pleasing to God. I've confessed, repented, and dealt with these "pests" in the past, but suddenly they show up again and try to invade my mind.

Philippians 4:6 advises us to guard our minds by fixing our thoughts on things worth thinking about. When I look at the list of adjectives, I see a description of Jesus. And I understand that the best way to keep unwanted pests out of my head is to concentrate on the One I most want to invite in. —DIANNE NEAL MATTHEWS

FAITH STEP: *Memorize Philippians 4:8. Whenever an undesirable thought or temptation enters your mind, use the verse to think about Jesus. How is He true, honorable, just, pure, lovely...?*

SUNDAY, MAY 14

My guilt overwhelms me—it is a burden too heavy to bear.
Psalm 38:4 (NLT)

SINCE I MENTOR TEEN MOMS, every week I get e-mails and notes from parents who discover their daughters are pregnant. It's a shock, to say the least, especially for parents who raised their children in Christian homes and taught their children Jesus's good plans for marriage and family. The parents who are most distraught are those whose daughters seemed to know better, but then strayed. It's enough to break a parent's heart! As hard as it is, the best thing a parent can offer is grace. If a young woman knows that sex outside of marriage is wrong, she'll be burdened with guilt. Grace helps her to bear that burden. Grace offered reminds her of Jesus's forgiveness. As Psalm 65:3 (NIV) says, "Though we are overwhelmed by our sins, you forgive them all."

The women from my mom's church reached out to me when I was a pregnant teen, and I was very defensive at first. They tried to talk to me, and I turned my back on them. Instead of getting caught up in the issue of whether or not having sex outside of marriage was okay (deep down I knew it wasn't), they extended love to me and my soon-to-be-born child. It's just what I needed most. I soon sought Jesus myself.

Grace teaches us that we all make mistakes, but Jesus loves us. Grace for a pregnant young woman also shows that she made a right choice in choosing life—a child is a gift. All of us make mistakes, and all of us appreciate grace. When you offer it to a young mom, you're blessing two people. —TRICIA GOYER

FAITH STEP: *If you know a young or single mom, find a way to reach out to her. Offer a word of kindness, a note, or even a small gift card. It will encourage her and make a huge difference.*

MONDAY, MAY 15

"What I'm trying to do here is to get you to relax, to not be so preoccupied with getting, so you can respond to God's giving." Matthew 6:31 (MSG)

LAST MAY, I ADOPTED A RESCUE DOG. Rue wasn't socialized, either to people or other animals. She is, as a result, fearful and bossy—a bad combination. At first, she was afraid of everything: a cookie sheet, a knock at the door, aluminum foil. She shied away, then fell back on her herding-breed attributes to take control of the situation. That she was confused and didn't know the situation was never out of control in the first place didn't faze her in the least.

She's like that person who feels threatened and, instead of retreating, decides to take over. Her training now is to realize her master has things under control so she has no need to take over. Rue is improving, but it's a long process. She's a stubborn girl with an established pattern of coping. She wants her own way. She's sure she's right.

I want something better for her. I want her to relax, knowing I'll take care of her. I'm glad she wants to please me, but I don't need her in a hyperalert state, thinking everything depends on her. I want her to realize I've got this. Rue needs to learn to trust.

This has hit pretty close to home as I work with her because she reminds me of myself, always trying to help Jesus make everything work out the way I think it should. Meanwhile in my Bible reading, I hear Him say to stop worrying. His Father knows my needs and will satisfy them. Like Rue, I can't quite believe that, so I keep trying to make stuff happen. When will I learn?

As with Rue, it's a process. —SUZANNE DAVENPORT TIETJEN

FAITH STEP: *Do you, like me, sometimes try to be the answer to your own prayers? Today, hand your anxious thoughts to Jesus. He can and will take care of you.*

TUESDAY, MAY 16

Confess your sins to each other and pray for each other so that you may be healed. . . . James 5:16 (NLT)

"GRANDMA, I CUT MY FINGER on a branch," said six-year-old Luke. He pointed at the bandage on his outstretched hand.

"Is it healing okay?" I asked.

"Yeah, but it's going kind of slow," he said. "That's because it got infected. I didn't tell Mommy when it happened because I didn't think she needed to know. But I should have told her sooner because she washed it and put medicine on it, and now it's almost better."

If only we, as adults, could learn so quickly.

Every time I speak at a women's event, at least one person confides a hurt. She hasn't told anyone yet because she doesn't think anyone needs to know. She often fears rejection if other people discover her secret: *What will they think of me? No one will want to associate with me if they know what I've done or what's happened to me.*

"I have learned now that while those who speak about one's miseries usually hurt, those who keep silence hurt more," said C. S. Lewis. I see this proven true time and time again. Those who suffer in silence suffer deeply. Those who tell someone what happened and how it affected them begin the healing journey.

That's why Jesus encourages us to speak up: "Share each other's burdens, and in this way obey the law of Christ" (Galatians 6:2, NLT). Silence prevents or, at the least, hinders healing. While it's wise to exercise discretion in sharing details, I've found that truth and transparency ultimately promote freedom. —GRACE FOX

FAITH STEP: *Wear a bandage on one finger for a day. Consider it a visual reminder to pray for people who are suffering in silence owing to fear of what other people might think.*

WEDNESDAY, MAY 17

God demonstrates his own love for us in this:
While we were still sinners, Christ died for us.
Romans 5:8 (NIV)

So OFTEN, I THINK, people feel like they want to hide from God. We'd like to clean up our act before approaching His holiness, and if we've given up on cleaning up our act, well, instead of asking for His help we'd just as soon avoid Him. It's as old as Adam and Eve in the garden. After they sinned, they hid, because they were ashamed. The beauty of that story is that God went looking for them, calling out, "Where are you?"

That same beauty is found in Romans 5:8. I read it the other day in a new way. Usually my focus is on Jesus when I read that verse. But this time I concentrated on the first part. Essentially, the meaning is this: God loved us a lot. He showed how much by sending His Son to die for us *while we were still sinners*. Not after we got our acts together. As if that's even possible.

Theologian and anti-Nazi activist Dietrich Bonhoeffer said it this way: "God does not love some ideal person, but rather human beings just as we are, not some ideal world, but rather the real world."

How appropriate that God came to us as we are—in flesh and blood. And He invites us to come as we are. In Jesus we see the ultimate bridge between holiness and humanity. His love covers our sins. We don't have to hide. —GWEN FORD FAULKENBERRY

FAITH STEP: *Is it hard for you to come to God without trying to hide? Remember, He loves you just as you are. Lay your heart bare before Him today.*

THURSDAY, MAY 18

But in fact God has placed the parts in the body, every one of them, just as he wanted them to be. If they were all one part, where would the body be? As it is, there are many parts, but one body.
1 Corinthians 12:18 *(NIV)*

THERE IS ALWAYS A PUZZLE in progress in our home. Currently there is one that is finished, two more are almost complete, and a fourth that was complete until I tried to slide it off the dinner table onto cardboard. It fell and broke apart, which didn't make my kids happy. After it tumbled, I got on my hands and knees and picked up every piece, knowing the puzzle wouldn't be complete if I missed one.

When I accepted Christ, I became a piece of His greater picture. My life transformed from dark to light, and my despair turned to hope. The whole picture of my life changed, and I began to see myself differently. There was a special place where I was needed, where I belonged.

It's true for each of us. Whether the piece looks common or is designed for a special purpose, we're all needed to work together.

As 2 Timothy 2:20–21 (NIV) says, "In a large house there are articles not only of gold and silver, but also of wood and clay; some are for special purposes and some for common use. Those who cleanse themselves from the latter will be instruments for special purposes, made holy, useful to the Master and prepared to do any good work."

Just like each puzzle piece has a purpose, so do we in Christ's kingdom. He always makes sure we fit into the perfect spot. And together we reflect a picture of Christ to the watching world. —TRICIA GOYER

FAITH STEP: *Thank Jesus for the special part you have in His kingdom. Think about all those you are connected with in special ways, and pray for them today.*

FRIDAY, MAY 19

He guided them with the cloud by day and with light from the fire all night.
Psalm 78:14 (NIV)

YEARS AGO MY HUSBAND AND I were traveling in the Blue Ridge Mountains in North Carolina. Clear, sunny skies accompanied us until our third day as we drove along the highway past Charlottesville. What happened next almost paralyzed us with fear.

As we rounded a curve on the interstate, a cloud of fog descended. We slowed, expecting the dense moisture to thin. Instead, visibility was near zero. We couldn't see a thing! We inched our way toward the taillights of the car in front of us. We had never felt so afraid and cried out to Jesus many times. After what seemed like hours, the fog faded.

During those long, tense moments, Jesus reminded me of a similar situation in the Bible. When God led His people out of slavery in Egypt, He led them by a cloud during the day to signify His presence. Wherever the cloud appeared—though evoking fear at the time—it led them to safety.

When a cloud descended over Jesus and three of His disciples at His transfiguration, fear filled the hearts of those disciples. But a voice from heaven soon calmed them, assuring this was a holy moment (Matthew 17:1–6).

Jesus calmed our fears that day, too, and convinced me that no cloud of difficulty could ever erase His light, His voice, or His protection in our lives. His presence would always go before us, behind us, and beside us to guide us. —REBECCA BARLOW JORDAN

FAITH STEP: *What clouds of difficulty have you experienced this year? Each time you see a cloud in the skies, thank Jesus for His presence and guidance in all kinds of "weather."*

SATURDAY, MAY 20

But those who hope in the Lord will renew their strength;
they will fly up on wings like eagles; they will run and not be tired;
they will walk and not be weary. Isaiah 40:31 (CEB)

I'VE NEVER MINDED HAVING a layover between airline flights. I can read, listen to music, work on my computer, walk, or people-watch. But one spring I discovered what it's like to be stranded on an airplane with nothing to do. While returning home from a conference, our plane taxied out, then sat for a half hour before taking off. A few days later, I flew to Tennessee to ride with my daughter and three grandchildren the rest of the way to our house in Texas. Our plane reached its destination on time, but we had to wait an hour and a half before disembarking. I felt exhausted.

Then there's the kind of waiting that's not physical, but of an emotional and spiritual nature. Maybe we're waiting to see an answer to a prayer that represents our heart's deepest longing. Or we yearn to see divine intervention in a relationship or situation that makes us feel trapped. We may begin to despair of ever seeing a loved one turn toward Jesus. Those types of waiting can drain us physically and emotionally—and maybe even shake our faith.

Isaiah talked about hopeful waiting in the Lord that renews and strengthens a person. I think that in order to get those results we have to guard our attitude. Do we believe that Jesus always keeps His promises? Do we trust that He wants the best for us? If we remember the source of our hope, we can allow Him to comfort and to nurture us. And we'll come through the waiting period stronger than we were before. —DIANNE NEAL MATTHEWS

FAITH STEP: *Have you grown weary of waiting for something? Ask Jesus to renew your strength and to help you soar like an eagle through this difficult time.*

SUNDAY, MAY 21

And if I go and prepare a place for you, I will come back and take you to be with me that you also may be where I am. John 14:3 (NIV)

AS A MISSIONARY, my daughter Leslie lives in the Czech Republic (former Czechoslovakia), and it's there she married a wonderful, Christian Czech man. Their wedding was held in a cathedral consecrated in 1131. Gothic in style, its main tower rises 330 feet. Inside, sunlight filters through stained-glass windows, and all the columns, walls, and ceilings are decorated. There are too many ornaments and statues to take in. As I sat there on my daughter's wedding day, I realized that even when this cathedral was being constructed, Jesus knew it would someday be part of my daughter's story.

Cathedrals were built, in part, to give illiterate people of the time a glimpse of Jesus's majesty, but no humanly designed structure on earth will compare to what Jesus has designed and crafted for us in heaven. As John 14:2–3 (NLT) says, "There is more than enough room in my Father's home. If this were not so, would I have told you that I am going to prepare a place for you? When everything is ready, I will come and get you, so that you will always be with me where I am."

A cathedral in Europe has been part of my daughter's story even before her birth, and a mansion in heaven is part of ours. Sometimes in life it's hard to understand—or face—all the heartache and hardship on earth, but it's important to keep praying and thanking Jesus for the beautiful eternity He's already designed. And especially for the forever love Who will be waiting for us when we cross through heaven's gates. —TRICIA GOYER

FAITH STEP: *Take a few minutes and try to picture what Jesus is preparing for you in heaven. It's hard to do with our limited imaginations, but focusing on our eternal home—even for a short time—helps us to put everything in perspective.*

MONDAY, MAY 22

---

*I will say of the Lord, "He is my refuge and my fortress,
my God, in whom I trust." Psalm 91:2 (NIV)*

RECENTLY, WE FOUND OUT that the small school our boys have attended since kindergarten will be closing. The boys will be starting a new school.

I have been reliving my own new-school moments, remembering the thumping of my heart and the tears as I watched my mom walk away. And the hope that I'd find a friend to eat lunch with. The hardest school change for me was in fifth grade when I switched from private to public. After a week of being sent home with stomach issues, my teacher, Mrs. Cox, took me into the bathroom to talk privately. I loved Mrs. Cox. She cared about me and my weird stomach. I could tell when she pointed to the bad words written on the wall and then covered them with her hand. She said, "I don't like these words either. But you? You are going to be okay." And she was right. I was. Soon the stomach cramps stopped. The light began to shine. I was going to be okay because Mrs. Cox said so.

That pep talk in the school bathroom grounded me in hope. And that is the place I am planting my feet now: in hope, trusting Jesus to provide great teachers and new friends for my boys.

The first week has been a little rough. The tears haven't subsided yet. There have been upset stomachs. But I know this: good things are almost always hard. And sometimes being launched in another direction launches us into trusting Jesus. And Jesus, being good, doesn't leave us alone. No matter what, we can lean into Him and know we are going to be okay. —SUSANNA FOTH AUGHTMON

FAITH STEP: *Write a note to yourself: "With Jesus, leaning into Him, I am going to be okay" and place it where you'll see it every day.*

TUESDAY, MAY 23

Ears to hear and eyes to see—the Lord made them both.
Proverbs 20:12 (CEB)

SO FAR, I'VE BEEN ABLE to get by with inexpensive reading glasses. They work well and cost so little that I can buy them in various colors and styles to match my fashion mood. If they get scratched, my heart doesn't sink very far.

Like most people who rely on reading glasses, I often wander the house wondering where I left them. Most recently, I got as far as our couples' Bible study meeting in a friend's home one night before realizing I'd left my glasses on the kitchen counter. I dug in my tote bag for a spare pair. Nothing.

I couldn't follow along in my Bible during the study, couldn't see my notes on the page.

"Want to borrow my readers?" a woman beside me asked.

"Yes, please!" All that was blurred instantly cleared.

In our relationship with Jesus, we want more than to borrow His glasses. We want to borrow His vision—the way He views people, life, eternal life, the way He sees us and those who have wronged us, the vision He has for loved ones we've prayed for "forever" who seem no closer to the Truth than they were years ago.

There's a song that says, "Give me Your eyes for just one second, [Jesus]. Give me Your eyes so I can see everything that I've been missing."

If you've ever had vision problems, you know the joy of slipping those lenses in front of your eyes and finally seeing clearly. How would our lives be changed if we routinely adopted Jesus's visual acuity?

—CYNTHIA RUCHTI

FAITH STEP: *In your prayer time today, ask Jesus to let you borrow His eyes so you can gain His perspective, especially on issues that have seemed cloudy or fuzzy to you.*

WEDNESDAY, MAY 24

God will protect you with his pinions; you'll find refuge under his wings.
His faithfulness is a protective shield.
Psalm 91:4 (CEB)

IT DOESN'T TAKE MUCH INTERACTION with people before we realize that many are fighting fierce battles on a soul-deep level.

Those watching someone they love slog through a life-threatening crisis. Those caught in the scorching heat of divorce. People struggling with changes in their aging parents. Victims of violence and unspeakable abuse. Parents of wayward children, troubled children, addicted children, estranged children...

So much pain. So many innocents caught in the crosshairs.

As deep as the pain pierces, because of what Jesus bore in His death on the Cross, we've been spared the full brunt. Jesus stands between us and the intensity of the impact. Our Protector. Our Deflector.

It may not feel like it. We believe the pain couldn't be any worse than it is. We're convinced we won't survive this latest blow. Yet, we do. In part because Jesus takes our pain upon Himself: "Surely he took up our pain and bore our suffering" (Isaiah 53:4, NIV).

The day is coming.

What do we do until then? Stay tucked tight behind our Shield and Defender, our Protector and Deflector. When the darts are flying, those closest to the Shield are the most protected and the toughest targets to hit. Still in the war, but not in the line of fire.
—CYNTHIA RUCHTI

FAITH STEP: *The mental picture of hunkering down behind a strong Shield comforts me when life is hard. Still in the war. Not in the line of fire. Who in your circle of friends and family needs this perspective today? Take time to share it.*

THURSDAY, MAY 25

He will cover you with his feathers, and under his wings you will find refuge; his faithfulness will be your shield and rampart.
Psalm 91:4 (NIV)

I AM GETTING READY to speak at a women's retreat. I'll be gone for five days, and I get to spend time with a dear friend. I am excited and hopeful about what Jesus is going to do.

But in the midst of that excitement, there is this thread of fear tightening itself like a cord around my heart. I never like leaving my boys. Before each trip I kiss their faces and hold them close and feel my heart fluttering in my chest. I can tend to get lost in the terrible mire of "what if" thinking. What if something happens to them while I am gone? What if something happens to Scott? What if something happens to me? What if they all get in an accident on the way home from dropping me off at the airport and then no one can get ahold of me since I am sipping ginger ale at thirty thousand feet? SO. MANY. FEARS.

But the truth is, I don't have to be afraid if I tuck myself under the wings of the One who loves me most. Jesus's heart is thrumming with love for me. I can rest, warm and safe. He is shielding me with His great faithfulness. I am fortified with His grace and mercy. He has encircled me with the mighty wall of His great strength and wisdom. I can step outside of the circle of love and live in fear. Or I can tuck in close and breathe in peace. Tucking into that safe place where Jesus is holding me close is a good place to be.
—SUSANNA FOTH AUGHTMON

FAITH STEP: *Wrap yourself in a blanket while you pray. Picture yourself tucked into the safe place near the heart of Jesus.*

FRIDAY, MAY 26

---

*If we confess our sins, he is faithful and just to forgive us our sins,
and to cleanse us from all unrighteousness. 1 John 1:9 (KJV)*

MY DAUGHTER ADELAIDE is the sweetest little thing. Out of all of the kids on the Triple F Ranch, she probably gets into trouble the least, which may be why that when she does, it's kind of a big deal.

The other day she and her siblings and cousins made a bad decision. Instead of being where they were supposed to be, which was in the yard, they went into our house with no adults home and made several messes. So they all got into trouble. Adelaide, who prides herself on making good decisions even when others don't, took it particularly hard.

That evening when it was time to make dinner, I asked her, "What are you in the mood for tonight?"

"I'd like a plate of forgiveness with a side of mercy."

I had to laugh, and she did too. "You're already forgiven. Don't you know that?"

"Yes, but I still feel yucky."

Can't we all relate? Sometimes when we do something wrong, it's hard to feel like we're forgiven. But we have to trust in the promise we have in Jesus. Feelings can be liars, but Jesus is the Truth.

This applies to all sorts of things. We may feel alone, but the truth is Jesus never leaves us or forsakes us. We may feel anxious, but He is our peace. We may feel unloved, but He promises nothing can separate us from His love. And no matter what we've done, Jesus promises to forgive us. —GWEN FORD FAULKENBERRY

FAITH STEP: *Pray this prayer: Jesus, I confess my sin of _____ to You. Based on Your promise in 1 John 1:9, I receive Your forgiveness now and choose to walk with You in newness of life. Thank You for forgiving and cleansing me. Amen.*

SATURDAY, MAY 27

We can make our plans, but the Lord determines our steps.
Proverbs 16:9 (NLT)

EXHAUSTION HIT ME after I'd worked for two years as the dean at a girls' high school. Ready for a change of pace, I applied as a volunteer at a summer camp—presumably for young girls. When summer ended, I planned to return to my job as dean for another year. Then I'd pursue a nursing degree and eventually head to an overseas mission field.

Imagine my surprise when I arrived at the camp to hear: "Grace, your application says you work with teenagers. Perfect! You'll be in charge of the teen girls in our leadership training program."

I didn't know whether to laugh or cry.

A guy named Gene Fox was in charge of the teen boys. He'd recently graduated with an engineering degree and had been accepted by a mission agency to work in Nepal for three years. He planned to leave for Kathmandu in January.

As ministry partners that summer, Gene and I spent every waking minute together. Days before camp ended, Gene asked me to marry him. I said yes!

I returned to my job and stayed one semester. Gene postponed his departure for Nepal. We married in February and landed in Kathmandu in July.

Both Gene and I went to camp thinking we'd mapped our future. Boy, were we surprised when Jesus flipped our plans upside down!

We can make our plans, but ultimately Jesus directs our paths. Our role is to walk surrendered and trust Him to work out the wonderful details. —GRACE FOX

FAITH STEP: *Take a prayer walk today. Surrender your plans, whatever they are, to Him. Invite Him to direct your path, and thank Him for being trustworthy.*

SUNDAY, MAY 28

*Jesus said to everyone, "All who want to come after me must say no
to themselves, take up their cross daily, and follow me."*
Luke 9:23 (CEB)

AT A CHURCH SERVICE, our pastor recognized a couple in the congregation who were celebrating their seventieth wedding anniversary. Everyone burst into applause as they stood up, the wife with a corsage on her shoulder and her husband's arm around her waist. The pastor invited them to say a few words, and they spoke about the importance of making Christ the center of their marriage and putting each other's needs ahead of their own.

Later, a young family who had decided to become members of the church took the stage. When the wife was asked if she knew Christ personally, she responded, "I do." Her response, along with the comments from the long-married couple, reminded me why the Bible often uses the marital relationship as a metaphor for our relationship with Jesus. Similarly, that older couple's marriage didn't last because they had said "I do" to each other seventy years earlier. It lasted because every day they tried to make their actions say, "I choose to love you and put you above all others."

Jesus requires that same commitment from us. Every day we choose whether or not to say "I do" to Him. Will we trust Him with everything that concerns us? Will we follow His will instead of our own? Are we prepared to love Him more than anyone or anything else? Our answers will determine whether we live a self-centered life or a Christ-centered one. —DIANNE NEAL MATTHEWS

FAITH STEP: *Today look for ways to say "I do" to Jesus. Use your words and your actions to demonstrate that you are committed to loving Him above all others.*

MONDAY, MAY 29

Rejoice with those who rejoice, weep with those who weep.
Romans 12:15 *(ESV)*

YESTERDAY, THE PASTOR ANNOUNCED that a member's husband had passed away. When I got home, I wrote a note to myself to make her a card. Each day, I saw the reminder and found reasons to avoid creating the card. I wanted to offer comfort, to let her know others cared. So what was causing my resistance?

I finally admitted that if I set aside time to make the card, to pray for her, and to write her a note, I feared I'd be immersing myself in the pain of loss. My inclination tempted me to look away instead, to avoid connecting with the suffering of another.

At last, I made the card.

Left to myself, I find it challenging to weep with those who weep. What a blessing that Jesus lives in me! He is the compassionate Shepherd who wept over Jerusalem, who entered into the grief of his friends when Lazarus died, and who cares about my tears as well. He can enable my heart to support those who are grieving, even when I feel uncertain of how to help.

Jesus didn't avoid human pain. He entered in and still does. He is beside every mother as she whispers a prayer for her child. He is holding each man whose shoulders groan under the weight of a job's relentless pressure. He wraps an arm around a woman who stands beside her spouse's grave.

When we invite Jesus to live through us, our arms can be part of the comfort He offers. Our humble words of love can echo with His compassion. —SHARON HINCK

FAITH STEP: *Dare to weep with someone who is weeping today. Ask Jesus to give you His heart of compassion and guide you in ways to show your love.*

TUESDAY, MAY 30

"The seed cast in the weeds is the person who hears the kingdom news,
but weeds of worry . . . strangle what was heard, and nothing comes of it."
Matthew 13:22 (MSG)

EVERY SPRING I WATCH my gardens eagerly for the first patches of green to pop up their heads: my trusted perennial flowers returning without fail. Inevitably, another batch of green invades the space alongside them. In the beginning, I had to inspect the area carefully to determine which plants were "enemies" and which ones were "friends."

After years of gardening, however, weeds are easy to spot. Still, if I get lazy and leave them alone, the weeds will eventually take over and strangle the good mature plants. The result is an overgrown mess, and the damage is almost impossible to reverse without ruining some of the beautiful perennials.

I've discovered weeds and worries have a lot in common with gardening. Through His Word, Jesus plants good perennial seeds in my life like love, hope, and faith. But worrisome thoughts involving pride, selfishness, and doubt are like weeds that can crowd out the good plants and spoil the garden.

I'm so grateful Jesus doesn't leave us defenseless. Our Master Gardener has given us a great way to dispose of those mental weeds as soon as they appear: We use our powerful God-tools . . . for clearing the ground of every obstruction and building lives of obedience into maturity (2 Corinthians 10:5–6, MSG). To the gardener, that's great news.

Excuse me, but I have some weeding to do!

—REBECCA BARLOW JORDAN

FAITH STEP: *Draw a picture of a garden. Label a few of the flowers with troubling thoughts that often bother you. As you confess them to Jesus, "clear them out" by erasing them or replacing them with positive thoughts.*

WEDNESDAY, MAY 31

The Lord is your keeper; the Lord is your shade on your right hand.
Psalm 121:5 (ESV)

SUMMERS IN ARKANSAS are intense. Hot, humid, with sunrays that physically hurt. If you were to visit me between May and October, you'd find me wearing sunglasses and a visor because direct rays near my eyes give me an instant headache. I appreciate any form of shade I can get.

Several years ago as summer was heating up, I reached my limit of no shade on our back deck. "Not one more summer without shade!" I told my husband. Two days later we had a canopy over a large section of the deck.

When we bought our current home, one of the selling points for me was the screened porch off the back of the house. Just looking at the shelter that porch offers on hot days already gives me some relief.

It should come as no surprise to me then why I love the many verses in the Bible about shade, shelter, taking refuge in the Lord, and being protected in the shadow of His wing.

When worries over finances, my kids, or my husband blaze like summer heat, I can bask in the Bible's reminders that Jesus is my shade. He protects and shelters me, not necessarily by removing the scorching trouble, but by covering me in the midst of it. Better than any sun umbrella could ever do, He always knows which direction I'll be hit, and He moves in ways I often can't see in order to guard me.

The summer reminds me to be grateful for Jesus's protective shade over me. His presence shelters from tempests, both seen and unseen. I welcome the shade of the Son! —ERIN KEELEY MARSHALL

FAITH STEP: *Find a figurine of a bird or a tree for your office or home as a reminder of your refuge beneath Jesus's sheltering wing or shaded by His presence. Pray Psalm 57:1.*

THURSDAY, JUNE 1

Jesus said to the servants, "Fill the jars with water," and they filled them to the brim. John 2:7 (CEB)

AFTER THIRTY YEARS, I'd given up hope of finding a water jug like the one my grandfather kept in his refrigerator. The jug wasn't fancy. Gray with a yellow lid. My siblings and I all remembered it as a symbol of our grandfather's love and affection for us, recalling his work-worn hands on that jug of cold water.

Recently, a box arrived from a cousin in Florida. The water jug. Not just one that looked like Grandpa's, but the very one he'd used. My cousin had found it while going through his father's—my uncle's—belongings.

I still marvel that after all these years, I have a tangible reminder of my grandfather and of my cousin's generosity and thoughtfulness. A simple water jug with so much meaning.

Jesus used common household water jugs to contain His first miracle, water into wine, the very first public hint that He was more than a man. He was the Son of God.

I'm in awe of the water-to-wine thread woven through the Gospel of John. Water into wine. Living Water at the well. Born of water and of the Spirit in the conversation with Nicodemus. Baptism. Wine at the last meal Jesus shared with His disciples before His betrayal and water that washed the disciples' feet as they waited for the wine.

Lack of wine for a wedding served as the initiation moment of His public ministry. And it started with a water jug. —CYNTHIA RUCHTI

FAITH STEP: *We may reach for a cup of tea or coffee when approaching time alone with Jesus. Tomorrow, make it a glass of cold water with gratitude that the Son of God gave His life for you.*

FRIDAY, JUNE 2

Then Jesus said to his disciples, "Whoever wants to be my disciple must deny themselves and take up their cross and follow me."
Matthew 16:24 (NIV)

I WAS TALKING TO my son Jack about buying presents for his brothers. We usually give the boys money to spend on each other for their birthdays. Jack said, "You only give us five dollars per person. That's not enough money to get them anything good."

"You know that you can actually save up your own money to buy your brothers better presents, right?" I said.

He grinned. "I know, but for some reason, I always end up finding something I want to buy for myself instead of saving the money and waiting to make them happy."

I laughed. "That's true of most people. We want to make ourselves happy first."

Sacrifice is not the easiest road to follow. It goes against our nature. It is so much easier to meet our own wants and needs than to deny ourselves and see to the needs of others. The thing is...that is exactly what Jesus did for us. He loved us so much that He denied Himself and offered Himself up as a sacrifice on our behalf. And in turn, He asks us to do the same. It is how we get to love Him back.

When we deny ourselves, we are following in His footsteps. We are journeying down the road of sacrifice. The funny thing is, when we follow in Jesus's footsteps, when we begin living out the life of sacrifice we were meant to live, He meets our needs better than we ever could. —SUSANNA FOTH AUGHTMON

FAITH STEP: *Ask Jesus to show you a way that you can focus on others today instead of yourself.*

SATURDAY, JUNE 3

When he [Jesus] looked out over the crowds, his heart broke. So confused and aimless they were, like sheep with no shepherd. Matthew 9:36 (MSG)

WHEN WE WERE SHEPHERDS, my daughter and I went to Shearing School. There we learned the physically difficult and emotionally daunting task of separating sheep from their fleeces. We were afraid we would cut the animals (we did) and ruin their fleeces (we didn't). After two days, we could shear a sheep in about twenty minutes, a task our shearer could do in four. We learned that the $3.50 per sheep we were paying her was a bargain and gave up any idea of doing it ourselves.

That isn't all I learned. Those sheep we practiced on, the shearer told us, were provided by a shepherd unworthy of the name. His sheep were bony and wild. Their fleeces went to market, where buyers would surely reject them for their lack of luster and strength. That shepherd needed the wool off his sheep, didn't care if they were hurt in the process, and wanted it done for nothing.

I think of that frightened flock every time I read today's verse. In the Amplified Bible, the words *confused* and *aimless* read "bewildered (harassed and distressed and dejected and helpless)." Those poor, unloved sheep were very like the people coming in droves to hear Jesus. Neglected by the indifferent religious leaders of their day, they listened to Jesus for three days. Until they ran out of food. Then, having fed their hearts and minds, Jesus miraculously filled their stomachs.

The Bible says Jesus, our Great Shepherd, will put us together, provide us with what we need to please Him, and make us into what gives Him the most pleasure (Hebrews 13:21). He loves us that much. —SUZANNE DAVENPORT TIETJEN

FAITH STEP: *Are you feeling harassed, distressed, dejected, and helpless? Take those battles to your Shepherd and let Him help you.*

Sunday, June 4

*This is love: it is not that we loved God but that he loved us and
sent his Son as the sacrifice that deals with our sins.*
1 John 4:10 (CEB)

A snippy customer service representative sighed heavily into
the phone the other day. She hadn't understood what I was asking
her to provide. Her reaction startled me with its harshness. I almost
responded with an attitude that matched hers. Instead, fresh from a
lesson like the one above about our love for Jesus being rooted in the
fact that He loved us first, I calmly reworded what I needed from her.
The woman's manner changed instantly. She apologized. At the end
of our conversation, we expressed our appreciation for each other.

We make choices every day to live in reaction to our fears, hardships, and people who fail us or to live in response to the love of
Christ. The first cripples and hamstrings us. The second sends us
soaring.

A companion verse to the above-mentioned 1 John 4:10 is
1 John 4:19 (CEB): "We love because God first loved us." It immediately follows the biblical teaching that reminds us, "There is no fear
in love, but perfect love drives out fear" (1 John 4:18, CEB).

We love God because we were loved first by Him, and we love
others because of the way we are loved by God, as expressed through
Jesus. So living in love means living in response to the love of Christ
rather than as a reaction to fear, disappointments, and how others
treat us.

Reactionary or responsive? We do have a choice. —Cynthia Ruchti

Faith Step: *Include in your morning routine this personal pep talk: "I am
loved by God and rescued by Jesus. I will respond to what life hurls at me from
that position of love, protection, provision, and strength."*

MONDAY, JUNE 5

For the word of God is alive and active. Sharper than any double-edged sword, it penetrates even to dividing soul and spirit, joints and marrow; it judges the thoughts and attitudes of the heart. Hebrews 4:12 (NIV)

RECENTLY WIDOWED, my sister-in-law Ruth was trusting Jesus in big and small ways. She felt His comforting presence in her grief and relied on Him for many practical needs.

One day she came home to find her bathroom occupied by wasps. Ruth had never liked dealing with insects, but she was alone now. So she grabbed a flyswatter and flailed at them. They kept escaping.

The next day when even more wasps invaded, she called a neighbor for help. Her neighbor came over and said, "Let me show you how I do it." She calmly placed the flyswatter over a wasp and then used a firm object to press down and dispatch the insect. From then on, Ruth's fear of the insects fell away and she's managed to vanquish them.

She told me that lesson helped her with another kind of intrusion: wasps of the mind. We all discover spiritual wasps buzzing nearby at times. Thoughts hissing, telling us Jesus has forgotten us. Lies that tell us we're worthless. Fears that insist disaster is imminent. If we try to ignore them, they remain, ready to sting. If we flail around fearfully, our panic rises. Instead we can look closely at the invader, find a scriptural truth to apply, and calmly place the Word over that mental wasp, allowing us to summarily squash it.

Through the inspiration of the Holy Spirit, Christ has given us His Word—a means to reveal our own thoughts and attitudes that need forgiveness and a constant reminder of His grace and power to banish lies. —SHARON HINCK

FAITH STEP: *Ask Jesus to show you a lie that has invaded your thoughts. Then search the Scripture for the truth.*

TUESDAY, JUNE 6

A gentle answer deflects anger, but harsh words make tempers flare.
Proverbs 15:1 (NLT)

I HELD THE PHONE to my ear and willed myself to stay calm. The closing date was days away, and because I'd been honest about some discoloration on our carpet in the house we were selling, the warranty company was digging in its heels about transferring the warranty to the new owners. According to the flooring company where we'd bought the carpet four years earlier, the carpet had a twenty-five-year no-exclusions warranty. But I was learning just how numerous the exclusions were.

My patience was exhausted over the upcoming move, and the woman at the warranty company was saying everything she could to fire up my anger.

Anger is like a snowball headed downhill, pulling up pieces of everything it tumbles over, gaining reckless speed and force until it's nearly impossible to control. When given free reign, anger is destructive and more difficult to stop the longer it is given headway.

Fortunately, life and Proverbs have taught me that the soft approach really is calming. Gentleness has the healing mark of Jesus's Spirit (Galatians 5:22–23). He tells me to learn from Him because He is gentle (Matthew 11:29–30), a spiritually mature trait that's echoed throughout the Bible.

I let Jesus's reminders of a gentle approach win over my powerful desire to set the woman straight. Our tones had already risen somewhat, but I was amazed how hers quieted after I adjusted mine.
—ERIN KEELEY MARSHALL

FAITH STEP: *Memorize Proverbs 15:1.*

WEDNESDAY, JUNE 7

You're here to be light, bringing out the God-colors in the world. God is not a secret to be kept. . . . If I make you light-bearers, you don't think I'm going to hide you under a bucket, do you?
Matthew 5:14–15 (MSG)

RECENTLY I WAS AT THE HOSPITAL, visiting a good friend, a member of our former church who was recovering from a serious infection. With her usual humility, she told me she felt like she wasn't of much use to God in her current situation. In reality, this energetic woman had been dubbed the "Encourager" (and probably the "Energizer Bunny") by everyone who knew her. She loved to do for others. But here, she felt like she couldn't light anyone's life.

"You're like a lightbulb—or a lamp," I said, trying to reassure her. "It doesn't matter where you are. You'll light up the room and anyone who is present."

No sooner had I spoken than an attendant entered the room, bagging my friend's garbage beside her bed. True to her nature, my friend offered a tender, generous thanks to the helper for keeping her room so spotless. I watched his face light up with pleasure at her expression of appreciation. I recognized heaven's hearty "Amen." "I rest my case," I said, grinning.

No matter where Jesus stations us, if we allow Him to be the true Light of our world (John 8:12), He will make us His personal light-bearers to those around us. As lightbulbs or lamps, our light is never hidden from others. In some way, we will shine for Him.
—REBECCA BARLOW JORDAN

FAITH STEP: *Is your inner "lightbulb" flickering? Has it burned out? Ask Jesus today to recharge your light and keep it burning brightly so others will see His light—in you.*

THURSDAY, JUNE 8

*"Nazareth! Can anything good come from there?" Nathanael asked.
"Come and see," said Philip.*
John 1:46 (NIV)

"COME AND SEE!" is echoed several times in the New Testament. Philip told Nathanael he had met the Messiah. "Come and see," he urged his friend. The woman at the well told her fellow villagers, "Come, see a man who told me everything I ever did" (John 4:29). After Jesus rose from the dead, an angel invited the women to "come and see" His empty tomb (Matthew 28:6).

"Nana, come and see!" I hear these words from my grandkids when they're excited to show me something. It might be a rainbow in the sky, an interesting beetle on the sidewalk, or their favorite cartoon character on television. Whether it turns out to be something beautiful, shocking, or gross, if they want to show it to me, then I want to see it.

There are times when Jesus wants to show us something new. *Come and see what will happen if you talk about Me to your neighbor. Come and see what you will learn if you commit to that Bible study or small group. Come and see how I can use you if you give up that unhealthy habit. Come and see how close we can be when you start each day with prayer.*

The invitation is being extended. How will you respond?
—DIANNE NEAL MATTHEWS

FAITH STEP: *Ask Jesus what new thing He wants to show you and keep your eyes open for His gifts.*

FRIDAY, JUNE 9

The apostles returned to Jesus from their ministry tour and told him all they had done and taught. Then Jesus said, "Let's go off by ourselves to a quiet place and rest awhile. . . . "
Mark 6:30–31 (NLT)

MY HUSBAND AND I MOVED to a different house several months ago. It's on the corner of a busy intersection, but you'd scarcely know it. The house sits back from the street, sheltered by a wooded lot.

Our driveway winds up a little hill between evergreens and shrubs. It leads visitors to our patio, which is bordered on the north by trees.

I love this place. It feels like a retreat center in the middle of the city. I liken it to a sacred space of sorts, a getaway where weary souls find rest.

Life's busyness and noise make it vital for us to withdraw occasionally. To sit in silence. To bask in nature's beauty. To focus on our heavenly Father's face and therein find renewal.

Jesus felt the need for escape too. Scripture mentions several occasions when He withdrew from the crowds and ministry responsibilities to be alone with His disciples or with His Father (Matthew 14:13, Luke 9:10, John 6:15–16). Sometimes He climbed into a boat and rowed away. Sometimes He climbed into the hills where He disappeared for hours. Scripture doesn't describe in detail what He did on those occasions, but it does say that He often escaped to pray.

Self-care matters. We're only humans, destined to discouragement and defeat unless we withdraw periodically to rest and refresh. Doing so isn't a luxury. It's a necessity. As someone once said, "Let's draw apart before we fall apart." —GRACE FOX

FAITH STEP: *What would a soul retreat look like for you? Check your calendar and then schedule one within the next month or two.*

SATURDAY, JUNE 10

It is dangerous to be concerned with what others think of you....
Proverbs 29:25 (GNT)

A DEAR FRIEND HAD BEEN TRYING to set up a meeting to introduce me to another of her best friends. I was looking forward to it.

When the woman arrived, she looked me over and politely shook my hand. Then she addressed our friend: "Is this your colleague?"

"Former. Yes," my friend responded.

"You never really talked about her, just her daughter."

My friend looked at me apologetically. For a reason I could not identify, I was unacceptable to the woman.

I still think about that woman and the sting of her rejection, but now with the grace of time it doesn't affect me as much. A quote from writer Zora Neale Hurston helps put such encounters into perspective: "Sometimes, I feel discriminated against, but it does not make me angry. It merely astonishes me. How can anyone deny themselves the pleasure of my company? It's beyond me."

Jesus was rejected too. He journeyed to His homeland, Nazareth, to teach in the synagogue, but "they were offended by Him" (Matthew 13:57, HCS) and He left without doing any miracles. It was their loss.

I certainly don't want to miss out on Jesus. —TARICE L. S. GRAY

FAITH STEP: *Run down a mental list of all the people you know who accept you for exactly who you are. It should make you smile.*

SUNDAY, JUNE 11

When your words turned up, I feasted on them; and they became my joy, the delight of my heart, because I belong to you. . . . Jeremiah 15:16 (CEB)

I COLLECT LISTS OF WORDS. Words I want to explore more deeply. Words I'd love to work into my next project because they say so much with so few letters. Words touted to be among the most beautiful ones in the English language, like *susurrous* (whispering, hissing) and *chatoyant* (like a cat's eye) and *mellifluous* (sound that is sweet and soothing, pleasing to the ear).

The comfort Jesus brings us through what He whispers to our hearts is mellifluous, pleasing both to the ear and to the soul. When we open God's Word and find a passage that speaks directly to that moment's need or we discover words of encouragement for a friend who is hurting, the words are like a feast. They provide what we are lacking and remind us that we belong to Him.

In that same fifteenth chapter of Jeremiah, a companion verse is heavily underlined in my Bible: "If you utter what is worthwhile, not what is worthless, you will be my spokesman" (Jeremiah 15:19, CEB).

How many worthless words do I utter? How often do I spew advice that isn't rooted in God's Word? How many times does Jesus catch me in the middle of sharing a prayer need that sounds more like gossip and then have to yank my chain to bring me back to the land of the uplifting?

Will your words and mine qualify us to remain His spokespeople? —CYNTHIA RUCHTI

FAITH STEP: *Sometimes setting two plates side by side—one healthy and full of nutrition, and the other piled high with harmful foods—makes our choice clearer. The plate of words Jesus offers is a feast, a joy, a delight. Consider what kind of meal your words would offer.*

MONDAY, JUNE 12

The righteous cry out, and the Lord hears them;
he delivers them from all their troubles.
Psalm 34:17 (NIV)

YESTERDAY OUR 2002 VEHICLE decided to take a break. From us. One hundred miles from home. Luckily, there was a repair shop close by. The repair shop hauled in the car while I texted my husband, Scott, who was back in the Bay Area: "Call me now! Car emergency!" When he called, he requested that I define "car emergency" in my texts to mean something like "Car Repair Emergency." That way he knows we are all alive.

Later, on the way home with Scott, I had a minibreakdown, mostly because I was scared about what the repair guy might say when he finally called. I sent up prayers like, *Okay, Jesus, how are You at healing engines?* and *Do You know of a car fairy who could drop off a new smell-free car at our house before we get home?* Thankfully, the car was able to be repaired.

I get so worried about how we are going to work everything out. The daily struggles of life can weigh me down. But...I don't want to get pulled down in the muck of anxiety that keeps me stressed and fearful. So I am trying to look up. To the One Who is not worried at all. In fact, He is not only *not* worried, He is already taking care of us, working everything together for good.

Jesus has a way of working things out, even when I'm stressed out and scared. He promises to deliver me from all of my troubles. Not some of my troubles. *All.* And I'm learning to keep my focus on Him and the promise of His deliverance. —SUSANNA FOTH AUGHTMON

FAITH STEP: *Meditate on Psalm 34:17. Remind yourself throughout the day that Jesus delivers you from all of your troubles.*

TUESDAY, JUNE 13

When the cares of my heart are many, your consolations cheer my soul.
Psalm 94:19 (ESV)

FIVE OF OUR SEVEN ADOPTED CHILDREN were adopted after age five. This means they had years of neglect, abuse, and being taught that wrong is right. It's hard to teach them to care for others first when they've had to fight to take care of themselves for so long. Instead they struggle with self-centeredness.

Their self-centeredness comes out in unexpected places, such as the "Happiest Place on Earth": Disney World. As one child gave us the silent treatment because she'd rather have been back at the hotel swimming, another child was stomping and pouting because of her sister's poor attitude. It proved to me again that happiness truly comes from the heart, not one's external environment.

Self-centeredness often comes from trying to carry all our own cares by ourselves. We think we are protecting ourselves, but the burden is heavy. The only cure is to know Jesus's consultations and comfort, and to know the care and comfort of those He's chosen to bring into our lives. Of course, to teach our children this, we need to turn to Jesus ourselves. We cannot give our children what we don't have spiritually, emotionally, and physically.

In the upcoming years, we'll continue to teach our daughter to care for *others* because we are already taking care of *her* needs. More than that, she can trust that Jesus will always be there to lean on. He—better than anyone else—can turn our unhappy days to some of the happiest on earth. —TRICIA GOYER

FAITH STEP: *Think of a person who tends to be self-centered and take time to pray for him or her. Ask Jesus to show you what He sees in that person and to give you compassion.*

WEDNESDAY, JUNE 14

Indeed, under the law almost everything is purified with blood, and without the shedding of blood there is no forgiveness of sins. Hebrews 9:22 (ESV)

DO YOU FAINT at the sight of blood? My husband comes close. It makes him extremely squeamish. I, on the other hand, don't have a problem with it. When Stella twirled a bit too fast in her pink tutu and crashed into the rock fireplace, I was the one who applied pressure to the wound that was spurting blood like a sprinkler. She has a little scar between her eyes, but I got the bleeding stopped without stitches.

As much as real blood doesn't bother me, I am somewhat averse to talking about the blood of Jesus. I feel bad about this because I know it's central to His sacrifice. I sing the songs about what can wash away my sin (nothing but the blood of Jesus) and how there's power in the blood. And even though I will myself to be respectful and reverent because I love Jesus, there's a part of me that wants to throw up. It's so barbaric. I understand why people in biblical times used blood language to make sense of what happened on the Cross. But we don't sacrifice animals to make peace with God anymore.

I was talking to my friend Bernie about this, and she said she used to feel the same way. But she's a doctor and deals with blood every day. So she's come to understand in a very tangible way how a person's life is totally connected to his or her blood. Now when she thinks about the blood of Jesus, she thinks about that—what it cost Him. That He literally gave us His life, and His blood gives us power over death. That's powerful. —GWEN FORD FAULKENBERRY

FAITH STEP: *What are some of the metaphors of our modern world that help you understand and connect with the Cross? Make a list and contrast those with the images used in the Bible.*

THURSDAY, JUNE 15

---

*He commanded and raised the stormy wind, which lifted up the waves
of the sea. . . . Then they cried to the Lord in their trouble, and
he delivered them from their distress. He made the storm be still, and
the waves of the sea were hushed. Then . . . he brought them
to their desired haven. Psalm 107:25–30 (ESV)*

ARKANSAS HAD CRAZY RAIN this month. The governor even declared
a dozen counties as disaster areas because of flooding. Facebook
posts showed trickling creeks turned into class-five rapids, a nearby
old mill was partly underwater from an overflowed river, and our
yard was halfway under water.

The waters subsided, but one video of a raging creek remains
stuck in my mind. The force was so powerful that no one could
stand up under it. It could have swept away most vehicles.

I love how creation points me to the Lord. Water, for example. I
need it to live; it refreshes me. But water can also redirect and consume and destroy. Those opposite roles remind me of Jesus and why
He came to earth and of my place with Him in eternity.

He called Himself a shepherd Who cares for His sheep
(John 10:14–15). Yet He also said, "For judgment I came into this
world, that those who do not see may see, and those who see may
become blind" (John 9:39, ESV). He calls me through His love to
help me understand that He wants to forgive me and lead me on
the best path for life.

But though I feel His love, I can also feel His justice. He takes His
holiness seriously. Jesus can be a deluge of love and grace as well as a
stream of truth and justice. Worship and honor well within me for
both of those realities. —ERIN KEELEY MARSHALL

FAITH STEP: *Write a note to Jesus thanking Him for His truth and grace, His
justice and goodness.*

FRIDAY, JUNE 16

But make sure that you don't get so absorbed and exhausted in taking care of all your day-by-day obligations that you lose track of the time and doze off, oblivious to God. Romans 13:11 (MSG)

I HAD A LOT TO ACCOMPLISH in the two days before a trip. I didn't just make one list—I had two or even three going, depending on how often I consolidated the jotted notes on random pieces of paper scattered around the cabin. I spent both days knocking out items from a list that, maybe not so mysteriously, kept getting longer.

I worked very hard and got it all done. When I finally laid down my tired body on the bed at night, I hurt.

The first day I attacked the list too early, starting as soon as my feet hit the floor. I skipped my daily Bible reading and prayer, telling myself I'd do it when I took a break. You'd think after all these years, I'd know better. Scatterbrained, forgetful, and klutzy, I'd have lost my way without that ever-evolving list.

The second day, I woke up almost afraid to begin again. This time, though, I took a deep breath and started with quiet time, even catching up the missed Bible reading from the day before. No, the day wasn't miraculously easy. I still worked very hard. And I still got frustrated when things refused to fall into place. But somehow even though I was tired, I was less frantic—more focused and peaceful.

Taking the time to connect first with Jesus always makes a huge difference. Slowing down and relaxing in His presence centers and grounds me. Every time. Every day. Trip or no trip.
—SUZANNE DAVENPORT TIETJEN

FAITH STEP: *You may believe that if you work hard enough, you can get it all done. Set down your list and give your day back to Jesus. Imagine Him working right alongside you today.*

SATURDAY, JUNE 17

Jesus replied, "No one who puts a hand to the plow and looks back is fit for service in the kingdom of God." Luke 9:62 (NIV)

EACH YEAR, MY HUSBAND AND I tackle a small section of the Superior Hiking Trail. We park our car at the end of the trail, then a shuttle drives us to the trailhead and drops us off. From there we're on our own. To reach our car, we have to complete the hike—no turning back.

I always like the first half of the hike. Provisions are organized in the backpack. Hiking boots are laced just right. I stride forward, eager to see what's around the next corner. After a few miles, reality sets in. Blisters form, muscles quiver from exertion, the trail switchbacks up again and again until my legs scream at me to stop.

When we welcome Jesus into our life, we begin with great enthusiasm. We volunteer at church, reach out to our community, pray boldly, and face challenges with eagerness. But just like the rigors of a hiking trail, the harsh realities of life can wear on us. Conflicts with those we're trying to serve can create blisters on our souls. Disdain for the message of the Gospel can surprise us and deplete our spiritual muscles. Remaining faithful in prayer for a situation that hasn't changed can feel like never-ending switchbacks up a mountain.

When fatigue threatens my resolve, it helps to remember that I'm "all in." Like on the trail, I've set a course where the only way to go is forward. Now my only reason for a glance back is to rejoice that Jesus has already taken me through paths that once seemed impossible. With that reminder, Jesus restores my enthusiasm. Squarely facing the goal, I can follow Him for another day. —SHARON HINCK

FAITH STEP: *Take a walk or a small hike today. Ask Jesus to deepen your commitment to following Him.*

SUNDAY, JUNE 18

*But thanks be to God, who in Christ always leads us in triumphal procession,
and through us spreads the fragrance of the knowledge of him everywhere.*
2 Corinthians 2:14 (ESV)

MY HUSBAND TRAVELS FOR WORK. When he travels internationally there are times when he's gone for seven or eight days. That's a long stretch for little kids. There are times when they are overwhelmed, tired, and emotional—and they just want their dad.

More than once I've found one of my kids in their dad's closet cuddling up to one of his shirts. "It just smells like him," they tell me. Their dad isn't there physically, but the fragrance of him helps to calm their nerves, to bring them peace, and to remind them of his love.

Isn't it amazing then that we, children of the Father, are the ones Jesus uses to spread His fragrance? Jesus is not here physically on earth, and so until He returns, we are His representatives. It is our calling to make Him known, and we do this when walking the victorious life we've already been given, triumphant because of Him.

When we exhibit peace during times we should be overwhelmed, show strength when we are tired, have rational thoughts when we are emotional, others will start to notice. And when they take a whiff of the joyful aroma of our lives, they will sense Jesus's fragrance too. Before long they will want to encounter Christ themselves. And when they do, His sweet fragrance will calm their nerves, bring them peace, and show them His unfailing love. —TRICIA GOYER

FAITH STEP: *Find a special fragrance to represent your walk with Christ. Wear it every day for the next week, and whenever you get a whiff, use it as a reminder that you are Jesus's fragrance to the world.*

MONDAY, JUNE 19

My dear children, I am writing this to you so that you will not sin. But if
anyone does sin, we have an advocate who pleads our case before the Father.
He is Jesus Christ, the one who is truly righteous.
1 John 2:1 (NLT)

IN 2008, A CHARITABLE ORGANIZATION asked me to become an advocate on its behalf by speaking up for children living in poverty. I believe in its mission to bring life in its fullness to children around the world, and my family had already sponsored kids in India for about ten years prior through this charity, so I said yes.

Becoming an advocate meant I threw my support behind this nonprofit and had no qualms about associating my name and reputation with it. My experience has given me the joy of helping nearly one thousand children receive education and medical care, but it's also given me a better understanding of today's key verse.

What does it mean that Jesus is our advocate? Synonyms would suggest He's our backer, our campaigner, and our activist. He throws His support behind us. Specifically, He defends our case before God when we sin. It's like He speaks up for us and says, "Not guilty. I already paid the penalty on their behalf."

If I've placed my faith in Jesus, then He's put His stamp of approval on me. Now I'm on the same team sharing the same mission.

I find this truth exhilarating! Praise wells within me as I ponder Jesus being my advocate. I feel well-loved knowing that the One Who is truly righteous speaks on my behalf and willingly associates His name and reputation with me. —GRACE FOX

FAITH STEP: *Do you feel shame for past failures? Remind yourself of the truth.*
Say, "Jesus is my advocate. He's already dealt with this."

TUESDAY, JUNE 20

If I ride the wings of the morning, if I dwell by the farthest oceans,
even there your hand will guide me, and your strength will support me.
Psalm 139:9–10 (NLT)

WHO NEEDS AN AISLE SEAT *when the view is this gorgeous?* I thought. Gazing through the small window, I marveled at the giant, puffy clouds that looked solid enough to float on, set against the bluest of backgrounds. Whenever a space opened up, I caught a glimpse of the green and brown patchwork of the fields far below.

As we began our descent, the captain warned about turbulence as the plane lurched and the view on both sides unnerved me: nothing but a sheet of solid whiteness. I gripped the armrests with each bump and shake, reassured by the knowledge that the aircraft lay in the hands of an experienced pilot.

Each of us will get knocked around by turbulence from time to time. We'll have days when everything is going smoothly, then *bam!*—an unexpected problem shakes you up: a job loss, a serious illness, bad news about a loved one, or an unforeseen turn of events that leaves you confused.

During those times, it's comforting to know we're in the hands of a Pilot we can trust. Jesus has the power and wisdom to guide us through every situation. The ride may get bumpy, but He has promised to bring us safely to our destination. —DIANNE NEAL MATTHEWS

FAITH STEP: *Think about where you are experiencing turbulence. Visualize Jesus taking your hand and guiding you to a place of peace, joy, and rest.*

WEDNESDAY, JUNE 21

A man of many companions may come to ruin,
but there is a friend who sticks closer than a brother.
Proverbs 18:24 (ESV)

MY HUSBAND AND I had been out of town for two weeks and were happy to get home. After we dragged our suitcases into the house late in the evening, I saw the voice mail light blinking on our answering machine. My friend Kathy had left a message saying she'd hoped to talk and that she was having a rough time. The message had gone unanswered for several days.

I quickly booted up the computer and sent her an e-mail to let her know why I hadn't responded and wrote myself a note to phone her as soon as possible. I hated the feeling of letting down a friend, especially when she'd reached out to me in a time of need.

As I pondered how unreliable I sometimes am, I was filled again with gratitude for our Savior who is ever-present. When we tell Him we need support or even just a friend to listen, He never misses the message. The world can be a dark place filled with hardships that break my heart. I watch the news and hurt for the suffering. It's hard to know the best ways to make a difference. It's even difficult to figure out how to shine a light in the shadows cast by the pain and grief in the lives of family and friends closest to us.

When our efforts seem so inadequate and flawed, it helps to remember that we aren't the Savior—but we can point to Him. And as Jesus empowers and guides, He will teach us how to be a better friend, the way He is to us. He is truly the friend who sticks closer than a brother. —SHARON HINCK

FAITH STEP: *Think of one friend who needs help or encouragement. Ask Jesus to guide you in specific ways to express your friendship.*

THURSDAY, JUNE 22

While suffering, He uttered no threats, but kept entrusting Himself to Him who judges righteously. 1 Peter 2:23 (NAS)

As a parent, one of the most hurtful things I experience is when I feel like my kids misunderstand my heart. It's not so much the questioning that bothers me. It's the attitude that goes with it—an attitude of distrust, like I'm trying to punish them rather than doing something good that they need. This is hurtful because I want them to know they can trust my heart of love—I'm doing what I do, ultimately, for their good.

I was trying to explain this to my son, how it makes no sense to distrust me when I have proven myself to be trustworthy every day of his life. Then it occurred to me that I do the same thing when I doubt God, which I'm sure I do to some degree every day. And hasn't He proven Himself, as the hymn says, "o'er and o'er"?

The key to trusting God is to follow Jesus's example. Imagine how unfairly He was treated, how it must have appeared that God didn't know what He was doing, as Jesus made His way to the Cross. But the Bible says Jesus entrusted Himself because He knew God would do what was right.

Unfortunately, my kids can't know that about me. The best I can do is try to do what's right. I'm going to make mistakes, but I need them to trust my love anyway.

We have a better deal than that. We know Jesus knew the character of God because He was God. He trusted God's love—and so can we.
—GWEN FORD FAULKENBERRY

FAITH STEP: *Are you going through something that makes it hard for you to trust God in this moment? As an act of your will, follow Jesus. Keep entrusting yourself, as He did.*

FRIDAY, JUNE 23

The Lord will fulfill his purpose for me; your steadfast love, O Lord, endures forever. Do not forsake the work of your hands.
Psalm 138:8 (ESV)

NEARLY EVERY DAY I receive a message or a Facebook post about teenage mothers or adoption. People know these topics are my passions. But it's not like I woke up one day and knew I wanted to dedicate my life to needy young people. The call came slowly over time. One young person I met. One prayer at a time, asking God to show me His heart.

So how does one know if God's calling him or her to a specific purpose? First, there's a burden on your heart you can't shake. Second, there is a specific person you know who needs your help. Third, there is a Scripture passage that encourages you to have faith and to step out. Finally, when you pray, you have a sense that God is asking you to act.

Of course, just because we feel the call doesn't mean following it is easy. We often feel as if we don't have time. We also worry if we're taking time away from others we care about. And most of all we feel that we can't do it alone.

We also need to understand that we can only serve others when we do so in God's strength. We don't need to have confidence in ourselves to step out and follow God's call. Instead, we need to put our confidence in God. If He's made us aware of a need, then He will also give us a way to follow through—not because we can do it but because He can. It's then that a passion is born. A passion for others and, most of all, a passion for Him. —TRICIA GOYER

FAITH STEP: *Which person or group would you like to serve? Write down what worries you about reaching out. Then after each worry write, "I can't, but God can." Keep that list and pray over it. Ask God to show you when to step out.*

SATURDAY, JUNE 24

He who was seated on the throne said, "I am making everything new!"
Then he said, "Write this down, for these words are trustworthy and true."
Revelation 21:5 (NIV)

THE OTHER DAY, MY MOM CALLED to talk about Jack's quilt. She is an amazingly talented quilter and has set out to make each of her eleven grandkids their own quilt. Jack is number five.

When we were with her this summer, she and Jack sat down together. First, she had him pick out a quilt pattern that he liked. And then he told her all of the different colors that he liked: black, turquoise, blue, lime green, yellow, gray. I couldn't see how these would be a good combination. But my mom has an eye for color combinations. She knows how to make pattern and color and texture work together to form something beautiful.

Yesterday she texted me a picture of the finished quilt. It is a thing of beauty. I couldn't believe how amazing it looked. How all of the different colors that Jack chose blended so well and so vibrantly. I showed the picture to Jack, and he said, "That is awesome!" Which is high praise coming from a fourteen-year-old.

The quilt reminds me of how the patchwork of our lives can become something lovely and treasured in the hands of Jesus. We just can't see it. We cannot see how all the goodness, the mess-ups, the weaknesses, the heartache, and the craziness of daily living can be transformed into a thing of beauty. But it can. And it is. And it will be. When we offer it up to Jesus. It is the reason He came to earth: to transform our lives into a thing of beauty, for His glory and our joy. He is making our lives something beautiful and new. —SUSANNA FOTH AUGHTMON

FAITH STEP: *Color a picture of a quilt. In the different squares, write down different seasons or areas of your life that Jesus is making beautiful and new.*

SUNDAY, JUNE 25

*Only let each person lead the life that the Lord has assigned to him,
and to which God has called him.*
1 Corinthians 7:17 (ESV)

OUR FAMILY ATTENDS an inner-city church in Little Rock, Arkansas, which means there are a lot of needs and many opportunities for outreach. There are some who serve in the food pantry and others who lead an afterschool club at a local, low-income apartment complex. One man helps immigrants with their legal paperwork; another man assists teens aging out of foster care. I serve young moms through a weekly support group.

Each of us is passionate about our ministry. Each of us is honored to share the good news of Jesus Christ with "the least of these." We are leading the life Jesus has called us to, and if you were to hear each of our stories, you'd discover that volunteers got involved with these ministries only after surrendering their own dreams and goals to Jesus. We each desired ease and comfort, but Jesus had different blueprints for our lives in mind.

In the Bible, we read: "God-of-the-Angel-Armies speaks: 'Exactly as I planned, it will happen. Following my blueprints, it will take shape" (Isaiah 14:24, MSG). The word "planned" here is translated "compare." The life Jesus called us to takes us out of our comfort zone. It's as if Jesus has weighed the different possibilities, looked at them from all angles, and then chose the best way. Jesus assigned a certain type of life for us not just for our benefit, but for the benefit of others who need to know Him. As we say yes to Him and follow after Him, we are blessed and in turn others are blessed in numerous ways. —TRICIA GOYER

FAITH STEP: *Write a list of five places where you could volunteer. Then pick one and schedule a way to give your time, skills, or resources in the next month.*

MONDAY, JUNE 26

God can pour on the blessings in astonishing ways so that you're ready for anything and everything, more than just ready to do what needs to be done. 2 Corinthians 9:8 (MSG)

"READY, SET, GO!" That childhood cry tugged at my memory one summer as I planned to leave for a mission trip to Peru. Although two decades had passed since my last mission adventure to Mexico, I prepared as best I could. I felt a little rusty, as my responsibilities primarily involved working with children, leading a vacation Bible school. Still, what could go wrong?

Plenty, apparently. As soon as we arrived, I learned we'd teach for two hours a day, not one. The day before vacation Bible school began, I ended up scrambling to teach a room full of children, ages five to thirteen, for an hour and a half during the worship service—all without preparation or props. The week included a fall and a swollen ankle, a trip to the ER, an earthquake, and a stomach virus. I uttered Samuel's childlike cry often to the Lord during that week: "Speak, God. I'm your servant, ready to listen" (1 Samuel 3:10, MSG), with a few "Help!" cries thrown in. But I kept teaching.

When the week ended, I learned that the word *ready*—and the word *blessing*—were strangely related. In spite of numerous challenges for which I'd been totally unprepared, seventeen children in our group decided to follow Jesus. What a joy to celebrate with them.

There are some things for which you can't prepare. But when you lay your expectations at the feet of Jesus and cry out to Him, "Ready, set, go!" He loves to pour on unexpected blessings in astonishing ways. —REBECCA BARLOW JORDAN

FAITH STEP: *Are you facing any challenges for which you feel unprepared? Take time today to thank Jesus that with each challenge will come His unexpected blessings.*

TUESDAY, JUNE 27

But seek first the kingdom of God and his righteousness, and all these things will be added to you. Matthew 6:33 (ESV)

MY HUSBAND, STEVE, has been in the construction industry for his entire career as a project manager for a commercial building contractor. A few months ago he started his own company. It's an ongoing faith journey as we trust Jesus to provide financially for our family and build this dream he has begun.

Jesus has used some painful situations to lead our family to this point of leaning on Him in new ways. Despite working hard, we've had promising doors close: a job loss, a sale of a beloved home, ragged weariness. But we can see how Jesus has been using those circumstances to teach us to rely on Him instead of our own efforts.

Now, as Steve prays for direction, his new theme is "from sole provider to soul of provision." As Jesus has drawn Steve to abide more in His provision, Steve's soul has been fed and freed as he's never experienced before.

Matthew 6 says a lot about focusing on Jesus's priorities and trusting Him to provide what we need. The Lord has been sinking these truths deep into Steve's and my hearts. Thus, our prayer was born, and we are learning to rely as never before on the Lord.

Jesus has creative ways to help us learn to lean on Him and hold an open hand in expectancy of His provision. It's a beautiful and big and sometimes scary way of life, and we're in it for the long haul.

We don't know what "all these things will be" that will be added to us when we seek Jesus's kingdom first. But we can rest in Him because He knows, He is faithful, and He promises never to forsake us.
—ERIN KEELEY MARSHALL

FAITH STEP: *How has Jesus shown you that He is your provider? Ask Him to fill your soul with His provision.*

WEDNESDAY, JUNE 28

Christ loved the church and gave himself up for her to make her holy, cleansing her by the washing with water through the word, and to present her to himself as a radiant church, without stain or wrinkle or any other blemish, but holy and blameless. Ephesians 5:25–27 (NIV)

IT'S UNFORTUNATE THAT the only household task I enjoy in its essence is ironing—something few people do anymore. On laundry day when I was little, clothes came off the line smelling lovely but they were wrinkly and stiff. We sprinkled them and stuffed them in a pillowcase to soften up, then pulled them out one at a time to press out the wrinkles. Special clothes—Sunday dresses, pinafores, dress shirts—were starched.

I begged to do the ironing, but my mother hesitated to let me get near her hot iron. Still, she let me try sooner than she wanted to. I liked the heat and the steam, the sense of rocking back and forth as I worked, the now-smooth results, and the feeling of accomplishment. It affected my world, changed things for the better.

When I think of that tiny work and how much joy I took in it, I catch a glimpse of the satisfaction Jesus must have felt in His infinitely greater work of loving us and giving Himself for us so that we could come before Him radiant and holy, free of even the tiniest spot or wrinkle. The Bible says Jesus did it "for the joy set before him" (Hebrews 12:2).

I still enjoy ironing. I'd like to find joy in all my work, but I'm not quite there yet. But I do take joy in pleasing Jesus and in doing any task well. That thought helps me do my best, "prepared and willing to do any upright and honorable work" (Titus 3:1, AMP).

Find the joy! —SUZANNE DAVENPORT TIETJEN

FAITH STEP: *Think of some kind of work you enjoy. Today, if you can, do it. Relax into it, use your senses, and enjoy whatever you like about it. Share your joy with Jesus.*

THURSDAY, JUNE 29

We take our lead from Christ, who is the source. . . .
Ephesians 4:16 (MSG)

SO OFTEN I FEEL LIKE Charlie Brown in *The Peanuts Movie*. In an effort to impress the Little Red-Haired Girl, he tries to do everything well, but ends up making a mess of things and feeling like a failure. He feels like he's not smart enough, strong enough, or cool enough. He tells a friend who is concerned about him, "I've come down with a terrible case of inadequacy."

A lot of people I talk to have the same problem. We're trying to balance families, careers, friendship, personal growth, and health, not to mention our spiritual lives. Sometimes it feels like there are so many demands, we can never meet them all. We pour ourselves out until there's no more energy left and still so much is required. Like Charlie Brown, it's easy to feel inadequate.

In such times, we must remember what Paul says in Ephesians. We take our lead from Jesus. He is the source. We can't meet everyone's needs, but He can. We can't necessarily respond to stress with peace on our own, but we can draw from the source of true peace. It may take more love than we feel we have at times to take care of others, but the One we follow *is* love. He has enough power to help us forgive. Enough strength for us to draw on to reach our goals. He is the source of wisdom, help, salvation, the source of all things good. —GWEN FORD FAULKENBERRY

FAITH STEP: *Are you like Charlie Brown (and me)? Do you have a case of inadequacy today? Go to the source. Ask Jesus to fill you with whatever you're lacking. In Him, there will always be enough for you to live the life He's called you to.*

FRIDAY, JUNE 30

---

*"The coming of the Son of Man can be illustrated by the story of a man
going on a long trip. . . . He gave each of his slaves
instructions about the work they were to do, and he told the gatekeeper
to watch for his return."*
Mark 13:34 (NLT)

MY FAMILY LIVED ON A SMALL ISLAND in British Columbia for eleven
years. In that area, homeowners wishing to holiday elsewhere often
invited local students to house-sit.

A couple I know traveled overseas for a few weeks one summer.
They hired a young woman to house-sit, left a chore list, and circled
their return date on the kitchen calendar.

My friends returned home a day earlier than planned. They found
their flower gardens overrun by weeds. Dirty dishes covered the
kitchen counter, and pots were piled in the sink. Towels littered the
bathroom floor, and the bathroom itself hadn't been cleaned. Imagine the house sitter's chagrin!

When I heard the story, I thought about Jesus and His promise to
return someday. We don't know the exact day or time of His appearance, but we know it's imminent. I want to be prepared.

For me, that means living every day in a way that honors Jesus. I
ask Him to make me supersensitive to sin in my life so I can address
it quickly. When He returns, I don't want to be embarrassed by
what He finds. I want to be ready so I can welcome Him with open
arms. —GRACE FOX

FAITH STEP: *What would Jesus find in your heart if He returned today?
Ask Him to show you what spiritual housekeeping needs to happen, so you can
welcome Him with open arms.*

SATURDAY, JULY 1

He made the entire human race and made the earth hospitable, with plenty of time and space for living so we could seek after God, and not just grope around in the dark but actually find him. . . . He's not remote; he's near. We live and move in him. Acts 17:28–29 (MSG)

MY KIDS RECENTLY RECEIVED RipStiks from their grandparents. RipStiks are like glorified skateboards that not only roll forward and back but also swivel. Just standing on them takes practice and balance, and that's before learning to move on them.

Mastering them is a whole-body technique that requires a willingness to fall often during the learning curve. It's about finding and keeping centered despite uneven pavement, road bumps, physical and environmental limitations, fear, and peer distractions.

Last week the kids made a course inside the house. Some of their pathways were tight, requiring fine turns. While learning to stay centered and focused, they also had to manage their own power so they didn't demolish my decor. I've been amazed watching their determination.

In a tactile way, watching them has reminded me of two spiritual disciplines: holding fast to Jesus, my Center, to remain steady despite the forces around me, and putting in the time to learn His rhythms in my life. There is a reason spiritual disciplines have their place in getting to know Jesus. The more time and focus I put into my relationship with Him, the more I'll see myself being steadied by Him and the more balance I'll enjoy in areas of life that used to knock me off-kilter.

Life is fast and full and sometimes furious, but I can manage the tight spots if I discipline myself to keep Jesus as my Center.
—ERIN KEELEY MARSHALL

FAITH STEP: *What rocks your balance? Name the situation or relationship and ask Jesus to keep you centered on Him, so you remain steady.*

SUNDAY, JULY 2

Then God said, "Let us make mankind in our image, in our likeness,
so that they may rule over the fish in the sea and the birds in the sky,
over the livestock and all the wild animals, and over all
the creatures that move along the ground."
Genesis 1:26 (NIV)

I HAVE THREE BOYS. And when people meet them for the first time they say things like, "Wow! They look nothing alike," and "They don't even look like you."

I have always felt that since I carried them in my body, my boys should slightly resemble me. No such luck. They also have very distinct personalities. They like doing different activities. They play different sports. They respond to different situations with their own outlook and wisdom.

There is a beauty to their individuality. I wouldn't want to change a thing about them. They are made in the image of the One who loves them the most, and I love them just the way they are. And Jesus loves the way that He made them. Different. Special. Unique.

He made you that way, too. My son, Jack, likes to say that you are completely unique...just like everyone else in the world. You have an outlook on life and Jesus's goodness that no one else has. Jesus loves who He made you to be: a child of the Most High. You are a joy spreader. You are a lover, not a fighter. You are a hope giver. You are a song singer. You are a soul lifter. You are a light bearer. Every time you step out the door, you have the chance to show off the beauty of Who Jesus is and how He made you to be like Him.
—SUSANNA FOTH AUGHTMON

FAITH STEP: *As you start your day, remind yourself, "I am made in the image of Jesus. I am a child of the Most High." It will change how you live out your day.*

MONDAY, JULY 3

Yet as soon as the priests who carried the ark reached the Jordan and their feet touched the water's edge, the water from upstream stopped flowing. It piled up in a heap a great distance away.... Joshua 3:15–16 (NIV)

THE FIRST TIME two of our grandkids saw the ocean, their expressions said it all: wide-eyed, mouths gaping with a loud "Wow!" The water's vastness overwhelmed them. We promised them they'd love it, but I wondered how they'd respond when they reached the water's edge.

As they tiptoed in, the waves began tickling their feet, begging for an adventure. Seconds later, they plunged into the cooling waters. Squeals of delight followed.

When Joshua and the people he led approached the Jordan River, I wonder if they felt the same way as my grandchildren. God had promised them the land beyond the Jordan. However, they faced a huge obstacle. The Jordan banks overflowed at that time of year. They must have felt overwhelmed.

But as God promised, as soon as the leaders' feet touched the water's edge, the obstacle fell away. The swift waters parted, and all the people crossed onto dry land. Can you imagine the squeals of delight from their children?

I remember times in my life when I, too, faced challenging situations. All required obedience and a step into unknown waters. I wish I could say I always obeyed.

Yet every time I trusted Jesus, without fail, He blessed. Not only did the waters part, but they also, with Jesus's grace, piled up higher than the eye could see. And I crossed over from doubt into delight.

—REBECCA BARLOW JORDAN

FAITH STEP: *Memorize Joshua 1:9. List any obstacles you're facing. Then ask Jesus to help you to trust Him and give you wisdom and courage.*

TUESDAY, JULY 4

For the sake of Christ, then, I am content with weaknesses, insults, hardships, persecutions, and calamities. For when I am weak, then I am strong.
2 Corinthians 12:10 (ESV)

I JUMPED AT THE CHANCE to be on the faculty at a major writers' conference. But intimidation set in after I discovered that I would lead a ten-hour class on writing devotions, teach a one-hour workshop, and be available for appointments. I spent a few months gathering material, preparing notes, composing handouts, and creating PowerPoints.

As I prepared, I strongly felt the need for prayer support, so I contacted a few close friends. By the time I boarded the plane, I had checked and double-checked all the class materials I needed. I so wanted to look professional; instead I felt scatterbrained: forgetting to cover something and having to backtrack. Running out of time or failing to advance the PowerPoint. But the worst happened on the last day: I forgot to include the handouts in my tote bag.

I gave the class a devotion to edit and raced across campus to my room. Later, I mentioned my embarrassment to a student. She reassured me that I shouldn't feel bad. "When you left," she said, "one woman said to another one, 'She brings peace, doesn't she?'"

How odd they perceived me like that, I thought. But really, it's no surprise. I've learned that I'm usually at my best when I'm weakest and needy. Because that's when I'm fully aware of my dependence on Jesus. When I allow His power to work through me, I see Him do things I could never have accomplished on my own. No matter how scatterbrained I feel. —DIANNE NEAL MATTHEWS

FAITH STEP: *Think of a struggle or a problem that makes you feel helpless. Then ask Jesus to fill you with His power.*

WEDNESDAY, JULY 5

Some fell in the weeds; as it came up, it was strangled among the weeds and nothing came of it. Some fell on good earth and came up with a flourish, producing a harvest exceeding his wildest dreams.
Mark 4:7–8 (MSG)

FOR YEARS OUR FAMILY LIVED in a country subdivision. The back of our house faced expansive fields where corn and soybeans grew. We wanted to landscape along the back edge of our property, but it lay so far from the house and the outside faucet that it was difficult to water. Then one summer my husband planted a line of hedge roses in hopes they would be low maintenance. They didn't exactly thrive.

One day I walked back to weed the roses, which had managed a few blooms. The largest and tallest flower made me stare for several minutes. Out of the weeds at the edge of the field, a green threadlike vine had crept through the dirt border, over the lower rung of the split-rail fence, and into the rosebush. It had grown upward and wrapped itself a few times around the rose stem under the bloom. That weed looked so sneaky and evil, I relished digging its roots out of the ground.

Jesus warned about a spiritual kind of weeding that needs to be done. I can let the cares of this earthly life and desires for material wealth and success crowd out God's Word so that it doesn't bear fruit in me. Even after I respond to the Gospel and become a follower of Jesus, these things still try to creep back into my life and strangle my spiritual growth. It's important to guard and nurture our relationship with Jesus by doing any necessary "weeding." Only then will we bloom and flourish the way He intends. —DIANNE NEAL MATTHEWS

FAITH STEP: *Evaluate what your mind has been focused on lately. Have any weeds crept in and tried to get a stranglehold on you? Ask Jesus to help you dig them out and replace them with His truth.*

THURSDAY, JULY 6

*Nehemiah said, "Go and enjoy choice food and sweet drinks, and send some
to those who have nothing prepared. This day is holy to our Lord.
Do not grieve, for the joy of the Lord is your strength."
Nehemiah 8:10 (NIV)*

MY SISTER, JENNY, is one of the most joyful people to be around.
I think it's because she loves life so much. It's not that she hasn't
had difficulties in life. She has. It's not that she hasn't had her heart
broken. She has. It's not that everything goes the way that she wants
it to. It doesn't. But she is not going to let that determine how she
walks out her days. If there is ever an opportunity to do something
fun, her response is always, "We must!" If there is a reason to celebrate, Jenny will say, "Do we need to go get some ice cream?" And
we usually do need to go get some ice cream because the more ice
cream the better. Jenny views life through a lens of joy. And when
you hang out with her, you get in on the joy.

It is how life should be as a Jesus follower. When we follow His
path, we get in on the joy of who He is. It is not that life can't be
difficult or heart wrenching. It can. It's not that life will go exactly
like we think it should. It won't. But there is so much joy to be had
in the presence of Jesus. He loves us so much. He has good plans
for us. He has surrounded us with grace and mercy. He is the lifter
of our head. He is our shield. He is our strong tower. He is our kind
shepherd. And He can be our joy. We should take Him up on it. As
Jenny would say, "We must!" —SUSANNA FOTH AUGHTMON

FAITH STEP: *Go buy an ice cream in celebration of who Jesus is and all He has
done for you.*

FRIDAY, JULY 7

*"Where is your faith?" he asked his disciples. In fear and amazement
they asked one another, "Who is this? He commands even
the winds and the water, and they obey him."*
Luke 8:25 (NIV)

THIS MORNING THE WIND IS COAXING my curtains into a dance as
they furl and billow. We've had several hot, humid days, but today
lower temperatures have allowed me to fling the windows wide.
The refreshing air invigorates me. I'd almost forgotten the joy of a
cool breeze.

Of course some wind is frightening. Tornadoes, hurricanes, or
typhoons can cause massive danger and destruction. In their small
boat, the disciples needed Jesus to calm the storm. They were
amazed to discover that the same Jesus Who walked with them on
dusty paths, broke bread with them, and rested in the shade of an
olive tree could also control the forces of nature.

We often cry out to Jesus when the winds of life are harsh. But
the same Jesus who can quiet the storm can also send an invigorat-
ing fresh breeze when we need it. Perhaps we need a creative way
to approach some problem at work or new energy to invest in a
challenging relationship. Perhaps we need a glimmer of hope that
our volunteer services are making a difference. Perhaps we just need
strength to lift our arms toward the heavens and welcome His touch.

Let's not wait for fierce storms to ask for Jesus to act in our lives.
Let's acknowledge what the disciples saw firsthand. Jesus has power
and can speak change into our lives. He can calm us when we are
storm-tossed or stir us when we're passive or lifeless. —SHARON HINCK

FAITH STEP: *Open a window. Breathe in the breeze and ask Jesus to send the
refreshing changes we need as we serve Him.*

SATURDAY, JULY 8

I prayed to the Lord, and he answered me. He freed me from all my fears.
Psalm 34:4 (NLT)

WHEN WE FIRST MENTIONED that we were thinking about adopting older kids, we got a lot of responses, and many of them were warnings, which at times filled us with fear: "I know a couple who adopted older kids, and they stole from them and made their life miserable." "Older kids you adopt will bully your younger kids." "If you mess up the birth order, your children will struggle and will be in therapy for life."

When I listened to the opinions of others, fear, confusion, and worries filled my mind. Yet when John and I prayed and considered Jesus's still, small voice speaking to our hearts, we knew adopting older kids was the right thing to do. And we realized that while people were trying to offer us advice, their advice was leaving Jesus out of the picture.

To be afraid is to picture the future without Jesus's protection. To be confused is to picture the future without Jesus's guidance and His Spirit. To be worried is to picture the future without Jesus's wisdom. John and I had to trust that if Jesus was leading us to adopt older kids, He would be there to help us with whatever happened.

Now that we have older girls living in our home, there have been numerous challenges, but all of these challenges have been tackled with Jesus's wisdom, guidance, and Spirit. Things don't have to be perfect to be right, even adoption—especially adoption. Things won't be perfect with any child, but we know that Jesus will be with us no matter what comes our way. —TRICIA GOYER

FAITH STEP: *Think about a decision you are trying to make. Write a letter to Jesus, telling Him that you trust Him and that you believe His wisdom, guidance, and Spirit will be with you today and into the future.*

SUNDAY, JULY 9

And I heard a loud voice from heaven saying, "Behold, the tabernacle of
God is with men, and He will dwell with them, and they shall be His people.
God Himself will be with them and be their God."
Revelation 21:3 (NKJV)

I STARTED A VERY AMBITIOUS Bible study at my church in which we
are reading through the entire Bible in ninety days. We met to discuss the first week's readings, which were basically Genesis through
somewhere in Leviticus. I am not particularly fond of Leviticus.

I am, however, fond of the detailed description of the tabernacle
given in Exodus. It is in places like this in the Bible where I fall in
love all over again with the mystery and majesty of the Word.

Consider this: the Old Testament tabernacle had one door. One.
One way in and one way out—the same door for sinners and saints
and everyone else in between. A coincidence that later Jesus would
call Himself the door? I think not. Then there's the brazen altar, where
a blood sacrifice was made to atone for sins. Remember Romans 5:8?
While we were still sinners, Christ died for us. Then there's the holy
place—illuminated by the menorah or lampstand. He is the light
of the world. The brazen laver, where the priest washed himself,
another picture of our need to be cleansed.

My favorite part, though, is the curtain that separated everyone and
everything from the holy of holies. On the night Jesus died, it was
torn in two. No more separation. The tabernacle of God is with us.
—GWEN FORD FAULKENBERRY

FAITH STEP: *Look up the guidelines for the tabernacle starting in Exodus 26.*
As you read through, sketch a picture of how you imagine it looked. Move through
it, stopping to appreciate the symbolism of all of the parts.

MONDAY, JULY 10

Who then will condemn us? Will Christ Jesus? No, for he is the one who died for us and was raised to life for us and is sitting at the place of highest honor next to God, pleading for us.
Romans 8:34 (NLT)

I'VE BEEN A JESUS FOLLOWER for fifty years, but the enormity of what He did for humankind never ceases to amaze me.

Imagine—the King of the universe could have commanded our allegiance, but He did not. The Creator could have programmed us like mass-produced robots to cater to His every whim, but He did not. The Holy One could have looked upon our miserable failures and banished us with His breath, but He did not.

Jesus, the Son of God Almighty—did something that boggles my mind. He made Himself nothing and assumed the humble position of a babe (Philippians 2:6–7). Then He did the unfathomable by willingly dying a brutal death on a Cross to take our place in order to set us free.

Jesus could have come to earth to pursue His divine rights. Instead, He yielded those rights for our sake. He died for us, was raised to life for us, and now sits at God's right hand where He pleads for us. Everything He did in life, death, and resurrection was about us.

Even as I write these words, I sit in awe of what Jesus has done for us. Amazement fills me; gratitude wells within me. "Thank You, Jesus, for Your mercy and Your love poured out for humankind." —GRACE FOX

FAITH STEP: *Spend a few moments pondering what Jesus has done for you. Sing a song to Him—a song of praise and adoration for this One Who loves you more than words can ever express.*

TUESDAY, JULY 11

He said to me . . . feed your belly and fill your stomach with this scroll. . . .
So I ate it, and in my mouth it became as sweet as honey. Ezekiel 3:3 (CEB)

"IF ONLY WE COULD KEEP her out of the plants. Eating dirt can't be good for her," my daughter-in-law said, sighing. We weren't talking about a mischief-making kitten or a new puppy. We were talking about my one-year-old granddaughter.

No matter what her parents and we grandparents did to protect her from it, the child found a way to get into the dirt and shove some into her mouth. Making mud pies took on a whole new meaning for a child who found them delicious.

Our concern both intensified and was allayed when her pediatrician listened to our description of her behavior and requested lab work. My granddaughter's condition was determined to be pica, an eating disorder that causes people to crave and consume nonfood items such as dirt, clay, paint chips, plaster, chalk, paper...

Her pica was rooted in an iron deficiency that was relatively easy to correct. What a relief. Not only were the plants safe again, but she also was kept from developing far more serious illnesses from the lack of nutrients and the dangerous things that lurk in dirt.

Sometimes we act like a child with pica. What we consume—by eating, listening, viewing, scrolling, thinking—has little nutritional value and the very real potential for harming our souls.

We know the root cause of our appetite for consuming what isn't even food. Left to its own devices, too often our flesh craves the opposite of what Jesus wants for us. —CYNTHIA RUCHTI

FAITH STEP: *How are your faith's eating habits? Craving anything unhealthy or downright dangerous? Time for a checkup and maybe some blood work? Check out Psalm 34:8: "Taste and see that He is good!"*

WEDNESDAY, JULY 12

"For my thoughts are not your thoughts, neither are your ways my ways,"
declares the Lord. "As the heavens are higher than the earth,
so are my ways higher than your ways and my thoughts than your thoughts."
Isaiah 55:8–9 *(NIV)*

MY HUSBAND WAS ASSEMBLING an aluminum storage shed in our backyard. I sat on the grass studying the instructions. After he screwed together several walls, I interrupted. "I think you did that wrong. The dark side is supposed to be on the inside."

Together we puzzled over the drawings and reread the ambiguous directions. My husband patiently agreed to try it my way. He disassembled everything and put the pieces together a new way. I was wrong. The shed was now inside out.

Sometimes I also try to grab the pattern of my life from the hands of Jesus and tell Him what He's doing wrong. His ways seem inside out when they're works in progress. I come up with better plans. Doesn't Jesus want me to step in to explain to my friend what she's doing wrong? Doesn't He want me to tell everyone what I believe are the root problems in my church? Doesn't He want me to stridently defend Him when someone questions my faith?

My way makes sense until the structures I build tumble down.

Instead, Jesus calls me to serve my friend with compassion as she struggles or to repent where I'm part of the problem in my church or to listen with love to a person full of doubts. His ways aren't my ways. When I trust that His love and His wisdom provide a better plan, I give Him room to work. —SHARON HINCK

FAITH STEP: *Write down one way in which you are trying to accomplish the work of Jesus, and ask Him if He has a different plan.*

THURSDAY, JULY 13

Enter his gates with thanksgiving, and his courts with praise!
Give thanks to him; bless his name! Psalm 100:4 (ESV)

ONE CHILD OVERFLOWED the toilet this morning. Another used all of my creamer to sneak coffee to school in a water bottle. It didn't work, and she left it in the car…where it spilled. The rest of my children have scattered you-name-it from one end of the house to the other. Still, I release a heavy sigh and I'm thankful. Thankful for running water. Thankful for coffee creamer. Thankful for their messes because these children finally have a forever home, and they are ours.

There is very little we can change in our lives in one minute's time. We can't change our home or our family struggles. We can't change our health in such a short amount of time, and we can't clean up the messes our kids make, but we can change our hearts. We do this by being thankful. Choosing thankfulness is like turning on a lightbulb in a dark room. Our choice to give thanks to Jesus and praise His name—even when the messiness of this life presses—pushes out frustration and anger from our hearts.

One Yiddish proverb says, "If we thanked God for the good things, there wouldn't be time to weep over the bad." When I take time to thank Jesus and praise Him in the midst of my busy, messy life, the messes don't disappear but my heart changes. Thankfulness helps me to appreciate all that I have and reminds me what really matters: my home, my husband and children, and mostly my relationship with Jesus. Today each of us can choose to be thankful no matter what is happening in our lives, starting now. —TRICIA GOYER

FAITH STEP: *Write down three things you are thankful for. Keep the list, and whenever something gets you worried, angry, or stressed, add something to the list. Or create a journal of thanksgiving and write in it throughout the week.*

FRIDAY, JULY 14

"And behold, a voice from heaven said, "This is My beloved Son, in whom I am well-pleased and delighted!" Matthew 3:17 (AMP)

MY DAUGHTER, MARIN, wanted to learn how to ride a bike without training wheels. She was five at the time and my oftentimes overly protective husband was admittedly nervous about letting his baby girl go. "She's too young," he said. "She needs the wheels to brace."

I insisted she was ready. So it became my task alone to teach her.

I suited her up with knee and elbow pads and a helmet and ran behind the bike holding the seat for weeks until I was certain she had her balance. I felt it first, her self-assurance and her composure, as she pedaled forward. Then I did it—I let go.

It felt like my heart took flight. I've never felt more proud about anything than in that moment. Marin rode three houses down all by herself when I finally yelled out, "You're doing it! Yay!"

I shouted for my husband to come outside and got my parents to FaceTime on my smartphone. I needed everyone to see her because she was something to see!

I can only imagine the feeling our heavenly Father had when His Son, Jesus, obediently followed John the Baptist into baptismal waters. He opened up the sky and spoke, as if to say, "Look at My Son. Isn't He something?"

It's the kind of pride a parent longs for. My hope is that my heavenly Father is proud of me. When I am obedient to His Word, whether being selfless with my neighbor or smiling through a painful ordeal, I do wonder and often wish that He's looking down on me, whispering, "Look at My daughter Tarice. Isn't she something?" —TARICE L. S. GRAY

FAITH STEP: *What are some of the things you've done in the past that you know were pleasing to God? Find ways today to do something else that will make God smile.*

SATURDAY, JULY 15

But seek first his kingdom and his righteousness, and
all these things will be given to you as well.
Matthew 6:33 (NIV)

HI, MY NAME IS SUSANNA... and I am a coveter. And lately I have
been wanting a lot of things. The worst part? The wants don't go
away. Every time a want is fulfilled, a new want arises in its place.

Case in point? We have two very old cars. One of them decided
to die. So we made the leap and bought another used car. But it is
a beautiful used car that is only five years old instead of fifteen. So
now we refer to our cars as the "new car" and the "ugly car." Not one
of us wants to ride in the ugly car. It smells like old milk. In fact,
we want to ditch the ugly car and get another new car.

See what I mean? Getting more doesn't make us want less. The
wants keep coming. They seem to empty us of all gratitude. They
suck the joy right out of our day, and we forget to thank Jesus for the
things He has given us, like the ability to breathe and move and live.

I think that's why He keeps bringing the wants to our attention. He
is saying, *You think this is what you want... but it isn't. What you really*
want is Me. What you need to look for is Me. What you need to focus on
is Me. If you are chasing after Me, everything else will fall into place.

It always comes back to Him: His deliverance, His mercy, His
grace. If we take care of putting Jesus first, He takes care of everything else. And if we are being honest? That is what we truly want.
—SUSANNA FOTH AUGHTMON

FAITH STEP: *What is something that you want right now? Offer it to Jesus in*
prayer and say, "Jesus, more than anything I want You."

SUNDAY, JULY 16

Jesus looked her in the eye. "Didn't I tell you that if you believed, you would see the glory of God?"
John 11:40 (MSG)

SOMETIMES I WONDER what Jesus is saying to me and wish He'd speak out loud to make it crystal clear. And sometimes He does.

Lazarus had died, and his sisters, Mary and Martha, were grieving and confused as to why Jesus hadn't shown up sooner to save him. They were good friends of Jesus's, so they'd heard Him talk and had had His attention in the past. And He had something specific to say at that moment. Of all the words of wisdom or comfort He could have said in reply to Martha's confusion, He spoke about the power and necessity of belief.

With life and death at stake, Jesus chose to talk about our role to believe Him.

He couldn't have been clearer or more concise. If they'd had neon lights back then, He might have broadcast this truth for Martha's—and our—benefit, so we couldn't miss it. If we make the conscious decision to believe, *we will see His glory.* Not maybe. Not...oh, He might get around to it.

We will see it. If we believe. And belief is always a choice.

Faith doesn't mean we will get everything we hope for, but it does mean we will see Jesus's glory: we will experience His power, love, and victory over death, which are His deepest desires for us and what we need most. —ERIN KEELEY MARSHALL

FAITH STEP: *Make an intentional search for a knickknack or keychain that has the word Believe on it. Put it somewhere visible to remind yourself of the promise to see Jesus's glory when you choose to believe Him.*

MONDAY, JULY 17

For he satisfies the longing soul. . . . Psalm 107:9 (ESV)

WHEN I CHECK SOCIAL MEDIA PERIODICALLY, I find illustrated Scriptures and meaningful quotes that feed my faith, strengthen my resolve, and give me plenty to ponder. I also stumble onto links to the world's cutest puppies, warmest socks, and reasons not to wear leggings. Many of us do this. We connect with friends, but we also can't scroll without seeing images that could disturb a sane person's sleep. We're kept up-to-date with prayer needs from half a world away, but our time spent on social media interferes with time to pray for those closest to us.

Recently I saw an image of an artsy coffee mug that was captioned, "All I need is Jesus...and a cup of coffee." At first glance, it seemed an innocuous tribute to the wonders of coffee and a micromini-devotional. But putting Jesus and coffee on the same plane?

"All I need is Jesus"—a stand-alone thought. Nothing added. All I need.

I did gain something of worth from that visual coffee-mug image, though. I'm starting the practice of toasting Jesus when I take a sip of coffee or tea throughout the day. When I pick up my mug, I hold it aloft, as if acknowledging Jesus's presence in a tangible way. "Here's to You, Jesus, and what You are capable of accomplishing in this difficult conversation I'm about to have." "A toast to You, Jesus, as the Sovereign One Who knows what I need in these next few moments as I open this bill, or answer the e-mail, or return this clinic's call for my test results."

I look to Him for everything, confident in His constant and powerful presence. —CYNTHIA RUCHTI

FAITH STEP: *Create a mug that says: "All I need is Jesus. The coffee's a bonus," or another message that reminds you He is the answer to everything you'll face. Raise the mug as your soul's reminder of His constant and powerful presence.*

TUESDAY, JULY 18

In him was life, and that life was the light of all mankind.
The light shines in the darkness, and the darkness has not overcome it.
John 1:4–5 (NIV)

I ARRIVED EARLY for an appointment. The office building sat near a channel of water with inviting benches. Taking a seat, I savored the sunshine on my face. A gentle breeze rippled the water. Suddenly, the sun's rays hit a specific angle and the surface sparkled as if covered with a million diamonds. The beauty was so spectacular that I gasped a prayer of thanks. What a privilege to glimpse such a profound moment in the midst of my mundane day!

A few minutes later, the ripples stilled, shadows shifted, and the scene reverted to normal water. If I hadn't taken a few minutes to pause, rest, wait, and watch, I would have missed a remarkable and transcendent moment.

Jesus is the light of the world. His light is evident everywhere we look. He invites us into times of remarkable transformation as He shines His grace into our lives in unexpected ways. We may glimpse Him in the beauty of the natural world, as I did that morning. Or we can hear His voice through the warm encouragement of a friend. Other times His light comes through gentle guidance whispered to our hearts in our quiet times.

When I'm caught up in my own agenda and schedule, I can miss the transforming beauty of Jesus's love at work. Days can grow dark and dull. His light is there, but I'm focusing on the wrong things.

Ask Jesus to open our eyes to the beauty of His grace and to notice all the ways He shines light into our experiences. —SHARON HINCK

FAITH STEP: *Notice a striking example of God's creation today. Study how that light enhances its beauty. Thank Jesus for His presence in your life.*

WEDNESDAY, JULY 19

Adopt the attitude that was in Christ Jesus. . . . He humbled himself by becoming obedient to the point of death, even death on a cross.
Philippians 2:5, 8 (CEB)

"EVERYTHING HAPPENS FOR A REASON." "It's all in God's plan." "Grin and bear it." "When life hands you lemons, make lemonade." I believe most people who use clichés or truisms mean well, but I'm not a fan. And I think we need to stop.

We have to be careful about reducing someone else's problems to part of God's plan or lemons they can turn into lemonade. If we're addressing something like I-planned-to-have-a-picnic-but-it's-raining-so-I-choose-to-play-in-the-puddles-instead, I can definitely support the lemons-into-lemonade scenario. It's called being positive. But if we're addressing a loved one's death or cancer or even the loss of a job, well, those are different matters entirely. I believe it's wrong to reduce pain and suffering like that to an overused saying. Sometimes life hands you lemons and you can't do anything fun with them. You might want to throw them back at life, but you can't. You might want to make lemonade, but the lemons are rotten.

Instead, we need to take our cue from Jesus, Who was humble. He didn't sugarcoat or shy away from the horror of the Cross. He faced it. He went there, trusting His Father and being obedient. Like Him, we can face hard things and go there with people, trusting the Father. We don't have to have an answer for everything. Christ in us is enough.

—GWEN FORD FAULKENBERRY

FAITH STEP: *Is there something a friend is facing that makes you uncomfortable? Someone searching for answers you don't have? Be there. Hold a hand, offer a shoulder to cry on, or child care, or even a meal. Give them what you have, which is Jesus's love.*

THURSDAY, JULY 20

Trust him at all times, you people. Pour out your hearts in his presence. . . .
Psalm 62:8 (GW)

ONE SUMMER EVENING YEARS AGO, our family was enjoying our backyard. Suddenly my three-year-old daughter ran to me, crying hard. Holly was in pain, but she couldn't tell me what was wrong. Frantically I searched for something to explain her distress. My attempts to comfort her did no good; I held my wailing child and fought back my own tears.

My husband looked around the garden where Holly had been playing and finally found a red hot pepper with teeth marks. When Holly had bitten into the pepper, the juice started burning her mouth; as she rubbed her face while crying, it got into her eyes as well. Wanting to soothe her pain, I kept giving her ice water. Later, a friend told me that ice water only makes it worse.

Sometimes people around us don't know the best way to help us when we're hurting. No matter how well-intentioned, their words and actions may prove useless. We might not have a clue what we need; we only know that we're in pain. Thankfully, there is Someone who understands and knows our deepest needs.

When Jesus walked the earth, He knew the needs of each person who crossed His path. He offered just the right words and touch required for comfort, healing, growth, or change. Today Jesus lives inside His followers; we can trust Him to know how to minister to us even when we can't see past our own pain and confusion. Jesus wants us to pour out our hearts to Him, knowing He will never give us the wrong response. —DIANNE NEAL MATTHEWS

FAITH STEP: *Is there something troubling your heart today? Pour out your pain and grief to Jesus, trusting Him to know exactly what you need and to lovingly provide it.*

FRIDAY, JULY 21

I'm all right with weaknesses, insults, disasters, harassments, and stressful situations for the sake of Christ, because when I'm weak, then I'm strong.
2 Corinthians 12:10 *(CEB)*

I SEARCHED THROUGH my supply of boxes the other day for something that would hold two dozen books being sent to a ministry for families of the incarcerated. The right-size box came in two varieties. One was flimsy. The other sturdy but battered. The flimsy box was sure to be poor protection for the contents. The sturdy box needed some shoring up—more packing tape on the edges and corners—but would easily weather yet another journey.

Among those who followed Jesus in the Bible were young and old, widows, crusty fishermen, businesspeople who were successful, those who had lost everything including their dignity, rich women, and one with so little money she only had to count to two when adding it up (Luke 21:1–4).

As has been true since biblical times, Jesus chooses the sturdy who may have been through a lot—collapsed corners, ragged edges, places that need patching—over the spiritually flimsy. The weak in *strength* qualify for service in His name. In fact, strengthening the weak or working with them in spite of their weakness brings Him the most glory. The weak in *character*, however, were of no use to Him.

When I think about the people in my life who have had a faith-building influence on me in Jesus's name, they all show wear from their journeys. But they're sturdy in character, so Jesus continues to use them to bless, encourage, and help others. —CYNTHIA RUCHTI

FAITH STEP: *Who is serving Jesus faithfully despite their journeys' wear and tear, the sturdy but bruised? Write a note to thank them for their admirable strength of character.*

SATURDAY, JULY 22

When the Lord saw her, his heart overflowed with compassion. . . .
Luke 7:13 (NLT)

MY HUSBAND AND I BELONG to a small group at our church that decided to help others who were less fortunate. Our pastor told us about a single middle-aged gal who struggled with mental health issues. I visited the woman in a psychiatric hospital and asked if we could lend a hand upon her upcoming release. She said, "Yes. My apartment needs a thorough cleaning."

After the hospital discharged her, we went to her apartment carrying buckets, rags, soap, and bleach. We rolled up our sleeves and worked for hours. We also rearranged furniture so she could move about more easily in her electric scooter, and we removed bags of garbage.

When the time came for us to leave, the woman expressed gratitude through happy tears. We left knowing we'd blessed her, and that knowledge blessed us in return.

Jesus modeled compassion, but He also demonstrated the need to couple it with action. On one occasion, He saw a funeral procession for a young boy—the only son of a widow. He felt compassion for the mother, and compassion stirred Him to do something to help her—He raised the boy back to life (Luke 7:11–15).

The action we take when moved by compassion depends on many variables. We can't rush to everyone's rescue, but praying for wisdom and guidance helps us discern how Jesus wants us to respond. Even the smallest action done with love makes a difference. —GRACE FOX

FAITH STEP: *What kindness can you offer someone in need today? Here are a few ideas: weed a flower garden, offer a home-cooked meal, take a friend out for coffee, or lend a listening ear.*

SUNDAY, JULY 23

"You are the light of the world. A town built on a hill cannot be hidden. Neither do people light a lamp and put it under a bowl. Instead they put it on its stand, and it gives light to everyone in the house. In the same way, let your light shine before others, that they may see your good deeds and glorify your Father in heaven."
Matthew 5:14–16 *(NIV)*

I WAS TALKING TO my cousin Beth the other day. "I am sure there were hard things going on then, too, but life seemed so much shinier. Hard things seem to take some of the polish off of life." We were discussing how the darkness in the world seems to press in at home and abroad. How so many people we know are struggling and hurting. Then we talked about how life seemed so bright when we were kids. How everything was good and how joy poured in.

Beth was quiet for a second and then she said, "I think it is up to us to make life shiny."

She is a wise woman. It is time to give the darkness a push back. We can't control what comes our way, but we can choose how much shininess we bring to this life. Being shiny is simply reflecting God's goodness onto the people around you. It only takes a little bit of light to pierce the darkness. You are a gifted human being full of the light of Jesus. All you need to do is get on out there and be you. There are words that you can say, things that you can do, hugs that you can give, that no one else in this world can. Let all that Jesus has created you to be, be unleashed. And the world will get brighter. Let's light it up! —SUSANNA FOTH AUGHTMON

FAITH STEP: *Take a night walk with a flashlight. See how much light it gives off and remind yourself that Jesus is glorified when you light up the lives of those around you.*

MONDAY, JULY 24

Be hospitable to one another without complaining.
1 Peter 4:9 (NRSV)

WE HAVE FRIENDS who have a lovely home with a large barn that they've completely remodeled into a charming reception area. "Let me know if you ever need to host an event," my friend Jennifer told me. "Jon and I want to use our place to bless others."

A while later we needed a place to hold our daughter's wedding reception. She got married in the Czech Republic, and we wanted to host a reception for her close to home for family and friends who weren't able to travel to Europe for the wedding. Jon and Jen were only too happy to let us use their place. In addition, they put in countless hours working in their flower beds to prepare for the day. The property was perfect for the small ceremony of the couple repeating their vows, taking photos, and the celebration with friends and family.

Because of the generosity of Jon and Jen, our family, friends, and especially my daughter and son-in-law were given a wonderful gift.

"Entertaining seeks to impress," writes author Jen Wilkin. "Hospitality seeks to bless." It's true that some of us have more than others. It's what one does with what he or she has that makes all the difference. We can either see the things we have as items to protect and keep for ourselves, or we can see them as things we can use to bless others. I'm so thankful to have generous friends. Seeing the reception photos is a reminder to me to give what I can, when I can, to those in need. —TRICIA GOYER

FAITH STEP: *Next time you hear of a friend's need, ask yourself, "What can I do to help and give?" Also, encourage others to help and give as they can too. You never know what chain reaction your generosity will start!*

TUESDAY, JULY 25

You are a chosen people. You are royal priests, a holy nation, God's very own possession. As a result, you can show others the goodness of God, for he called you out of the darkness into his wonderful light. 1 Peter 2:9 (NLT)

OUR FAMILY LOVES agate hunting along Lake Superior. During the day, agates are ordinary-looking rocks you might walk past without noticing, but at dawn and dusk, the sunlight slants down to strike an agate at just the right angle to set it aglow. If you see a rock looking as if it is lit from within, hold still and lock your eyes on it. Don't rush to pick it up without getting a fix on its location, because the angles between you, the agate, and the sun change when you move.

There, in a mosh pit of multicolored stones, hides the odd one out. It's irregular and rough, not smooth and round like the others. You've found a jewel, its translucent bands formed when many-colored molten silica flowed into a tiny opening in age-old cooling rock. Agates are identified by their translucence. Light shines through them. An agate is just a rock until sunlight hits it. It has no light of its own.

Nor do I.

But when light shines through me, empathy, kindness, humility, and compassion mark my life. I respect others and let myself be wronged instead of hitting back. I tell the truth and seek peace. When people ask why, I explain that I'm reflecting what I see the Lord doing.

Jesus, the Living Stone, is also the Light of the World. He shines through broken people into a broken world. And by that light many will seek Him. Let Him shine. —SUZANNE DAVENPORT TIETJEN

FAITH STEP: *Read Peter's letters as you picture him writing them. Does he seem different from the way he came across in the Gospels? What made the difference? How have you changed since meeting Jesus?*

WEDNESDAY, JULY 26

"The Lord reached down from above and took me;
he pulled me from the deep water."
2 Samuel 22:17 (NCV)

WHEN I CHECK MY NEWSFEED, I normally scroll through quickly. But one day I stopped and stared at an image on a friend's page. Over the next few days I returned to the post, time after time, to have another look. After some research, I learned that the image I found so fascinating was a painting by an artist named Yongsung Kim. *Save Me—the Hand of God* portrays the story of Peter and Jesus walking on water as recorded in Matthew 14:22–33. Kim gives the perspective of Peter looking up after sinking fully into the sea.

For a while I wondered why I felt so drawn to the image, considering that I've struggled with a fear of water all my life. I've almost fainted during movie scenes of people in danger of drowning. Yet, strangely enough, this scene soothes my spirit.

I think it's because the painting centers on Jesus and not on the scene as a whole. He bends down close to the water, feet planted on the surface. His outstretched hand reaches into the water, offering instant safety. And although the surface of the water slightly blurs His face, His expression of serenity and compassion comes through.

These days a framed print of Kim's beautiful painting hangs in my home office. It reminds me where I need to keep my eyes during the storms of life. Instead of looking at the raging waves around me, I need to focus on Jesus and on His outstretched hand that, whenever I feel myself start to sink, is always there. —DIANNE NEAL MATTHEWS

FAITH STEP: *The next time you feel as though you're drowning in doubt, fear, or a tangle of problems, imagine the face of Jesus looking down at you and His hand extended to lift you up.*

THURSDAY, JULY 27

Walk by the Spirit, and you will not gratify the desires of the flesh.
Galatians 5:16 (ESV)

I WASN'T WEARING a "JESUS IS MY FRIEND" T-shirt or sporting a WWJD bracelet. Nor did I have a fish symbol on my luggage. Neither was I approaching the curbside airport check-in with my hands folded in prayer. Nothing—supposedly—marked me as a follower of Jesus.

The attendant was patient as I dug for my ID. We shared a few moments of conversation as he printed my boarding passes and tagged my luggage.

When I reached for a tip to express my gratitude for the attendant's quick and congenial handling of the check-in process, I felt compelled to give him four times what I would normally tip. It's not that I didn't need that money, but the sense was so strong, it was unmistakably Christ's love compelling me.

The attendant smiled, thanked me, and said, "You're walking by the Spirit." Not, "You're so generous" or "I appreciate this" or "Isn't that nice of you!" He knew I had not acted according to my head but had acted according to the Spirit of Christ. And he directed the gratitude where it belonged—to Jesus, Who compelled me. I hadn't invented a generous idea. I'd listened to the generous Spirit.

The attendant has probably forgotten the exchange. I can't. It's a reminder that how I act—more than what I wear or the words I say or the message on a bracelet—speaks loudly about whether I am walking by the flesh or walking by the Spirit.

There is nothing more rewarding than staying in step with Jesus.
—CYNTHIA RUCHTI

FAITH STEP: *Watch for opportunities to be Jesus-generous today, with no ulterior motive other than to know you're walking by the Spirit.*

FRIDAY, JULY 28

*Can a mother forget the baby at her breast and have no compassion
on the child she has borne? Though she may forget, I will not forget you!*
Isaiah 49:15 (NIV)

THIS MORNING I HELD my brand-new grandson. He stirred, stretched, sneezed, then nuzzled into my shoulder again. His gossamer hair caressed my face as I sang to him. The intoxicating scent of "new baby" filled my breath. I rocked gently, wanting to hold him forever. Time stood still. A perfect moment of total love.

As I prayed for him, a yearning welled up in me, so strong it hurt. I ached for him to be blessed, to know the love of Jesus as he grew, and to be protected.

And in that consuming love, tenderness, and longing, I caught an echo of the love Jesus has for each of us.

My grandson can't help his family with their chores or earn money to buy groceries. He doesn't produce anything—except dirty diapers. In fact, the constant needs of one infant can turn a whole household upside down. Yet we all adore him.

On days when we feel we haven't accomplished anything of worth to offer Jesus, it is a comfort to remember that He cradles us with unconditional love. He adores us. He will never forget us. His love isn't based on anything that we can do for Him. He loves us because we are His and He is love.

As my grandson sighed and settled softly under my chin, I was reminded that we can rest in perfect peace, knowing He takes joy in holding us. We bring Him glory just by receiving His tender love.
—SHARON HINCK

FAITH STEP: *Look at some baby pictures. Thank Jesus for loving you when you are helpless and needy. Ask Him to remind you throughout the day that He never forgets you.*

SATURDAY, JULY 29

God . . . saved us and called us to a holy calling, not because of our works but because of his own purpose and grace, which he gave us in Christ Jesus before the ages began. 2 Timothy 1:8–9 (ESV)

IN THE OZARK FOOTHILLS of northwest Arkansas and southwest Missouri, a number of caves sit tucked away in rocky bluffs. Some are small; others are elaborate.

My family toured the Bluff Dwellers Cavern in Noel, Missouri. History tells us that the Bluff Dwellers had a very established way of life in this region.

Inside the cavern, we saw Crystal Lake and other sources of trickling water that still carve through the rock. *Amazing* doesn't even begin to describe it. The most phenomenal sights—miraculous, really—were the layers of sea fossils and shells that made up the immense walls of many passageways. The guide pointed to horizontal layers, each about six inches thick, that showed evidence that the sea floor once reached this area of Missouri—which, incidentally, isn't anywhere close to the ocean. I'm no scientist, but I witnessed evidence of the Lord's fingerprints throughout history.

I felt small and humbled inside that dark labyrinth, but I also felt secure, held tight. My Jesus, Who was with the Creator at creation, Whose role as Savior was established before the first sin in Eden, and Who invites me to talk with Him and trust Him each day, knows every inch of that cavern's history, just as He knows everything about the people who lived there long ago and about me today. That truth can bolster my faith in His wisdom and purposes for me. The Lord Who knows the intricacies of the earth's depths calls personally to me each day of my life. —ERIN KEELEY MARSHALL

FAITH STEP: *Spend a few minutes outside today, and look for Jesus's fingerprints in the world around you.*

SUNDAY, JULY 30

Fix these words of mine in your hearts and minds; tie them as symbols on your hands and bind them on your foreheads. Teach them to your children, talking about them when you sit at home and when you walk along the road, when you lie down and when you get up.
Deuteronomy 11:18–19 (NIV)

I HAVE A FRIEND, Paul, who writes and speaks about how to lead with a story. His basic premise is this: people understand concepts in terms of stories. He thinks it's the best way to communicate anything, especially something you're trying to teach your children, and I tend to agree with him. My students and my kids relate better to a story than any abstract idea I may be trying to instill.

The most important story we have, of course, is the story of Jesus. As the old hymn goes, "Tell me the story of Jesus, write on my heart every word. Tell me the story most precious, sweetest that ever was heard." Those words just underscore what the Bible teaches in Deuteronomy. God's Word—the Logos—Jesus—is to be fixed in our hearts and minds. His story is the lens through which we see the world. He's what we teach, preach, and live. He's in every moment of our story, and He is the story our lives are telling to others. Make it a good one! —GWEN FORD FAULKENBERRY

FAITH STEP: *Who needs to hear the story of Jesus from you today? Call that person and meet for coffee or tea. Get the story out!*

MONDAY, JULY 31

*But Jesus told him, "No! The Scriptures say, 'People do not live
by bread alone, but by every word that comes from the mouth of God.'"
Matthew 4:4 (NLT)*

MY DAUGHTER, CALIANNE, is a connoisseur of toppings. Just this
morning we joked with her about eating the streusel off the top of
her blueberry muffin and leaving the rest. At birthday parties she
licks the frosting, leaving the cupcake, and her pointer finger loves
to trail through the syrup covering pancakes and waffles. She's a
toppings girl after my own heart. I get it. In fact, a friend and I
joked once that we will run a bakery in heaven and we'll sell all
flavors of frosting by the barrel.

I'm guessing that may be fine with Jesus in heaven, but living off
the top layer of spiritual food on earth, skimming a verse a week, or
going to church once a week and not following up personally with
time with Jesus doesn't let me get very deep with Him. It would be
like tasting the icing but skipping the depths of the cake's goodness.

Living by every word that comes from the mouth of God implies
that I need to ingest every word, not just parts and parcels. I need
the entire Word to keep me growing and in tune with Him.

Living this way also implies that I'm investing the time to pause
with Him for those healthy meals of His Word. Investing the time for
ingesting the whole Word—that's what it takes to feed off of real spiritual nourishment, not just the toppings. —ERIN KEELEY MARSHALL

FAITH STEP: *Make some muffins and schedule time to read through an entire
book of the Bible this week. Ask Jesus to help you stay in tune with His Spirit's deep
work in you, praying over 1 Corinthians 2:10 (MSG): "The Spirit, not content to
flit around on the surface, dives into the depths of God, and brings out what God
planned all along."*

TUESDAY, AUGUST 1

Anyone who belongs to Christ has become a new person.
The old life is gone; a new life has begun!
2 Corinthians 5:17 (NLT)

A FEW WEEKS AGO my kids got it in their heads that we needed to make gelatin. We hadn't had any for several years, but suddenly, according to them, we had to have it.

I agreed to their request, but being me, I had to "healthify" it because that's just what I do. In this case it meant making the juice version of Knox Blox to reduce the sugar and food coloring. Although I've been having flashbacks to the eighties, I'll admit it's been sort of fun to play with something old made new.

On a life-changing scale, Jesus loves to make our old selves into new creations. With His own Spirit within us, He brings new life to us and creates something healthy and whole from the unhealthy us.

On days when I can't seem to win over a negative attitude or conquer my impatient nature or allow my spirit to rest peacefully in Jesus's plans, I remember the simple lesson of the healthified Knox Blox. The more time I spend with Jesus, the more weary I am settling for anything less than His new version of me that I catch glimpses of now and then.

Someday all the old, worn-out aspects of me will be gone, and I'll be free of them forever. Until that part of eternity arrives, I'm thankful that I can be reminded of Jesus's recreating power through the simplest of childlike lessons. —ERIN KEELEY MARSHALL

FAITH STEP: *Make some healthy gelatin. Sprinkle four packets of unflavored gelatin over a cup of cold juice in a dish. You can add a little sugar if desired. Stir in three cups of boiling juice and chill until set. Thank Jesus that His kind of new-ness is soul-filling deliciousness!*

WEDNESDAY, AUGUST 2

*"My Father's house has many rooms. . . . I am going there to prepare
a place for you. . . . I will come back and take you to be with me
that you also may be where I am." John 14:2–3 (NIV)*

I GAVE MY HEART TO JESUS at a young age. Excitement grew as I
learned that Jesus loved me so much, He had died for me. I had no
idea at the time what would follow, but I eagerly embraced Jesus's
teachings. As a child, my knowledge of His promises was limited to
His forgiveness, peace, and joy.

It was almost a year later, however, that Jesus promised much more
than my incomplete understanding of a joyful life and the absence of
turmoil. That's when I learned that when Jesus rose again, He went
to "prepare a place" for me. That's when the truth hit me: Jesus also
promised me life *forever*—a home with Him in heaven.

Jesus's disciples often spoke and acted with the same childish limitations that I have. They eagerly sought joy and a peaceful life, free
of trouble and Roman rule. But not until after Jesus's death, burial,
and Resurrection did they finally understand Jesus's last words to
them. He wanted more—so much more for them. Forgiveness?
Check! Peace and joy? Check! But also a forever life with Him: a
prepared place for all eternity. When persecution began, that promise took on new meaning, even as their passion and joy increased.

The older I get, the more I appreciate Jesus's promise to all who truly
know Him. On this earth with Jesus at our side, we can experience peace
and joy, even in the most turbulent and distressing times. But what makes
our stay on earth even more precious is the sweet reward that follows this
life: home forever with Jesus. —REBECCA BARLOW JORDAN

FAITH STEP: *Thank Jesus today that He has promised to give you not only
peace in your heart here on earth, but a home forever with Him.*

THURSDAY, AUGUST 3

"All who want to save their lives will lose them.
But all who lose their lives because of me will save them."
Luke 9:24 *(CEB)*

SOME OF MY FAVORITE CONVERSATIONS are with young people learning to gain a firmer grip on their faith. The other day I had a conversation with a young woman facing a tough decision about how she was treated at work. "If I talked to them like that, they'd give me the 'Suck it up, Buttercup' speech."

"But you're the Jesus person in the group."

"Being Jesus is hard."

"Yes. That whole 'take up your cross' thing."

"It's crazy heavy. And then I'm like, 'Blah, I feel so weak that I can't do it by myself.' But God never meant for us to do it alone. So then I'm like, 'Oh yeah. In my weakness, He is made strong.' And it's just this never-ending cycle of surrender."

I've camped on her words for days: "It's this never-ending cycle of surrender."

The young woman who'd sent me the text messages did the right thing by taking up her cross and embracing "this never-ending cycle of surrender," tapping into the promise that "all who want to save their lives will lose them. But all who lose their lives because of me will save them" (Luke 9:24, CEB).

My last message to her read, "Thank you for getting uncomfortable for Jesus." —CYNTHIA RUCHTI

FIRST STEP: *When was the last time you did something uncomfortable because you were convinced Jesus would approve or that He was urging you to act? Is it time for another round in this cycle of surrender?*

FRIDAY, AUGUST 4

But the word of God continued to spread and flourish.
Acts 12:24 (NIV)

I RECENTLY CAME ACROSS this verse about the early followers of Jesus. By itself, the statement doesn't seem too remarkable. Disciples told others, the Holy Spirit stirred hearts, more and more came to know Jesus. Hooray!

What does strike me as noteworthy is everything that leads up to this verse. Those who followed Jesus were facing danger. Peter had been imprisoned, then freed by an angel. An evil king called himself a god. A few chapters earlier, the apostles were conflicted about which Jewish laws needed to be obeyed.

Persecution, hostility, corrupt leaders, even disagreement and confusion within the Body of Christ. Sound familiar?

There are days I wring my hands and moan about the difficulties in our time. What a joyful reminder to find this short verse.

In spite of a society that ignores or even mocks the love of Christ, the Word continues to increase and spread. In spite of leaders who fall or fail, the Word continues to increase and spread. In spite of uncomfortable disagreements with our sisters and brothers, the Word continues to increase and spread.

Our journey together in following Jesus will sometimes include glorious miracles (like Peter's rescue). But even when it doesn't, each day we can place ourselves willingly into the hands of Jesus. We can ask Him to show us how to join in His work of increasing and spreading the love of God. —SHARON HINCK

FAITH STEP: *List a few things that seem to be squelching the love of God today. Draw a huge cross over them all and thank Jesus that nothing can stop His loving work.*

SATURDAY, AUGUST 5

Those who look to him for help will be radiant with joy;
no shadow of shame will darken their faces. Psalm 34:5 (NLT)

REGISTRATION FOR A WOMEN'S RETREAT was about to begin. The planning committee had invited me to a prayer time to kick off the event. That's when Wanda showed up.

Wanda's natural beauty astounded me. Her blue eyes shone and her smile lit up the room. But her beauty was more than skin deep. This woman glowed from the inside out.

"You're the epitome of radiance," I said to her. "What makes you glow?"

Wanda told me how her husband had become a drug addict and gone to prison for five years. She raised their two children alone. Things looked hopeful on his release, but he relapsed and they lost their home. He left and began living on the street. Their marriage ended in divorce.

"My life hasn't turned out the way I thought it would," said Wanda, "but I've found strength and hope and joy in Jesus. Every morning, even when I was raising small kids alone, I met with Him at four o'clock. He reassured me of His love and held me together when my world was falling apart. If I glow, it's because of time spent in His presence."

Wanda reminded me of Moses. He spent time with God and it showed on his countenance (Exodus 34:29–30).

Spending time with Jesus makes a difference. What do people see when they look at me? Do they see worry on my face? Or do they see the peace that Jesus brings? I want people to see Jesus in my countenance. —GRACE FOX

FAITH STEP: *Do you know someone whose face shines with the light of Jesus? Call that person and ask her to tell you her story.*

SUNDAY, AUGUST 6

---

*Blessed be the God and Father of our Lord Jesus, the Messiah! He is
our merciful Father and the God of all comfort, who comforts us in all our
suffering, so that we may be able to comfort others in all their suffering,
as we ourselves are being comforted by God. 2 Corinthians 1:3–4 (ISV)*

JACK HOLCOMB UNDERSTOOD SUFFERING. Known as the gospel
tenor with a "tear in his voice," the singing preacher lost his wife
early in their marriage, then eventually remarried and had a daughter. Days after his eighteen-month-old girl fell off a high chair and
died, her body was lost in the ruins of a tornado that struck the
funeral home. Eventually she was found by searchers. Through all
of this, Jack battled heart disease. At the age of forty-six, he finally
succumbed to the disease.

When my husband and I discovered one of Jack's albums years
ago, we knew nothing of his painful past. At first hearing, his vocal
tone seemed mournful and sad. But something else filtered through:
Jack possessed a joy, a deep passion for Jesus that allowed him to
triumph over his pain. Jack ministered to others, sharing his own
comfort rooted in a relationship with Jesus, the One who suffered
for us and Who comforts us in our suffering.

I've felt that same comfort from Jesus in my own times of sorrow.
Although I'll always feel the loss, Jesus has replaced my initial pain
with joy and a tenderness that makes me desire to encourage others
in their struggles.

Because Jesus comforts us, we, too, can testify to the biblical truth:
"Weeping may endure for a night, but joy comes in the morning"
(Psalm 30:5, NKJV). —REBECCA BARLOW JORDAN

FAITH STEP: *Watch for opportunities to express comfort to others in the way
Jesus leads you: a phone call, a meal, or a personal note or visit.*

MONDAY, AUGUST 7

In the beginning was the Word, and the Word was with God, and the Word was God. The same was in the beginning with God. All things were made by him; and without him was not anything made that was made.
John 1:1–3 (KJV)

LAST SUMMER AT AN OBSERVATORY in Sun River, Oregon, I looked right at the sun. They have a special telescope through which you can gaze directly at our closest star without frying your eyes. The friendly observatory staff helped me to see sunspots and a solar flare that appeared about an inch long but would fit five Earths in its span. I went back after dark to use their telescopes to see Jupiter and Saturn (and its rings), along with galaxies, nebulae, and new stars forming. The unimaginable expanse of space holds some of the loveliest things I've ever seen. I was awestruck.

Jesus made that—all of it! And not just that, but "everything, absolutely everything, above and below, visible and invisible, rank after rank after rank of angels—*everything* got started in him and finds its purpose in him. He was there before any of it came into existence and holds it all together right up to this moment" (Colossians 1:16–17, MSG).

This Jesus, God Himself, who made the galaxies, set aside all of His power and glory to come to our planet to be born as a baby because we were lost and in need of Him. He was God, but came to earth in a form much safer for us to look at.

The Maker of the sun, because of His great love for us, came so that we might have life and have it to the full. We can trust Him. Look at the Son! —SUZANNE DAVENPORT TIETJEN

FAITH STEP: *Tonight, if it's clear, go outside and look up. Pray or keep a holy silence under the stars before the One Who made them.*

TUESDAY, AUGUST 8

I have not kept this good news hidden in my heart, but have proclaimed your loving-kindness and truth to all the congregation. Psalm 40:10 (TLB)

"I HAVE GOOD NEWS," the voice said. "You've been selected to receive a one-hundred-dollar credit on your next bill." I'd never heard of this promotion, but my phone showed that the call came from my cell phone company. I thanked him and verified my account. A few minutes later, I received a text that the address on my account had been changed. Immediately after, I got another call from customer care. The man asked about the text and laughed as he told me he had hit the wrong button. He apologized and assured me he had corrected the situation and applied the credit to my account.

The next month I received my bill, with more than an extra thousand dollars on it. Someone had gone into a store, added ten new lines to my account, and purchased a smartphone for each new number. My carrier's fraud department explained "ghost calling," enabling a person to make any number show up on someone's caller ID.

All of the deception, fraud, and phishing going on these days can make us cynical. We don't want that spilling over into our faith. Some of what the Bible says about Jesus sounds too good to be true. He paid the penalty for our sins so we can be forgiven. He loves us unconditionally and offers us grace for daily living. He will never leave us and is preparing our perfect eternal home.

When it comes to biblical truth about Jesus, there's no fraud involved—only good news that keeps getting better.
—DIANNE NEAL MATTHEWS

FAITH STEP: *Write down one thing about Jesus that you have a hard time believing for yourself. Beside it, write TRUE in large letters. Ask Jesus to help you embrace this truth and live it out today.*

WEDNESDAY, AUGUST 9

*Because of the Lord's faithful love we do not perish, for His mercies
never end. They are new every morning; great is Your faithfulness! I say:
The Lord is my portion, therefore I will put my hope in Him.*
Lamentations 3:22–24 (HCS)

I THINK EVERY PERSON who's married has a time when they wake
up one day and ask, "What have I done?" I was so confident when
I married John because he is a wonderful Christian man, but I discovered that no one was perfect—especially not my new husband!
Worse yet, I learned that marriage brought out all *my* imperfec-
tions. When conflict came up, I retreated. When John spoke unkind
words, I lashed out at him. Every time he disapproved of me, I felt
defeated. Even little things became big things, and I wondered if it
would just be easier to run away.

Thankfully, over the years, Jesus showed me that these issues were
mostly my issues. Growing up in my home, conflict was avoided
or hidden, and so I thought that anytime we disagreed it was a big
deal. Also, I learned that it was possible to disapprove of someone's
behavior and still love them—and John did love me. These weren't
lessons that I learned overnight. I learned them morning by morning
when we woke up, offered forgiveness, and were willing to start again.

Sometimes with Jesus we've felt that we've hurt Him too much.
We think we've pushed us over the edge of His grace. But, thankfully, God's mercies are new every morning. No matter how bad a
day we've had, we can wake up the next one and start again.
—TRICIA GOYER

FAITH STEP: *Get a sticky note or small notecard and write out
Lamentations 3:22–24. Post it someplace that you will see in the morning,
and each day thank God for His mercies and His faithfulness.*

THURSDAY, AUGUST 10

---

*Every good and perfect gift is from above, coming down from the
Father of the heavenly lights, who does not change like shifting shadows.*
James 1:17 (NIV)

I LOVE GIVING PRESENTS. It is one of my favorite things. The other
day, I was considering what birthday present to give my mother-
in-law, Sandy. I was trying to think of all the things that she loves.
Jewelry. Good smelling soaps. Cute clothes. Fun decorations for her
home. She changes her décor with the seasons. It gave me a lot to
ponder. Did I want to go with a topiary for her mantel? Or maybe
she would like another sparkly shirt? She loves sparkles.

The reason Sandy is so much fun to buy for is because she is a gift
giver too. She loves giving gifts, and she appreciates getting them.
She buys me new socks for every season. I have socks for Halloween,
Christmas, and Valentine's Day. When I look at the socks, I know
that Sandy is thinking about me and she loves me. The reason we
both like to give gifts is because giving gifts is fun. It is fun to see
the joy on the person's face when they open a good gift. It broadens
the heart with love when you are given a gift from someone who has
taken the time to consider you.

Gift giving is really Jesus's idea. He started it all by giving us the best
gift: Himself. And He didn't stop there; He just kept right on giving.
His love. His grace. His peace. His hope. His joy. And as we follow
in His footsteps, He keeps blessing us with new gifts every single day,
new mercies every single morning.—SUSANNA FOTH AUGHTMON

FAITH STEP: *Grab on to today's perfect gift of mercy and know beyond a
shadow of a doubt that you are loved. Who in your life likes getting gifts? In the
spirit of Jesus and His love, surprise them today with a gift and let them know that
you love them.*

FRIDAY, AUGUST 11

*These words that I command you today shall be on your heart. You shall
teach them diligently to your children, and shall talk of them when
you sit in your house, and when you walk by the way, and
when you lie down, and when you rise.*
Deuteronomy 6:6–7 (ESV)

I CAN'T KEEP THE GRASS out of my house. No matter how many
times I ask the kids to take off their shoes inside, grass from the
yard still trickles in. I can sweep one afternoon, but by the next
morning the floors will be littered with trails from the outdoors. It
drives me crazy!

In the same way, outside influences ooze in.

The world's not-so-godly trails will find their way into my life,
and I need to take a proactive approach to keep them from getting
ground deeply in my heart.

Today's verses came from the Old Testament, long before Jesus or
I walked the earth. But the advice is timeless and important for all
of us.

When I prioritize Jesus in my home, my life sparkles with His
Spirit, and the world's negative trails don't become grunge in my
inner life. Themes on TV or discussions on social media that don't
align with biblical truth can be filtered through His Spirit's wisdom
so that I can maintain clearheaded thinking about what Jesus wants
me to believe and how He wants me to live.

I can leave a trail of godliness behind me by keeping Jesus's words
on my heart and making Him the heart of my home.
—ERIN KEELEY MARSHALL

FAITH STEP: *Next time you clean the kitchen or living room, invite Jesus to
dwell fully in your home so that His holiness and grace will fill every inch.*

SATURDAY, AUGUST 12

Jesus called the Twelve to him, and sent them out in pairs. He gave them authority and power to deal with the evil opposition. He sent them off with these instructions: "Don't think you need a lot of extra equipment for this. You are the equipment. No special appeals for funds. Keep it simple." Mark 6:7–9 (MSG)

A FRIEND TOLD ME that while on vacation, he rented a hybrid car. He drove to his hotel without any problem, but when he got in the car a few hours later, the car wouldn't start. He kept pumping the gas and turning the ignition to no avail. After several frustrating minutes, he was about to call a tow truck. But first he put the car in gear, just to see if that would help. The car drove fine.

He laughed as he remembered that hybrid cars use silent battery power to start the engine. The noisier gas power only begins once the car is moving. When he initially turned the key, the car was running. He just couldn't hear it until he pulled forward.

Sometimes we wait for the Holy Spirit to fire us up. We look for proof He's with us, like my friend looked for the roar of a gasoline engine. We forget that Jesus already placed the Holy Spirit in our hearts. His presence becomes evident as we move out in faith.

I suspect the disciples didn't feel powerful enough to confront and conquer evil when Jesus first sent them out. If they had sat down and waited for feelings of strength or for amazing signs to hit them, they may have missed out on the beautiful mission that Jesus appointed. Instead they headed out, perhaps feeling nervous and a bit underprepared. Miracles and transformative experiences met them.

As we heed Jesus's call to take on the ministry He appoints for us, miracles and transformative experiences will meet us too.

—SHARON HINCK

FAITH STEP: *Tell Jesus that you are willing. Ask Him to show you a new adventure to undertake for Him. Then step out in faith.*

SUNDAY, AUGUST 13

You have everything when you have Christ. . . . Colossians 2:10 (TLB)

SUNDAY MORNINGS BORDER on chaos for me. I hit the ground running—literally—trying to get in a little exercise before the day takes over. Then it's shower, wake up kids, throw down breakfast, try to look presentable, and attempt to get to church in time to practice with the Praise Team for that morning's songs. Sometimes by the time I take my seat at the piano I am already "worn to a ravelling," like Beatrix Potter's tailor of Gloucester, who had no more twist.

I need more time, I think. Or perhaps more discipline. More sleep. More preparation for the music. More cooperation from the band members (my kids). More money would be nice. Then I wouldn't have to work so hard and be so tired on Sundays. More clothes would be good because then it would be easier to pick out what to wear. Of course I need to lose a little weight and then my clothes would fit better. I've got to run more and eat less. At the very least, I need more coffee and I need it *right now*.

These are the thoughts swirling around in my head when we start to sing. All of the things I need. Then I start to listen to the words I'm singing: "You are the one thing. Jesus, You are the one thing that I need."

I keep playing, but close my eyes. Everything else fades, except the truth that I have everything when I have Jesus. Certainly, we have needs and He can help us sort those out. But at the core of all our longing, Jesus is the one thing we really need.

—GWEN FORD FAULKENBERRY

FAITH STEP: *Write down a list of all of the things you think you need right now. Then, for perspective, put down the pencil and close your eyes. Meditate on the name of Jesus and allow Him to bring stillness to your soul.*

MONDAY, AUGUST 14

"Ask and it will be given to you; seek and you will find;
knock and the door will be opened to you."
Matthew 7:7 (NIV)

YESTERDAY MY THREE CHILDREN asked me why we don't have any food. That would be because they ate it all. I keep telling them, "We have a certain budget for groceries...you can either eat all the food I get in one day or you can spread it out, say, over the whole week, like normal, sane, regular-eating people." Scott says, jokingly, that we should offer them one meal a day and then lock them out of the house and let them forage for the rest. I feel it would be wrong to unleash them on the neighbors since we brought them into the world and all. I am trying to nurture their young bodies. I just didn't realize I was growing giants. As soon as food comes into the house, it is devoured. I have started yelling out things like, "You cannot eat a whole loaf of bread!" and "Back away from the peanut butter!"

I am so thankful that with Jesus, provisions never run out. He never says, "Oh, I am so sorry...we are all out of grace today." Or "You really should have stocked up on mercy yesterday because I've got nothing for you." Or "Are you sure you need more love? Because I am fresh out. No more love. Check back tomorrow."

His stores of grace and mercy and love? Unending. New every day. Bountiful. Overflowing. We can run to Him every hour of every day, and He will meet us with open arms and say, "I have every single thing that you will ever need." —SUSANNA FOTH AUGHTMON

FAITH STEP: *What do you need today? Ask Jesus to supply it. He has all that you need and more.*

TUESDAY, AUGUST 15

Once again there was a battle between the Philistines and Israel. David went down with his men to fight against the Philistines, and he became exhausted.
2 Samuel 21:15 (NIV)

WHEN A YOUNG WOMAN asks for help where I volunteer, I jump up to do something. I love being able to make a difference.

But asking for help for myself? That doesn't come so easily. I don't want to appear weak or needy. I want to show that I have my act together. I want to display what a Christ-follower should look like: someone full of faith and empowered by Jesus to do great things for His kingdom. But is that what being a Christ-follower is really about? Standing strong, alone? Not at all.

Over the last year, Jesus has shown me that even strong people have moments when they are weak and need help from others. I've learned that Christ's grace is truly sufficient for me because His power is made perfect through my weakness (2 Corinthians 12:9). This is especially true in community. When John and I brought more children into our home through adoption, our church and friends didn't wait for us to ask; they just stepped up and helped. It was a huge blessing!

In our society, we are quick to place people in two categories: those who give help and those who need it. In truth, we all need help at times. Our needs allow the community of believers to experience the joy of giving and serving in Jesus's power. It connects us all with one another and often provides care beyond what we even knew we needed. —TRICIA GOYER

FAITH STEP: *Write down one area where you need help. Ask, "What has kept me from seeking help in this part of my life?" Step out in humility and ask for help. Also, reach out to someone who may be too embarrassed to ask.*

WEDNESDAY, AUGUST 16

*And you no doubt know that Jesus of Nazareth was anointed by God
with the Holy Spirit and with power, and he went around doing good. . . .*
Acts 10:38 (TLB)

TWENTY-EIGHT-YEAR-OLD EUGENE YOON wanted to make a difference in someone's life. But he never dreamed God would answer his prayer in such a dramatic way. One day a video crossed his news feed about a man named Arthur who'd been paralyzed. When Eugene saw that story, he felt God leading him to be part of Arthur's solution. But how could he help this young man to walk?

Eugene discovered a machine called an exoskeleton device that cost $80,000. Somehow, he hoped to raise enough money to buy one for the young man. Eugene left his lucrative job with a research company and hiked from the California border to Canada, posting videos and raising money on social media.

The first time Eugene watched Arthur walk with the new machine, he knew his act of kindness had been worth it all.

Random acts of kindness are nice: spontaneous moments of generosity. But intentional acts of kindness are even better: preplanned, faith-filled determination that refuses to surrender until the blessing has been delivered.

Jesus's actions were never random. He went about doing good, opening doors for faith to walk through, always bringing glory to His heavenly Father.

Like Eugene Yoon, we, too, can make a difference by doing good if we listen, watch, wait, and ask Jesus to use us to bless others.

What a way to live! —REBECCA BARLOW JORDAN

FAITH STEP: *Ask Jesus to help you go about doing good this week. Then watch for ways that He will answer.*

THURSDAY, AUGUST 17

*Whatever you do, do it enthusiastically, as something done
for the Lord and not for men.*
Colossians 3:23 *(HCS)*

DURING A FAMILY VACATION, I walked through a souvenir shop with my daughter and grandkids. My daughter exercised great patience as five-year-old Roman darted around, rushing up to show her his latest find and asking, "Can I get this?" Holly answered "yes" twice.

As we checked out, he said, "Mom, you just jack-fired my mind."

"Jack-fired your mind? What do you mean?" she asked.

"You jack-fired my mind by letting me get both of these toys."

We laughed about Roman's created word but found it came in handy when we wanted to express joyful amazement. For example, one night I didn't have time to tell my grandkids a whole bedtime story. I ended by promising, "Tomorrow night you'll find out what the children saw on the other side of the pond, and when you do, it will jack-fire your mind!"

Sometimes normal words are just not adequate. The truth is, no words can fully describe the wonder of Jesus. His willingness to leave His heavenly home, His mercy and unconditional love for me no matter how badly I stumble.

Words aren't enough to express my gratitude to Jesus either. That's why it's important to let my actions show Him how I feel. Any daily activity becomes an act of praise and worship when I'm doing it for Jesus. Then my life becomes a message that words alone cannot express. —DIANNE NEAL MATTHEWS

FAITH STEP: *Think about something Jesus has done for you that "jack-fires" your mind. Now decide how you will express your gratefulness and adoration through your actions.*

FRIDAY, AUGUST 18

Jesus replied, "Anyone who drinks this water will soon become thirsty again. But those who drink the water I give will never be thirsty again. It becomes a fresh, bubbling spring within them, giving them eternal life." John 4:13–14 (NLT)

LAST YEAR I TRAVELED to Egypt for two weeks to teach and encourage Christian brothers and sisters there. Temperatures hovered in the nineties, and our lodging had no air-conditioning. The unrelenting heat left me feeling parched. I drank the coffee, tea, and juice that my hosts graciously prepared. But nothing quenched my thirst like water. I craved it.

Truth be told, I didn't always love water. I wanted other, tastier drinks. I've enjoyed it only since becoming more health conscious in recent years. The change happened when I began to better understand its many vital roles like transporting nutrients throughout the body's system and improving circulation and blood flow. I wanted to thrive physically, so it only made sense that I wouldn't withhold water from my body or try to satisfy my need for it with something less effective.

In the same way, Jesus is my Living Water. He satisfies my deepest needs for purpose, love, and freedom. I might try to quench my spiritual thirst with substitutes like money, work, hobbies, relationships, and material possessions, but I soon find they leave me empty—they are less effective. They can never quench my thirst as Jesus can.

Only Jesus can nourish and sustain us. As I drink deeply today by spending time in His presence, engaging with Him in the Word and through conversational prayer, and practicing His presence moment by moment, He restores and refreshes my soul. —GRACE FOX

FAITH STEP: *Pour a glass of water and sip from it throughout the day. Each time you drink, praise the Living Water for satisfying your deepest needs.*

SATURDAY, AUGUST 19

Be to me a rock of refuge, to which I may continually come; you have given the command to save me, for you are my rock and my fortress. Psalm 71:3 (ESV)

AFTER A BREAK at a women's retreat, I returned to my table to find a rock at each place. No one else was back yet, so I examined everyone else's rocks. They were just smooth stones, emblazoned with crosses, like you might find at any craft store. I saw several I liked better than my own. Mine was off-white, wobbly, and had this big brown gash that cut into the cross. A lovely mottled stone sat across from me. Without thinking too much about it, I traded.

Immediately I struggled with guilt. What—was I a thief? By then others were coming back, so I checked that no one was watching and switched the rocks again. I felt better, but I still didn't like mine.

Soon everyone arrived, found their rocks, and settled in to listen to the next talk. As the speaker wrapped up, I absentmindedly picked up my ugly rock and discovered that it fit my palm as if carved to my shape. Amazing! Could it be specifically for me?

Doubtful, I asked some of the others at my table to try out my rock to see if it fit anyone else's hand. It did not.

Looking at others' gifts and comparing comes all too easily to me and reveals how much time I spend looking out for myself. I should know I don't need to. I am like the Israelites who "drank from the spiritual Rock that followed them, and the Rock was Christ" (1 Corinthians 10:4).

I kept that rock to remind me of how well Jesus knows and loves me and to Whom it is I want to continually come: Jesus, my Rock and my Salvation. —SUZANNE DAVENPORT TIETJEN

FAITH STEP: *Do you sometimes forget how intimately Jesus knows you? Take a walk today, heart and eyes open, and look for something that reminds you of His love for you as a unique individual.*

SUNDAY, AUGUST 20

In Him we live and move and . . . have our being. . . .
Acts 17:28 (AMP)

LAST NIGHT I SPOKE at a meeting of the Altus Sunset Rotary Club. Sometimes meetings like this are a snooze-fest, but with these folks, it was more of a party. There was great food and drinks and loud laughter. There was a crew of all different ages and backgrounds, who don't just do good in the world, they *are* the good. It oozes from them. I think I was hugged five times before I even made it to my seat.

The Rotary Club wanted to hear about my books and the writing craft, which was so nice of them. They endured my speech gracefully. Then one man asked me a question that really made me think. I'm still thinking about it this morning. He asked, "What inspires you?"

There are so many cookie-cutter answers to this question. So many rainbows and unicorns. So many legitimately inspirational people and verses and books that come to mind. But what I told him truly is the essence of why I write. Life inspires me when I let it, when I invite it, when I'm still enough to be present in my own life, paying attention to its beauty and imperfection. Everything becomes spiritual. Elisabeth Elliot wrote, "In every event He seeks an entrance to my heart," and I believe that. It doesn't have to be a big event. It can be the dishes or the laundry. The funny things my kids say. A raindrop on a leaf. My dad's text messages. Stretch marks. My students. Fog over the river. My nieces skipping down the path. Writing forces me to be still and let Jesus—Who is Life— inspire me. —GWEN FORD FAULKENBERRY

FAITH STEP: *What inspires you? Whatever helps you get still enough to hear His voice, do that today.*

MONDAY, AUGUST 21

"You are the light of the world—like a city on a hilltop that cannot be hidden. No one lights a lamp and then puts it under a basket. Instead, a lamp is placed on a stand, where it gives light to everyone in the house." Matthew 5:14—15 (NLT)

MY SIX-YEAR-OLD GRANDSON, Luke, recently modeled his new sunglasses for me. I smiled and told him he looked like a spy.

A few minutes later, I saw him peeking at me from around a corner in the house. "Hey, young fellow," I said. "What are you doing?"

"*Shh*," he said. "I'm a secret agent. I have to be careful not to blow my cover."

I laughed and played along, but his words—spoken in complete innocence—convicted me. They caused me to think about my faith in Jesus and my willingness, or lack thereof, to talk about it with people who don't share my beliefs.

Truth be told, I sometimes hesitate to talk about Jesus because I'm afraid to offend or I fear being considered a religious whacko. In essence, I'm more concerned about maintaining my cover than about introducing others to Jesus and the new life He promises.

Jesus calls His followers "the light of the world." I'm not to maintain a safe cover that hides my faith; I'm to lovingly but boldly let it be known to all. Sometimes this happens through my words as I tell of the difference He's made in my life. Sometimes it happens through my attitude and actions—caring for others in practical ways, forgiving those who hurt me, putting others' needs ahead of my own, and giving thanks in difficult situations.

As Christ's follower, I'm not here to play the role of a secret agent. I'm to be His ambassador in a hurting world. —GRACE FOX

FAITH STEP: *Light a candle. Spend a few moments thinking about Jesus and His love for you, and then invite Him to make you a bright light for Him in your community and beyond.*

TUESDAY, AUGUST 22

A tree is known by its fruit. Matthew 12:33 (CEB)

Do you ever feel you've been labeled unfairly? I'm a Christian and, technically, Southern Baptist, but those labels concern me because of what they've come to mean to many people. I want them to mean that I love Jesus and everyone else, and I'm here to be a problem solver, caretaker of the earth, and reliever of suffering. I want them to mean that I'm Bible literate. Culture engaged. That I have no agenda—just grace. I want them to mean that I struggle with doubt and failure, and that's okay.

But on the world stage I think those labels mean a lot of undesirable things.

I'm from a small town in the South, and I'm white. I want that to mean that I love fried food, country music, and black people. That I'm friendly, hospitable, and kind. That I know the value of simple things like sitting in the porch swing with my husband, watching our kids chase fireflies. That I'm a hard worker. That I know how to garden and can tomatoes. I want it to mean I'm proud of Flannery O'Connor, Maya Angelou, and Johnny Cash and ashamed of the South's heritage of hate. I'd never live anywhere else but Arkansas, and yet I'm embarrassed and so sorry for the dark parts of our history.

Jesus was unfairly labeled at times in His day, and certainly He still is today. He's been called a liar and a lunatic. A disturber of the peace. A coward. A fake. His response? Eyes on the Father, shoulder to the plow. He said a tree is known by its fruit, and He practiced those words, not concerning Himself with labels. I'm trying to follow His example. —GWEN FORD FAULKENBERRY

FAITH STEP: *Look up Galatians 5:22, and commit it to memory. Cultivate these fruits in your life today, and quit worrying about labels.*

WEDNESDAY, AUGUST 23

Some Pharisees from the crowd told him, "Teacher, get your disciples under control!" But he said, "If they kept quiet, the stones would do it for them, shouting praise." Luke 19:39–40 (MSG)

I'VE ALWAYS LOVED to make up rhymes and jingles. As a child, I wrote a short song about Ponce de León, which I kept expecting a folk-singer to discover. As a young mom, I once had a rhyme-a-thon with my younger son that lasted through dinner. When I became a nana, I got more serious about songwriting. It started with a soothing song based on my granddaughter's name and every positive adjective I could think of. It came in handy when trying to change the diaper on her squirming bottom. When my grandson was one week old, I made up verses to sing while showing him his reflection in the mirror. My second granddaughter received a custom-made lullaby using her name plus her siblings' names and middle initials.

My grandchildren don't mind that my voice is not concert-worthy; they don't insist on deep, profound lyrics. I believe they simply respond to the love behind my efforts.

And I believe the same thing about Jesus. Since the Bible repeatedly urges us to "sing to the Lord," I've been enjoying making up little verses to sing to Him. I offer them as prayers while making my bed, pulling weeds in the yard, or just gazing at the night sky.

If I ever feel inadequate in my praise-giving, I remember the above verse in which Jesus told the Pharisees that if His followers stopped praising Him during His entry into Jerusalem, the rocks would do it. Now, I'll never be asked to lead worship music from a stage, but I feel sure I can do a better job than a rock. —DIANNE NEAL MATTHEWS

FAITH STEP: *Think about what you would like to say to Jesus right now. Make up a tune to accompany those words. Or try setting Scripture verses to music.*

THURSDAY, AUGUST 24

But who can endure the day of his coming? Who can stand when he appears? For he will be like a refiner's fire or a launderer's soap. Malachi 3:2 (NIV)

THE CRUMPLED SATIN BLOUSE rested under a pile of off-season clothes in my cedar chest. I'd forgotten I owned it and pulled it out with the joy of unearthing a little treasure. The fabric was wrinkled with such deep creases I wondered how to salvage it.

I took out my little-used iron and set to work. It required tremendous heat and pressure to work away the crinkles. With patience, the blouse returned to life.

There are times when certain habits or patterns become deeply ingrained. Our souls can be creased with worry, stained with envy, wadded into a hopeless mess of selfishness. Is it any wonder that Jesus allows some heat and pressure to touch our lives?

Much of the suffering we face comes from the natural results of our world. Illness, crime, harsh weather—we don't need to view these as God's personal judgment. Whatever the source of the refining fire, Jesus can use it to shape us, to have deeper compassion for others, and to bring Him glory.

Peter describes suffering this way: "These have come so that the proven genuineness of your faith—of greater worth than gold, which perishes even though refined by fire—may result in praise, glory and honor when Jesus Christ is revealed" (1 Peter 1:7, NIV).

Feeling like crumpled fabric under the heat and weight of refining is uncomfortable. I pray that the suffering in my life won't be wasted, but that Jesus will use it to smooth some of the rough places in my life and create praise, glory, and honor. —SHARON HINCK

FAITH STEP: *Iron something today and ask Jesus to apply pressure to places that need changing in your life.*

FRIDAY, AUGUST 25

"Behold, I am making all things new." Also he said, "Write this down, for these words are trustworthy and true."
Revelation 21:5 (ESV)

MY DAUGHTER AND I entered an antique shop that leaned more toward a junk shop. Rusted, crumbling, moldy items filled every surface, every corner, even hung—cobweb-draped—from the ceiling.

Minutes earlier, we'd walked wide, carpeted aisles of a more upscale—and cleaner—antique store. Now we stood in a shop that made us sneeze. "I'm allergic to the mustiness of dying things," my daughter said. I agreed.

Her words stirred the beginnings of a reflection far clearer than what we saw in rippled windows and grime-fogged mirrors. I began to see that Jesus is also essentially allergic to the mustiness of dying things.

Jesus celebrates remembrances, in keeping with His Father's heart and His New Testament teachings: "Remember Me"; "remember this moment"; "recall what has been done for you." But musty, dusty, dying things are not His domain. Life is His forte. The sentence "Behold, I am making all things new" appears as some of His final words in the Bible.

What will we do with the reminder that if our thought-life remains mired in dusty, musty, decaying junk shops, we're lingering in places that make Him itch and sneeze? —CYNTHIA RUCHTI

FAITH STEP: *Is there a specific area of your thought life that resembles that dusty, moldy, overcrowded antique store? Invite Jesus to don His hazmat suit and join you in tossing the useless, dusting off the salvageable, and applying His truths to mold removal.*

SATURDAY, AUGUST 26

You have been believers so long now that you ought to be teaching others. Instead, you need someone to teach you again the basic things about God's word. You are like babies who need milk and cannot eat solid food.
Hebrews 5:12 (NLT)

THIS YEAR WE HAD FOUR NEW GIRLS move in with us from foster care. In the past six months we've worked on table manners, picking up after themselves, and eating appropriate amounts of food. They went from neglect of living in a group home where the food was locked up to having free access to the pantry. They went a little crazy with their access to food, to say the least.

But what's harder is dealing with their hearts and emotions. Many days I'm weary from their emotional pain. I've heard, "Hurt people hurt people," and it's hard being on the receiving end, especially since I wasn't the one who hurt them.

One day I asked a friend to pray. She said, "I felt Jesus telling me to tell you, 'This too shall pass.'" Tears came to my eyes. Why? I've seen the girls' outward comportment change, and this reminded me that Jesus was also working on their hearts. I no longer have to worry about these girls overeating. And with therapy, patience, and love, I'm trusting these outbursts will soon be a thing of the past too.

It also makes me think of how far *I've* come. When I first turned to Christ, I didn't understand the basics of His Word. Just as Jesus was patient with me, I can be patient too. No one changes overnight, but daily guidance can make all the difference. —TRICIA GOYER

FAITH STEP: *Do you know a family who has adopted or is fostering children? Offer to babysit or provide them with a meal. Caring for those who give so much to hurting children is a beautiful way to love.*

SUNDAY, AUGUST 27

*The people were amazed and said, "What kind of person is this?
Even the winds and the lake obey him!" Matthew 8:27 (CEB)*

WHICH ARE THE SCENES from the Bible you'd time travel to if you could? Near the top of my list would be when Jesus stilled the storm. One of the accounts of that event is recorded in Matthew 8:24–26: "A huge storm arose on the lake so that waves were sloshing over the boat. But Jesus was asleep. They came and woke him, saying, 'Lord, rescue us! We're going to drown!' He said to them, 'Why are you afraid, you people of weak faith?' Then he got up and gave orders to the winds and the lake, and there was a great calm" (CEB).

The disciples woke him, begging Him to rescue them, which suggests that they hoped He could. Jesus called them people of weak faith because they weren't *sure* He could.

When storms rage around us and every wave leaves us gasping for air, what do we believe about Jesus? That He's sleeping, inattentive, disinterested? Or does our faith thin out, leaving us wondering if He has the power to change things?

Jesus gave orders to the tumult, and there was great calm. The wind and the waves were more obedient and responsive than His followers. The storm recognized His voice and His authority. The wind understood His power. And the lake and gusts didn't just quiet down a little. They grew impressively calm. Subdued. "You win, Jesus. You always win."

Oh, to hear His voice and obey Him as quickly as the wind!
—CYNTHIA RUCHTI

FAITH STEP: *To what storm in your life is Jesus speaking, "Peace. Be still"? When anxious thoughts rise, beat them back with the declaration, "Every storm in my life must bow to the Name and the authority of Jesus Christ."*

MONDAY, AUGUST 28

Because Jesus was raised from the dead, we've been given a brand-new life and have everything to live for, including a future in heaven. . . . God is keeping careful watch over us and the future. 1 Peter 1:3–4 (MSG)

SEVERAL YEARS AGO I was redecorating and realized just how much I love the airy coastal look. Being surrounded by fresh whites and summery blues, greens, and yellows sends refreshment breezing into my spirit. So I subscribed to *Coastal Living* magazine. Even the sight of the colorful covers lifts my spirit.

I didn't realize my subscription had renewed until recently when I saw a new charge for it on my credit-card statement. Apparently I had signed up for auto-renew. Although I was surprised, I was glad not to have to think about sending a payment on time before my subscription lapsed.

Jesus's refreshment and the lightening promise of eternity with Him are always on auto-renew for His believers. If we've put our trust in Him as our Savior, we can trust that our "subscription" will never lapse. In fact, it cannot.

When I'm honest with myself about my tendency to take Jesus's salvation and His presence in my life for granted, it's reassuring to know I don't have to rely on myself to keep my salvation. I don't have to renew it. There is no new payment for another year's worth of saving grace or peace or hope or love. All of Jesus is always mine through no ability of my own. When I signed up with Him, He guaranteed He would handle my "subscription" always. That truth is refreshment like no other.
—ERIN KEELEY MARSHALL

FAITH STEP: *Treat yourself to an hour or more doing something that refreshes you. Spend at least a few minutes of that time praising Jesus for His ultimate refreshment and an auto-renewed salvation.*

TUESDAY, AUGUST 29

He stripped all the spiritual tyrants in the universe of their sham authority at the Cross.... Colossians 2:15 (MSG)

ANY TIME I STRUGGLE with doubt, which is often, if I'm honest, I can trace its roots back to the problem of evil. If God is all-good and all-powerful, then why do bad things happen? Bad things being anything from my dog dying to the genocide in Rwanda.

It's an old and common problem. A lot of people smarter than I have tried to solve it, through attempts both philosophical and theological. But when you get right down to it, none of the arguments matter. The explanation that we have free will and live in a fallen world is precious little comfort to a mother grieving her dead child or a man on his fourth round of chemotherapy.

Teaching a class on world religions raises many questions, but ultimately leads me back every time to Jesus and the Cross. There's an anchor for my soul in the above verse and in what American writer and theologian Frederick Buechner observes in *Wishful Thinking*. Unlike other religions, Buechner says, on the problem of evil, "Christianity ultimately offers no theoretical solution at all. It merely points to the cross and says that, practically speaking, there is no evil so dark and so obscene—not even this—but that God can turn it to good."

People who sugarcoat the Christian life have no concept of what it really means to believe in Jesus. Like Buechner writes, the choice to be a Christian is the choice to stare evil in the face and still have hope. To believe there is a purpose for it, that it will be used by a loving God for our good. That's the message of the Cross. —GWEN FORD FAULKENBERRY

FAITH STEP: *Do you struggle as I do with doubts? Don't run away from Jesus, but toward Him. Fall in His arms today and surrender to the hope that is found at the Cross.*

WEDNESDAY, AUGUST 30

"Your spirit, not your size, makes the difference."
Luke 9:48 (MSG)

THE AVERAGE PERSON may feel too ordinary to do anything considered special or of great value in our world. While most of us would like to make a difference, what can one person do anyway?

Through a recent mailing, I learned that fifteen-year-old Gabe and his eleven-year-old sister Livvy approached life differently from most of us. A couple of years earlier, those two had scrolled through a Samaritan's Purse gift catalog and decided they wanted to help renovate a missionary hospital in a needy area overseas. But how could two young kids accomplish something that huge?

They set to work baking. Selling thousands of cakes and cupcakes eventually earned them $35,000. Their gift paid for a new maternity ward, which opened two years after their initial dream. They not only traveled there for the dedication, they baked cupcakes for everyone as well. The first baby born in that maternity center was named after Gabe.

Jesus was teaching one day about the importance of using our talents. He said when His disciples stand before Him in heaven, He will unveil the "difference" their lives have made for Him on earth. To those questioning Him that day, Jesus surprised them: "Whenever you did one of these things to someone overlooked or ignored, that was me—you did it to me" (Matthew 25:40, MSG).

It's not our size that makes a difference but our willing spirits. Gabe and Livvy learned that lesson early in life. I'm praying that I will learn it too. —REBECCA BARLOW JORDAN

FAITH STEP: *Ask Jesus to give you a dream of how you can make a difference for Him. Then offer yourself and your abilities for Him to use any way He wants.*

THURSDAY, AUGUST 31

"Peace I leave with you; my peace I give you. I do not give to you as the world gives. Do not let your hearts be troubled and do not be afraid." John 14:27 (NIV)

ON THURSDAY NIGHTS I gather with a group of women at the church I attend. We eat together. We talk about life. I talk about Jesus and share the struggles of parenting. They are young women, ages thirteen to twenty-three. I am twice their age, yet they've become dear friends. The differences don't stop there.

I am white. Most of them are not. I'm married, but only a few of them are. I have a house, a car, money in the bank. They have none of these things. What brings us together isn't any outward appearance or station in life. Instead, we are brought together by our brokenness. They are teen moms, anxious and concerned about their futures. I was a teen mom, and through Jesus's help, I overcame the fear, shame, and worries. I've walked down the path they're now treading on.

There is a lot I cannot offer these young women: daily help with their homework, good jobs, parents that care for them, or a boyfriend who will love them. But what I can offer is what I found—peace. Peace that comes from Jesus. Peace that says, "He will be with me through all my challenges as a mom."

The peace we have as believers in Christ is something we can share with those just like us or those who are very different. The best way to offer this peace is to find a common brokenness with the person and then share how Jesus ministers to that brokenness with loving care. We are all broken in some way, but thankfully, together, we can discover the peace that Jesus brings. —TRICIA GOYER

FAITH STEP: *Do you know someone struggling? Consider your past struggles and how Jesus helped you. As you share your story, make sure to highlight the peace you found in Jesus—inner peace even in the midst of the struggles.*

FRIDAY, SEPTEMBER 1

Being confident of this, that he who began a good work in you will carry it on to completion until the day of Christ Jesus. Philippians 1:6 (NIV)

YEARS AGO, I fell in love with quilting. I watched a quilting show on television and followed the instructions to learn different squares and patterns. I started small, making quilted potholders and Christmas ornaments as gifts. Then as our tenth wedding anniversary approached, I decided to surprise my husband with a full-size sampler quilt, complete with an embroidered wedding verse and our names and wedding date.

Making several squares, I started out well. A few edges didn't match up perfectly, and some points in a star or arrow were a bit blunted. But the colors were beautiful, and each new pattern was fun to learn. However, my life was busy with work, school, and children. My quilting supplies waited in a bin for months at a time. Our tenth anniversary came and went. Every now and then, I'd pull out the fabric and make one more square.

Years later I pieced together all the squares and completed the backing, filling, and quilting. What I thought would be a short-term project wasn't finished until our seventeenth anniversary.

There are days when I feel like my life is a fabric bin full of half-finished projects. I take comfort in this verse from Philippians. Unlike me, Jesus doesn't abandon His work for months at a time. He works in our lives constantly. He begins a good work and, piece by piece, creates new purpose, new means of service, and conforms us to the pattern He envisions. He never gives up on us. —SHARON HINCK

FAITH STEP: *Choose one task that's been waiting for your efforts and work on it today. As you make a little progress, thank Jesus for faithfully bringing His plans for your life to completion.*

SATURDAY, SEPTEMBER 2

"Come to me, all you who are weary and burdened, and I will give you rest."
Matthew 11:28 (NIV)

I HAVE NEVER BEEN very good at resting. If there is a moment to think of how I should take better care of my body or mind or spirit, it is usually sucked away by my children or a deadline or something to do with church or making the next meal.

I have friends who take great care of themselves...who go away for a night to a retreat or go for a daily run or take a class to help them recharge. Not me. I prefer to run myself straight into the ground.

It's not the best choice. These days I can barely keep my eyes open. I am not just tired in body...I am tired in spirit, with some back spasms added into the equation. I have walked with Jesus long enough to know that I have stepped away from His grace and goodness, letting life creep in and overwhelm me. I think the back spasms are mostly Jesus saying, "Why don't you lie down? No...really...I mean it...LIE DOWN."

So today I am lying down. With an ice pack. And I am sipping tea and doing deep breathing exercises and mostly I am realizing that I need to sidle up to Jesus and invite Him one more time to flood the desert-dry places in my spirit with His life-giving water so that I can soak up His grace and swim in His peace and breathe. Then I'll be able to find that place to rest in His love, which is a great spot to take a nap. —SUSANNA FOTH AUGHTMON

FAITH STEP: *Take time today to "lie down" in the presence of Jesus and let Him rejuvenate your heart, mind, and body.*

SUNDAY, SEPTEMBER 3

Your name, O Lord, endures forever, your renown, O Lord, throughout all ages. Psalm 135:13 (ESV)

ONE OF MY FAVORITE TIMES of the week is when I'm worshipping with my economically diverse church family on Sunday mornings. We go to a multiethnic church. We have homeless people singing alongside state senators. We have many people from various countries singing in their own languages—all of us in the same sanctuary together.

Sometimes as I worship I imagine at that moment people all over our country and throughout the world are doing the same thing. Together our voices are raised in a beautiful symphony to Jesus. And I consider how praises have gone up through the generations and around the world.

It is good for us to see Jesus as our personal Savior. Someday in heaven we will stand before Him alone and there will be no excuses or pointing fingers. Yet it's also important to remember Jesus's reign over nations, ages, and generations. He is *our* Lord—not just from this century, not just from this nation. This means we can offer what we have to others, no matter where they come from or their language or background. Jesus is for ALL of us. He always has been, and He always will be.

As Psalm 72:17 says, "May his name endure forever, his fame continue as long as the sun! May people be blessed in him, all nations call him blessed!" It's something to remember and consider next time we're worshipping Jesus. It's remarkable that we—during this time and in this place—can be considered part of the "all" who will praise His name through all generations. —TRICIA GOYER

FAITH STEP: *Think of a friend who is different from you—in race, in age, or in economic background. Reach out to that person today with a kind word. Tell that person you are thankful for him or her—thankful that you can seek Jesus together.*

MONDAY, SEPTEMBER 4

But those who hope in the Lord will renew their strength.
They will soar on wings like eagles; they will run and not grow weary,
they will walk and not be faint.
Isaiah 40:31 (NIV)

WHEN PREPARING FOR a speaking event with Isaiah 40:31 as its theme verse, I researched basic principles of flying that enable eagles to soar. I'd probably learned them for a test in fourth grade, but I had set the facts aside to retain the wonder that a bird as large as an eagle—or a 747—can get off the ground. Wise King Solomon's list of "things too wonderful to understand" started with "the way of an eagle in the air" (Proverbs 30:19, KJV).

Basic dynamics of flight tell us that air flows over wings with lower pressure than air moving under the wing. The difference in air pressure causes lift. A bird—or plane—with air moving over its wings is *pulled* up from above and *pushed* up from the pressure below. Thermal currents of heated air provide a boost in an eagle's ability to soar with a minimum of effort. Sustained flapping uses twenty times more energy than soaring. So it's not surprising that an eagle will spend as little as two minutes out of every hour in the air flapping. Soaring conserves energy.

That familiar verse in Isaiah says that those who wait upon the Lord rise up with wings like eagles. Not flapping wings. Soaring. Letting life's pressures from beneath us and the tug of Jesus from above lift us into the air.

Too wonderful to understand, but true. —CYNTHIA RUCHTI

FAITH STEP: *Have you thanked Jesus for providing liftoff? Any number of pressures may be pushing against you. Thank Him today for making flight possible, for enabling you to soar, despite those pressures.*

TUESDAY, SEPTEMBER 5

I want to know Christ and the power that raised him from the dead. I want to share in his sufferings and become like him in his death. Then I have hope that I myself will be raised from the dead. Philippians 3:10–11 (NCV)

THIS IS A BOLD CLAIM from the apostle Paul. I wonder if I share his urgent devotion to knowing Jesus on such an intimate level. No, really, I don't wonder. I'm pretty sure I don't. I don't like to suffer. At all. And yet suffering is not optional for us here on earth, is it? We can be bitter about that or we can be like Paul and see what we have to gain from the experience. In short, I think what we have to gain is redemption.

What does it mean to know Jesus—to share in His sufferings and become like Him in His death? None of us are likely to be physically crucified. But every time we suffer, through great loss or the myriad of tiny deaths we die every day, we get a taste of how Jesus suffered on the Cross. And because He rose again, we have hope that our death—our thousand deaths—will also be redeemed.

I have a friend who always says, "Another thing to die to," when something happens to disappoint him. We laugh about it, but in a way I think he sees it as an opportunity. Like so many other things in the kingdom of God, it's such an otherworldly way of looking at death and disappointment. An opportunity? The theology lines up with Paul's. If we want to know Jesus, we must recognize death experiences for what they are—a chance to know Him better. To learn to hope in the Resurrection. The whole process of suffering makes us more like Jesus. So it makes it worth it. —GWEN FORD FAULKENBERRY

FAITH STEP: *Pray this prayer: Lord Jesus, give me eyes to see my suffering as a gateway to redemption. Let me not become bitter but entrust myself to the One Who is just. Please use this opportunity to make me more like You. Amen.*

WEDNESDAY, SEPTEMBER 6

Clay doesn't talk back to the fingers that mold it, saying, "Why did you shape me like this?" Isn't it obvious that a potter has a perfect right to shape one lump of clay into a vase for holding flowers and another into a pot for cooking beans? Romans 9:20–21 (MSG)

"I DON'T THINK people will ever say those things about me," I lamented to my husband as we returned home recently from a woman's funeral.

Her home was spotless, and her kitchen was filled with mouth-watering smells of typical country fare. Their huge vegetable garden in earlier years had produced a large supply for seemingly endless feasts. Even her husband confirmed that his wife had filled the freezer with homemade dinners, just for him.

I contrasted my own habits and cooking efforts. My once shiny furniture often betrays a layer of dust. With kids grown, the meals in my freezer are leftovers. I still cook but primarily to live healthier. Grumbles often escape with meal planning, not because I don't like doing it or that I don't love my husband; I simply don't enjoy cooking alone. And I like other things so much more!

To his credit, my husband considers us a team and shares the load often. That day, he readily refuted my faulty comparisons, reminding me of all he loves about me and assuring me I was all he needed.

A pot of beans or a vase of flowers? Each one meets different needs. Comparing ourselves to others—in their lifetime or from their eulogies—flies in the face of Jesus's assurance. His Word says that the Lord created each one of us "wonderfully complex" (Psalm 139:14, TLB). Who are we to argue? —REBECCA BARLOW JORDAN

FAITH STEP: *Read Psalm 139 each day this week. Thank Jesus for creating you just the way He planned.*

THURSDAY, SEPTEMBER 7

If you don't turn your lives around and become like this little child, you will definitely not enter the kingdom of heaven. Matthew 18:3 (CEB)

BABIES DON'T GET SO BUSY that they forget to eat. They stop everything—even fun times or sleep or their mother's sleep—when their tummies tells them they're hungry. Single-mindedly, they'll voice their displeasure at the hunger situation until it is satisfied.

I wonder if part of what Jesus meant when He said we were to have the faith of a little child meant letting our thirst for Him drive us toward His Word and His presence until we are fully satisfied.

Although impatience is a response that runs contrary to the Bible's teaching, insistence—like that of a nursing child with milk on its mind—marks the life of a Jesus follower who will bypass distractions in order to have those needs fulfilled.

Is it like this at your house? You head for your Bible and the cozy chair reserved for time alone with the Lord, feeding on His Word and focusing on Him. On the way, you notice the answering machine blinking, or the washing machine beeping that it's time to move wet clothes to the dryer, or the cup of tea that needs reheating, or the glitter spilled during yesterday's craft project, or notification of a social-media message.

An hour later, you have yet to sink into that cozy chair and "eat." Two hours later...

What infant would be so easily distracted from its mission? The child's hunger is reason enough to let everything else in its world fade away. In our hunger for Jesus, let's be like little children today.
—CYNTHIA RUCHTI

FAITH STEP: *Resolve to "come as a child"—focused and determined—to the answer to your soul's hunger—Jesus.*

FRIDAY, SEPTEMBER 8

He says, "Don't be afraid, because I have saved you. I have called you by name, and you are mine." Isaiah 43:1 (NCV)

As MY GRANDDAUGHTER helped me get ready for a book signing, she turned over one of my books and looked at my picture on the back cover. "Nana, are you famous?" she asked.

I laughed and said, "No." Then I remembered how excited Lacey gets seeing one of my articles online or a link to one of my books on Twitter. She had told me a couple of times, "I just love seeing you in action." I didn't want to disappoint her, so I added, "Well, there are a lot of different levels of being famous."

"Oh," she said, nodding, "and you are on the lowest level." Lacey seemed satisfied with that, but I found myself wondering exactly which rung of the ladder I clung to.

No matter how pure my motivation is, it's only natural to enjoy being appreciated. It's not always easy to watch others being applauded while I labor on in relative obscurity. After all, the more widespread and well known my work or ministry becomes, the more lives can be touched. Unfortunately, my desires and ambitions can pull my focus away from the One I serve.

Right after that conversation with my granddaughter, I heard a pastor share about a little boy's misunderstanding of the Lord's Prayer. "Our Father who art in heaven," he began, "I know you know my name." Even if no one on earth has ever heard of me, the fact that the King of kings knows my name is more than enough.
—DIANNE NEAL MATTHEWS

FAITH STEP: *The next time you feel unappreciated, undervalued, or overlooked, thank Jesus that He knows your name and considers you worth dying for. List a few of the blessings your relationship with Him brings into your life.*

SATURDAY, SEPTEMBER 9

Two blind men were sitting by the roadside, and when they heard that Jesus was going by, they shouted, "Lord, Son of David, have mercy on us!"
Matthew 20:30 (NIV)

MY HUSBAND AND I have had the adventure of owning a series of old cars. No matter how much love, care, and money we poured into them, they seemed determined to cause trouble.

More than once, we found ourselves stranded on the side of the road (or bridge or driveway) when they stopped moving.

Being on the side of the road provokes a helpless and sometimes scary feeling. In the time before cell phones, we had to make decisions about walking miles to get to a phone or hoping someone would stop for us.

Our lives can be as unpredictable as those old cars. We can be working, serving, and thriving when suddenly we're knocked to the side of the road. However we got there, we shiver on the roadside, watching everyone else zoom past.

When our old car would break down, my husband and I often met interesting people. We experienced the generosity of others and the faithfulness of Jesus in the midst of our need. When the blind men waited on the roadside, probably feeling forgotten, Jesus met them. If you have any area in your life where you feel forgotten or stranded, be assured that Jesus reaches out to those that others pass by. He also invites us to be alert to those who have been sidelined, so we can serve in His love. —SHARON HINCK

FAITH STEP: *Think of a friend who has been knocked out of the flow of life. Reach out to her or him today—a phone call, an e-mail, a letter, a visit, or a gift—and let Jesus pour out His love through you.*

SUNDAY, SEPTEMBER 10

There is no fear in love. But perfect love drives out fear, because fear has to do with punishment. The one who fears is not made perfect in love.
1 John 4:18 (NIV)

OUR THIRD SON, ADDISON, has always been a little on the shy side. As a toddler, he could hardly make eye contact with anyone without bursting into tears. As he got older, preschool musicals were his Achilles heel. He would take one look at the audience, lay down on the stage, and weep. It is difficult to get a good picture with your child lying prostrate. But in kindergarten, he told Scott and me, "I have decided I am not going to be shy anymore." And with a great amount of determination, he got up with his class on Grandparents Day and recited a poem with his class without a single tear. He told us, "I just kept looking at my teacher."

Fast forward to this year, and he has come a long way. Fourth grade has been a big year for Addie. He switched schools, gave his first oral report, and is even playing in a bell choir with his class. The bell choir is still making him a little nervous. He asked me the other day, "Mom, can you just pray that I do okay playing the bells? I just want it to go okay."

Conquering our fear is no small thing. And usually we need backup. Prayers. Encouragement. And Jesus. He is the one who casts out all our fear. We just have to do what Addie did and keep looking at our Teacher. When we keep our eyes on Jesus, He keeps us in a place of peace. He tells us the truth about who we are. We are His. We are loved. We are safe in Him. —SUSANNA FOTH AUGHTMON

FAITH STEP: *What is a fear that you need to give to Jesus? Offer it to Him in prayer and ask Him to remind you who are in Him.*

MONDAY, SEPTEMBER 11

Day and night they never cease to say, "Holy, holy, holy,
is the Lord God Almighty, who was and is and is to come!"
Revelation 4:8 (ESV)

WHAT GRABS YOUR ATTENTION and could fill your days if you had such luxury? Reading? Working? Tennis?

We tend to have more activities and responsibilities than we can keep track of. Squeezing in a favorite pastime doesn't happen as often as we'd like.

Imagine then that our favorite activity in heaven—worshipping Jesus—will be the one we'll get to do always. Right now most of my worship happens like corn kernels in a hot pan: the thought heats up in the morning as I rush to get myself and the kids ready for school, to fix breakfast and lunches, to make sure the puppy isn't using the kitchen floor as her potty. I pop up a quick, inner "Hallelujah, Amen" toward the heavens as my thoughts are swarmed by what else is waiting for my attention.

Other eruptions of worship get snippets of my focus throughout the day until I fall into bed and breathe a quick thanks and a few requests before falling asleep. Worship is something I have to remind myself to prioritize.

But in heaven, worship will be primary. Never rushed, never forced, never requiring effort to focus our distractible minds.

I can only imagine 24–7 worship as a someday thing. But Jesus invites me today to pause more frequently for that most important activity. —ERIN KEELEY MARSHALL

FAITH STEP: *Stop and worship Jesus for five minutes. If necessary to help build the habit, put a worship prompt on your phone for the next week.*

TUESDAY, SEPTEMBER 12

Jesus asked, "Didn't I heal ten men? Where are the other nine?"
Luke 17:17 (NLT)

I TREASURE MY GRANDKIDS' RESPONSE to my little tokens of love for them. Freshly baked cinnamon buns or chocolate chip pancakes garner big hugs and sticky kisses. A bottle of bubbles or a package of stickers generates giant smiles and giggles. And always—no matter what the gift is—they say thank you.

Their parents have trained them to express gratitude, and as their grandmother, I've grown accustomed to them doing so. You could say I expect it from them. If they forget, I give them a gentle reminder: "Aren't you forgetting something?"

"Oh yeah," they say. "Thank you!"

Jesus expects us to say thank You too. We learn this from the story of the ten lepers. When only one leper expressed gratitude for restored health, Jesus appeared surprised. "The other nine—where are they?" He asked.

In the nine's defense, they'd run off to do what Jesus had told them to do—present themselves to the priest so he could declare them clean according to Old Testament law (Luke 17:14). He hadn't told them to say thank you first, had He? Why then was Jesus surprised when the nine ran away without expressing gratitude? Because He expected them to say thanks without needing a reminder.

Jesus lavishes tokens of His love on us every day. Forgiveness, peace, comfort, joy. These gifts and countless more warrant our gratitude. Let's remember to say thank You. He treasures our response.
—GRACE FOX

FAITH STEP: *Name three evidences of Christ's love for you. Take a moment to thank Him for these gifts.*

WEDNESDAY, SEPTEMBER 13

*"He pays even greater attention to you, down to the last detail—
even numbering the hairs on your head!" Matthew 10:30 (MSG)*

THIS MORNING AS I UNTANGLED my just-washed hair, I stopped twice to empty twisted clouds of hair from my brush. It's fall, and I shed a lot. I looked up, calling out, "Recount!"

I can't imagine why anyone would care about my moment-to-moment hair count, but Jesus said God keeps track. It can't even be hard for Him (but it boggles my mind).

While I was still contemplating that God knows every single hair on my head, the phone rang. The accountant from the dentist's office said our insurance hadn't paid for a procedure done 363 days ago, and she needed some information from me so she could resubmit the claim before the one-year deadline. My husband had called out of the blue for an appointment, and when she pulled up his chart, she found the nonpayment. Two more days and the bill would have become our responsibility. "It's a good thing he called today!" she chirped. I agreed. It's been an expensive season, with taxes falling due and unexpected car repairs. That dentist bill would've put us in the hole.

No, it's not a big thing, as problems go, but that's kind of the point. God, the Father, cares deeply about you, me—each one of us. All the little things. Jesus said, "Every detail of your body and soul—even the hairs of your head!—is in my care; nothing of you will be lost" (Luke 21:18, MSG).

Today, because I was already thinking about a God Who numbers the hairs on my head, I recognized—this time, anyway—the loving care He gave me. May I see it more and more. —SUZANNE DAVENPORT TIETJEN

FAITH STEP: *You may be having a difficult time and can't see the hand of God in it anywhere. Ask Jesus to show you one instance and wait quietly before Him today.*

THURSDAY, SEPTEMBER 14

Blessed is the one who finds wisdom, and the one who gets understanding, for the gain from her is better than gain from silver and her profit better than gold. She is more precious than jewels, and nothing you desire can compare with her. Proverbs 3:13–15 (ESV)

AS SOON AS THE ADOPTION PAPERS were filed for our newest four children, I started homeschooling them. We use a literature-based curriculum.

My eleven-year-old was screaming with excitement when the boxes of books started arriving in the mail. Sometimes she'd finish more than one book in a day, and it showed. Whenever a topic came up, she always had a bit of useful information to add to the conversation. I know that her love of books will get her far, but there is a greater wisdom I long to impart to my daughter.

As 1 Corinthians 1:18–19 (NIV) says, "For the message of the cross is foolishness to those who are perishing, but to us who are being saved it is the power of God. For it is written: 'I will destroy the wisdom of the wise; the intelligence of the intelligent I will frustrate.'"

The message of Christ's saving grace doesn't make sense to most people—especially those who are wise. The love of Christ isn't logical, and sometimes it's hard to figure out.

While I want my daughter to continue to read and learn from books, I'm doing all I can to teach her that the wisdom of Jesus is more important than man's. The best part is that we don't need bookshelves to contain it since Jesus's wisdom can reside in our hearts.
—TRICIA GOYER

FAITH STEP: *Choose a chapter of Proverbs and write down some of your favorite verses. Then pick one proverb to memorize and ask Jesus to bring His wisdom to your heart.*

FRIDAY, SEPTEMBER 15

*Work willingly at whatever you do, as though you were working
for the Lord rather than for people.*
Colossians 3:23 (NLT)

I REMEMBER MY "WORK HISTORY" as a child and teenager, and I wasn't always a willing worker. Maybe I was obedient more often than not, but I thought my parents were asking too much when they expected me to do the job cheerfully on top of just getting it done. It seemed to me, the fact that I'd stopped what *I* was doing in order to do something *they* wanted should have been enough.

They said that when I had kids of my own, I'd understand. They were right about that too. Not only did my children act just like I did when doing their chores, but by that point in my life, I'd worked alongside some individuals whose attitudes made it clear they'd rather be anywhere else. I'd seen coworkers fail to make eye contact or remember to thank their customers. On the other hand, I'd also had the experience of walking into a restaurant and being greeted by someone with a genuine smile, an enthusiasm for the food on the menu, and an interest in making sure our dining experience was a good one.

We who follow Jesus represent Him in our work. It's all too easy to lose our outward focus and settle for being self-centered complainers or even slackers. If we allow having a bad day to be an excuse for giving less than our best and failing to love others through our work, we contribute to someone else having a bad day too.

We are the hands and feet of Jesus where we do our work. With Christ's help, we can also be His loving smile. And that could be just what someone needs today. —SUZANNE DAVENPORT TIETJEN

FAITH STEP: *Play a little game today. Pretend that Jesus will come to you in the face of someone you encounter. Look for Him as you love them.*

SATURDAY, SEPTEMBER 16

*If you wake me each morning with the sound of your loving voice, I'll go to
sleep each night trusting in you. . . . Teach me how to live to please you,
because you're my God. Lead me by your blessed Spirit
into cleared and level pastureland.*
Psalm 143:8–10 (MSG)

A SMALL DREAM OF MINE came true recently. I'd been anticipating it
for two decades. I introduced my kids to the *Anne of Green Gables*
movies. Since my teens, I've been waiting to have kids old enough to
appreciate Anne's quirks.

As we watched, I couldn't help quoting some of the best lines
before Anne (with an *e*) said them. How about some of these gems?

"Fortunately for you, Josie, the only thing you've ever had to wear
twice is a sour expression."

"I wouldn't want to marry anybody who was really wicked, but I
think I'd like it if he could be wicked and wouldn't."

And then there was Anne's response to Morgan Harris's compli-
ment ("I'll bet no one's ever told you how becoming red hair can be
in the moonlight"): "Actually, lots of people have."

It's been great to hear again that "bosom friends," as Anne would
say, are always together in spirit. And finally, "Tomorrow is always
fresh, with no mistakes in it." I often remind myself of that truth.

I'm ever so grateful for the biblical basis in those words. In fact, the
Bible says that Jesus gives us a new start each morning. A fresh beginning every twenty-four hours—who could have asked for such mercy
and grace and hope? He knew we'd need our hope renewed that often!
—ERIN KEELEY MARSHALL

FAITH STEP: *Thank Jesus for today's mercy and the new hope He will bring
with the risen sun. After all, He is the risen Son.*

SUNDAY, SEPTEMBER 17

*"In your anger do not sin": Do not let the sun go down while
you are still angry. Ephesians 4:26 (NIV)*

I COULD SEE THE PASTOR beginning to lose his patience. A parishioner sitting in a pew in the middle of the church was heckling him during the sermon. "That's not what the Bible said!" he barked.

"I think we see things differently," the pastor responded calmly.

"No, the Bible is plain as day," the parishioner rebutted.

"We'll have to agree to disagree," the pastor said.

The man was finally quiet.

It was more drama in Sunday service than I'd ever witnessed. But it got me thinking about the times I had questioned what I'd heard or read from a religious leader. There were times I'd become angry about the interpretation of Scripture or the context in which God's Word was being used. I'd get mad, not just at what was said but also at the fact that I didn't feel I could speak about it.

But as I've wrestled with the Word, I've learned to take time to ask God what He means in a specific passage or within the context of a sermon. When I feel I can't let something go, I pray for wisdom. Typically I find that even if I'm still lost, a prayer can bring peace to the disagreement.

Jesus angered the Pharisees who insisted the Sabbath was sacred when He took time on that day to heal the sick. Their anger turned to bitterness, and their relationship with the Savior was damaged. Anger can be blinding. It made the Pharisees blind to the presence of God in their midst.

In my nightly prayers, when I feel a twinge of anger, I try my best to bring it to Jesus and to exchange it for His peace. —TARICE L. S. GRAY

FAITH STEP: *Anger is a burden. Write down what angers you and have a friend pray over it with you.*

MONDAY, SEPTEMBER 18

*For it is by grace you have been saved, through faith—and this is not from
yourselves, it is the gift of God—not by works, so that no one can boast.
For we are God's handiwork, created in Christ Jesus to do good works,
which God prepared in advance for us to do. Ephesians 2:8–10 (NIV)*

OUR THREE-YEAR-OLD GRANDDAUGHTER loves to help in the
kitchen, so her parents gave her a child-friendly knife and cutting
board. When my husband and I were visiting and making a batch
of chili, her mommy got out her daughter's tools so she could sit at
the table with me. My husband cored a bell pepper and spread it
out for her. While I chopped onions, our granddaughter carefully
diced up the pepper. Later she helped me rinse the beans and add
them to the slow cooker.

That night at supper, she was delighted when we told her daddy
that she had helped make the chili. She couldn't read a recipe, buy
the produce, brown the ground beef, or create a meal all by herself.
Her parents provided the tools and raw ingredients. My husband prepared the pepper. I supervised each moment and guided her. But she
felt the joy of participating.

In the same way, Jesus gives us a gift that we could never create
by our own efforts: salvation. He prepares good works for us to
do. He guides us to the place where we can serve and empowers
us each step of the way. We are as dependent as a three-year-old
in the kitchen. There's no room for boasting in any step along the
way. But there is plenty of room for joy. At the end of our lives we
can—with the same joy as a little child—tell our heavenly Father,
"I helped." —SHARON HINCK

FAITH STEP: *Think about a good work that Jesus has led you to do. Thank
Him for preparing the task in advance and empowering you each step of the way.*

TUESDAY, SEPTEMBER 19

*"What is the price of two sparrows—one copper coin? But not a single sparrow
can fall to the ground without your Father knowing it. . . . So don't be afraid;
you are more valuable to God than a whole flock of sparrows."*
Matthew 10:29, 31 (NLT)

RECENTLY I RETURNED HOME after being away for two weeks. The
fridge was empty of the basics: milk, fruit, and fresh veggies. I
headed to the grocery store. On the way I decided to stop at the
gym for a workout. Unfortunately, while on the treadmill, I suffered a sciatic injury. I could barely hobble, but—like a glutton for
punishment—I refused to go home without buying food first.

My favorite grocery store has carts that require a quarter to unlock
them for use. I always carry quarters, but this time I couldn't find
one. How would I ever manage the groceries? I limped toward the
entrance praying, *Jesus, help me.*

I stepped into the store. Lo and behold, an empty unlocked cart
sat three feet away. I waited and watched for a couple of minutes,
but no one claimed it. It seemed invisible to shoppers and staff
alike.

"Thank You, thank You, Jesus," I whispered. I pushed the cart
around the store feeling very loved indeed.

Jesus cares about the birds, and He cares about His children far
more. He's present, aware of, and eager to help us with every detail
of our lives. No concern is too small for Him. Not even that of a
shopping cart. —GRACE FOX

FAITH STEP: *Identify one detail that is on your mind today. Thank Jesus that
He cares about those things that matter to you. Ask Him to help you with it.*

WEDNESDAY, SEPTEMBER 20

Since prayer is at the bottom of all this, what I want mostly is for men to pray—not shaking angry fists at enemies but raising holy hands to God.
1 Timothy 2:8 (MSG)

THE APOSTLE PAUL took a disciple under his wing named Timothy. At the beginning of his letters to the young associate, Paul admitted that "grace mixed with faith and love poured over me and into me," overcoming his background of persecuting those who followed Jesus. "And all because of Him," he added (1 Timothy 1:14, MSG). Paul said he was proof of Jesus's patience "to those who are right on the edge of trusting him forever" (1 Timothy 1:16, MSG).

I thought about Paul's words when listening to depressing news and watching the early presidential debates last year. I agreed with many statements, spoken and unspoken: the world was growing more dangerous; times were changing; life was still precious. No matter who I listened to, each had a solution for the world's dilemma. At times, I felt both angry and discouraged but still reached for hope.

Inevitably I asked Jesus, "What's my part? What do I do?" Paul's letter to Timothy encouraged me to keep being faithful and to pray, not "shaking angry fists at enemies" or involving myself in needless controversy, but "raising holy hands" to Jesus.

It's easy to walk the fence of faith, give up hope, or close our ears and eyes to our world's condition at times, believing, "What will be, will be." But in the meantime, we pray, never ceasing to encourage others to look to Jesus, who is our hope. —REBECCA BARLOW JORDAN

FAITH STEP: *Make a list of leaders or people you know who are walking the fence in their beliefs. Pray for each one by name this week.*

THURSDAY, SEPTEMBER 21

[Jesus] will transform and fashion anew the body of our humiliation to conform to and be like the body of His glory and majesty, by exerting that power which enables Him even to subject everything to Himself.
Philippians 3:21 (AMP)

THE OLDER I GET, the more I am aware of human frailty. I think when we are younger, if we're healthy, there's the sense that we're invincible. Bulletproof. I don't know that I ever consciously thought that; I just know that with each passing year, I become more aware of how untrue it ever was in my life or anyone else's.

It's not only my own body that makes me aware of this through its creaking and cracking. It's the people around me. My dad, whom I've always thought of as the strongest man alive, tires a lot more easily than he once did. My mom, who used to stand on the back of a horse in parades, gets around much more carefully. And then there are my friends. One has been battling stage-four breast cancer, a fight that has taken her to the edge. Another, diagnosed with multiple sclerosis, has gone from needing a cane to using a wheelchair in the past five years. We don't want to think about what could be next.

While Jesus always ministered to people's physical problems, the focus of His ministry was on their spiritual conditions. That's our focus too—it's what lasts. But I am grateful for verses like the one above, which speaks to the transformation of our bodies. It puts in a nutshell the whole story of Jesus's death and resurrection. And it promises that just as in our bodies we must follow Him in death, we will rise again with new bodies, as He did. —GWEN FORD FAULKENBERRY

FAITH STEP: *Copy Philippians 3:21 and slip it into your pocket today. Every time your body reminds you of its limitations, claim the promise that Jesus is transforming you into His likeness—both physically and spiritually.*

FRIDAY, SEPTEMBER 22

Cast all your anxiety on him because he cares for you. 1 Peter 5:7 (NIV)

I NEVER CONSIDERED MYSELF an anxious person, but the more kids we add to our home, the more anxiety I feel. I've lain awake at night thinking about homeschooling more children, about sibling relationships, and about emotional and academic shortcomings in my kids. I've worried about not having enough grocery money and setting up dentist appointments—seven dentist appointments. Nearly every time I see a blank space on the calendar, I worry I'm missing something important that we're supposed to be doing.

Since becoming a Christian, I have known there were "big" things I should take to Jesus in prayer, but as the years have passed I've learned that Jesus cares about all my little anxieties too. He listens to my prayers about which homeschooling curriculum to buy just as well as He listened to my prayers for my grandfather when he was dying of cancer. There aren't big anxieties or small ones in His eyes. We are urged to cast *all* of our anxieties on Him. Or as Philippians 4:6–7 (NLT) says, "Don't worry about anything; instead, pray about everything. Tell God what you need, and thank him for all he has done. Then you will experience God's peace, which exceeds anything we can understand. His peace will guard your hearts and minds as you live in Christ Jesus."

Do you have anxieties? Turn them over to Jesus. Thank Him for His answers, and soon His peace will guard your heart and mind. These are free gifts from Jesus, but it's our job to turn over whatever burdens us for the peace that only He can give. —TRICIA GOYER

FAITH STEP: *Create a prayer jar. Get a jar and set it in a special place. Whenever you have an anxiety or worry, write it down and put it into the jar as a symbol of offering it up to Jesus.*

SATURDAY, SEPTEMBER 23

"When the Son of Man comes, will he find faith on earth?" Luke 18:8 (ESV)

FAMILIAR WITH MIDWESTERN SIGNS of winter's approach, I perked up when a TV show mentioned the Alaskan version. In Alaska, when fireweed blossoms reach the top of their stalks, residents know to count on only six short weeks until winter. The plant is a beautiful sign of summer when it starts to bloom and a warning about winter's approach. If it blooms early, Alaskans hurry to stock up on firewood, fuel, and food for the long winter.

Hearty Alaskans know the value of careful preparation for winter. Those caught unaware will pay a heavy price.

Jesus gives us few details about His return. No fireweed blossoms. No save-the-date for our calendars. But He does tell us what He hopes and expects to find when He does return: faith. Fearless, relentless faith like that of the woman in Luke 18. Jesus used the persistent widow's prayer in a parable to teach us to "pray continuously and not to be discouraged."

We won't be caught unaware or unprepared for the moment of His return if we live faithful and faith-filled, day in and day out. If He comes on a Sabbath morning, He may find many of us in church, singing praises, giving, listening to God's Word. What if He comes on a random Wednesday afternoon? What then? Will He find faith at work?

To guarantee preparedness, we must let faith hem and define us 24–7. Jesus did not teach Sunday morning faith, but persistent, consistent, relentless faith that can't be caught unaware. —CYNTHIA RUCHTI

FAITH STEP: *Think of one thing that might have to change so that no matter what hour of the day, what day of the week, or what year, when Christ returns, He'll find you living faithfully. What can you do today to transform that one into none?*

SUNDAY, SEPTEMBER 24

[Martha] had a sister, Mary, who sat before the Master, hanging on every word he said. Luke 10:39 (MSG)

RECENTLY IN SUNDAY SCHOOL, we were talking about listening. Someone said it was hard to tell if people are listening to you when you can't see their eyes.

Most mothers have had their faces physically pulled in the direction of the child who has something important to say. I certainly have. We all watch the eyes of our listeners. Do they get what we're saying? Do they agree? Disagree?

Jesus longed to be heard. He told people to listen before He launched into His stories. He proclaimed, "Who has ears to hear, let him hear." Most people didn't. When they listened at all, many heard what they *thought* Jesus was saying instead of what He actually said. As Good Shepherd, He said the appropriate response of His sheep was to listen to Him. Unfenced in a dangerous world, sheep won't survive long if they're not listening to their shepherd. Jesus wants us to listen to Him because He has the words of life.

In Mary, Jesus found a good listener in a busy household. She sat at His feet, undistracted, receiving His life-giving words. We know Jesus appreciated it because He praised Mary for listening instead of getting up to help her sister.

Listening well turns clamor into background noise. It's a gift to the speaker, costing time, thoughtfulness, and the effort of paying attention. I heard singer/songwriter Michael Card say, "The best way to love someone is to listen to them." I'm working on loving like that. —SUZANNE DAVENPORT TIETJEN

FAITH STEP: *Tune in today. Listen wholeheartedly to your pastor or teacher, to loved ones and friends, to the stranger on the plane. Look at them and hear them.*

MONDAY, SEPTEMBER 25

I don't say this out of need, for I have learned to be content in whatever circumstances I am. I know both how to have a little, and I know how to have a lot. In any and all circumstances I have learned the secret of being content.... Philippians 4:11–12 (HCS)

IT USED TO BOGGLE MY MIND when I read how Adam and Eve fell into sin even though they lived in a perfect environment (Genesis 2–3). God created them, blessed them, and gave them a beautiful garden in which to dwell. They enjoyed intimate fellowship with Him and with each other. How could that not be enough? But they no longer felt content with their circumstances once seeds of doubt about God's goodness were planted. They wondered if He was withholding good from them.

I have to admit that I'm not so different from Adam and Eve. It doesn't take much to allow discontent to creep into my mind. I momentarily forget that, through Christ, I have "every spiritual blessing that heaven has to offer" (Ephesians 1:3, GW). How can that not be enough?

Discontent can lead to an insidious form of dissatisfaction that erodes my trust in my Creator. I begin to feel like I'm in conflict with God because He doesn't have my best interests at heart. If left unchecked, this dissatisfaction will infect every area of my life.

So for today, I plan to keep my focus on all the blessings I have in Jesus. I will thank Him for who He is, for what He has done, and for what He will do in the future. And I hope that will bring me one step closer to learning the secret of being content in any circumstance . . . and keep me from my own fall.
—DIANNE NEAL MATTHEWS

FAITH STEP: *The next time discontent creeps into your mind, make a list of the blessings you have through your relationship with Jesus.*

TUESDAY, SEPTEMBER 26

This is the day the Lord has made; let us rejoice and be glad in it.
Psalm 118:24 (HCS)

I OFTEN CATCH MYSELF THINKING, *I'm really going to enjoy life when...* The sentence ends according to what I perceive to be my most pressing need: lose weight, get healthier, meet this deadline, make friends in our new neighborhood, pay off this loan, find a new job, move closer to family. Won't it be great when...?

I know that life on this earth will never be perfect, yet I still fall into the trap. The problem with always focusing on something I want to happen? I fail to appreciate what is happening around me.

During my last visit to my daughter's house, we failed to do half of what we'd planned. But one evening, despite the disappointments, I sat on the steps with my baby granddaughter held tight in my arms, looked up at the twilight sky, and whispered, "Lord, thank You for this moment."

Even in the midst of disappointment, sickness, loneliness, or grief, Jesus has arranged special moments, things He wants us to see or do. He may want to show us evidence of His presence through the beauty of nature or provision for a need. He may arrange for us to cross paths with a person who needs a loving touch from us or who can offer us encouragement.

There's nothing wrong with wanting our circumstances to improve or looking forward to special events, unless that desire clouds our ability to see what Jesus is doing right now. I never want my focus on tomorrow to make me miss what He has planned for me today.
—DIANNE NEAL MATTHEWS

FAITH STEP: *Fill in the blank: "My life will be better when _____." Now release that desire into Jesus's hands and ask Him what He wants you to see or do this day.*

WEDNESDAY, SEPTEMBER 27

The Lord is good to all; he has compassion on all he has made.
Psalm 145:9 (NIV)

WHEN MY FRIEND SHELLY died of ovarian cancer three years ago, a pebble of doubt buried itself deep inside my soul. I didn't realize it then, but over time I began to doubt Jesus's goodness. The way I'd once prayed: "Jesus, whatever you want? That's what I want!" seemed to wither away before the words could make it to my tongue. Because now I wasn't sure if I wanted what He wanted. I still loved Him. I just didn't trust Him.

But in this new wild season, something has begun shifting in me. Jesus is transforming me, asking me to think about who He is and how He has remained faithful all along. *All along.* Which shows me again just how good He is.

The sweet oil of the Scriptures laced with hope are loosening the knot of doubt in my spirit. I'm rediscovering truths like: "God is light; in him there is no darkness at all" (1 John 1:5, NIV). And I'm finding myself saying, one more time, "Whatever you want? That's what I want."

And He is speaking to my spirit: *How about you give Me all your fear, anger, doubt, questions, grief, and pain, and I will wrap you in My peace.... And overwhelm you with My love.... And show you My goodness.*

Life is difficult and heart-wrenching and sorrowful at times. It is beautiful and brilliant and hopeful too. And Jesus is good. I want Him to know I want in on what He's doing. Whatever that is. So I'm praying a new prayer these days: "I am open." It's a prayer small on words and big on hope. —SUSANNA FOTH AUGHTMON

FAITH STEP: *Practice saying this prayer to Jesus, "I am open."*

THURSDAY, SEPTEMBER 28

---

*Jesus answered, "Everyone who drinks this water will be thirsty again,
but whoever drinks the water I give them will never thirst. Indeed,
the water I give them will become in them a spring of water welling up
to eternal life." John 4:13–14 (NIV)*

SOCIAL MEDIA SITES make me thirsty. I know that may sound weird, so let me explain. I love seeing updates and photos that friends post online. I want to rejoice in their adventures and successes. But when I'm feeling grief about losses in my own life—conferences I can no longer attend, career paths I've had to relinquish, family I miss—watching other people celebrating can ignite my sense of emptiness.

I've begun to realize that no matter how much I've tasted the water of this life, the minute it stops pouring in, I'm thirsty again. Thirsty for more interaction, more productivity, more appreciation. I end up comparing my life to that of others and wanting more for myself. My selfish human nature creates a thirst that can never be slaked.

Does anything stir up unhealthy thirst in your life? Have you found that no matter how much you draw in and drink, you're never fully satisfied? Let's ask Jesus to help us thirst for something better.

Jesus offers the water of life. His love can quench our emptiness, our restless yearning, and our discontent. He fills us with Himself. With His perspective, we can love others instead of giving in to envy. He refreshes us, so we can serve others with joy. He releases a never-ending spring in our souls. —SHARON HINCK

FAITH STEP: *Take a drink of water and thank Jesus for His water of life that truly satisfies. Ask Him to increase your thirst for Him.*

FRIDAY, SEPTEMBER 29

Share each other's troubles and problems, and so obey our Lord's command.
Galatians 6:2 (TLB)

MY HUSBAND STOOD in the doorway of my office one recent rainy morning. "Do you have a minute?"

His finger over his lips silenced me as I followed him to the kitchen window. Through the slit in the blinds I saw six small doves huddling together on our porch swing. Their feathers ruffled as the porch chimes swung in uneven rhythm to the howling wind. I didn't know if the birds feared the storm. But instead of battling the weather, they drew close together for warmth and shelter under our patio covering.

That picture remained with me the rest of the day as I thought of the body of Christ all over the world, "feathers" ruffled with fear—and the storms that affect their lives. How do we survive these storms?

Later, I imagined Jesus tapping me on the shoulder and whispering, "Do you have a minute?" Then He reminded me of those doves, huddled together. I began to watch the news more attentively. Invariably, in a disaster, no one remained alone. People drew together in clusters, comforting one another, weeping together, helping each other—just like the body of Christ.

Sharing others' problems may mean offering a hug, a hammer, or a meal. Or simply huddling together, drawing warmth and encouragement from each other in the storms. Because we are always stronger together in Christ. —REBECCA BARLOW JORDAN

FAITH STEP: *Pray for the body of Christ around the world. Ask Jesus to show you how you can encourage others in your own church or neighborhood during stressful times.*

SATURDAY, SEPTEMBER 30

*But it is the spirit in a person, the breath of the Almighty,
that gives them understanding.*
Job 32:8 (NIV)

TWENTY YEARS AGO I made a decision to drop out of college. Then a young mom with two children and one on the way, I believed college was just too much to manage. I hoped that when my kids started school I'd go back to school myself, but that didn't happen. Instead, I began homeschooling. I also took an interest in writing. While my kids napped, I worked on articles and novels. I attended writers' conferences and met with other writers. I had big dreams, with very little education.

Unfortunately I met rejection for many years, and there was a time that I felt like giving up. I was certain I was wasting my time. And that's when I turned to Jesus in prayer. I relinquished all of my hopes, dreams, and writing ideas to Him. As I prayed, Jesus reminded me of the little girl who checked out more books at the library than she could possibly carry home. Jesus reminded me of the stories I made up in my head. He showed me that He'd planted these seeds in my heart, even as a child. Writing wasn't my idea but His.

Over the years I've written over fifty books, and I've depended on Jesus for every one of them. I don't have a college degree, but He leads me to the right information and research. I've met amazing people who've led me along the way. When I turn to Jesus, He gives me understanding. His presence was there at creation, and it's in each of us as we strive to follow the plans He's uniquely designed for each of us. —TRICIA GOYER

FAITH STEP: *What did you enjoy doing the most when you were young? What brought you joy? Pray and ask Jesus if there are dreams He has for you that He wants to fulfill. Then relinquish your dreams and ask to follow His.*

SUNDAY, OCTOBER 1

He has made everything beautiful in its time. He has also set eternity in the human heart. . . . Ecclesiastes 3:11 (NIV)

IN THE SOFT LIGHT OF THE MORNING I sit with coffee and quietness. My three-year-old girl sleeps. Rain falls and fog settles over the mountain in front of me like a bridal veil. The old cat pokes about the deck, unenthused by the food my son hastily dumped into her bowl.

The moment before, a sort of beautiful chaos. A fifteen-year-old girl whose last question was "Do you like my outfit?" A twelve-year-old quarterback, the cat feeder, who snapped at me in his haste, then stopped to say he was sorry—quick hug—and out the door. Another girl, eight, dressed up in red, white, and blue for some patriotic-themed day at school, a braid and a bow, hugs and kisses and innocence. A fourteen-year-old German, lent to us till the end of October, bewildered by warm fall weather, distracted, tired from last night's American football game. And my husband, the coach, their ride.

This is a snapshot of an ordinary life, an ordinary morning in an ordinary house. I live in an ordinary town in an ordinary state on an insignificant planet. And yet, Jesus sees me. He is with me. He has set eternity in my heart.

This knowledge transforms an ordinary morning into a thing of wonder. A morning with Jesus gives me eyes to see this ordinary place as a place full of purpose and possibility. He gives me ears to hear my family, a heart to know and love them well. And He fills me—even me—with His spirit. So I can walk through this ordinary day in extraordinary grace and peace. —GWEN FORD FAULKENBERRY

FAITH STEP: *As you spend your morning (or evening or whenever) with Jesus, ask Him to give you eyes to see, ears to hear, and a heart to know His purpose for your (extra)ordinary life.*

MONDAY, OCTOBER 2

Therefore, if anyone is in Christ, the new creation has come:
The old has gone, the new is here!
2 Corinthians 5:17 (NIV)

LAST NIGHT WAS one of those nights when I nearly lost my mind because the children wouldn't listen. I yelled at them and put them to bed without kisses... not that they wanted any from me. My back was so tense that I had to go do stretches on my bedroom floor. It was there, laid out, that I cried and asked Jesus to forgive me. I don't think He is superfond of my yelling. But He is always quick to show me the parts of me that He would like to change— and then He helps me make those necessary changes.

When I am in Jesus, I can't hide from who I am. Sometimes it's ugly. But addressing my old self is how He begins to bring in the new. He can't work on an area of my heart if I keep it to myself.

Slipping into that old skin of anger and selfishness is so much easier than asking Jesus to make me new. But the new me is what I really want. I have to be willing to invite Him into the mess of my life and say, "Okay, what does being 'new' look like in this moment?" and "Can You change this hard part of my heart?"

The best part is that when I ask Jesus into my life, the change has already begun. I am recognizing my need for His life-changing grace and mercy. My heart is turning toward Him. And something lovely happens... I can feel the old parts of myself start to fall away. And I begin to look and act and sound more like Him... a new creation. —SUSANNA FOTH AUGHTMON

FAITH STEP: *What is a part of your old life that you need to invite Jesus into? Ask Him to change your heart and continue His work of making you new.*

TUESDAY, OCTOBER 3

"Who among you by worrying can add a single moment to your life?"
Luke 12:25 (CEB)

"I WOULDN'T WORRY ABOUT THAT," I overheard one woman telling a friend, dismissing her concern as trivial. The friend's response startled me: "Oh? What *would* you worry about?"

Her question penetrated the flippant "Aw, don't worry about it" with a moment of introspection. We all worry. If that concern wasn't significant enough, what is?

What's your worry trigger? Worry triggers show us where we're not trusting Jesus. If we're honest with ourselves, we could point out the places without much coaxing. We may not worry over finances, but if something threatens our children's safety or happiness… We may weather our own medical crises with calm detachment, but if a parent or spouse is hospitalized with an undiagnosed condition… We might fly without fear but worry when our teen is out past curfew…

What are we supposed to do with the worry that comes so naturally to many of us? Jesus didn't leave us without an answer to that question. It's shared three verses later in Luke 12. "If God dresses grass in the field so beautifully, even though… it's thrown into the furnace, how much more will God do for you, you people of weak faith!" (Luke 12:28, CEB).

If worry is ineffective and Jesus promises that God cares about our situation more than we could imagine, worry is left without any wind in its sails. —CYNTHIA RUCHTI

FAITH STEP: *Name your worry trigger. Write it down. Is it your children, health, finances, future, all of the above? Which of those factors did Jesus fail to cover in His teachings? None. Stick the note with your worry trigger in the spot in your Bible where you find Luke 12:28. Lean on its truth.*

WEDNESDAY, OCTOBER 4

"For if you forgive other people when they sin against you, your heavenly Father will also forgive you. But if you do not forgive others their sins, your Father will not forgive your sins." Matthew 6:14–15 (NIV)

MY WRITING CAREER BEGAN IN 1999. My speaking ministry started about five years later. I never sought it. Word of mouth spread, and soon invitations arrived regularly. I felt scared and inadequate, but it seemed obvious that God was opening doors, so I responded by saying yes.

A close relative—someone whom I'd served in various ways when she faced health issues—watched the developments from a distance. She began making hurtful comments and questioning my motives. Things climaxed when she said, "I don't want anyone to know we're related."

My heart broke. I desperately wanted her to apologize, but no apology came. The more I replayed her words in my mind, the more wounded, angry, and imprisoned I felt.

Healing began when I chose to forgive. "To be a Christian means to forgive the inexcusable because God has forgiven the inexcusable in you," C. S. Lewis wrote. I found that to ring so true. Jesus empowered me to forgive by reminding me of His example. He'd forgiven me for offenses more times than I could count, and He wanted me to extend the same kindness to others.

Years passed. One day—quite unexpectedly—this relative said she was sorry and asked for forgiveness. Responding with an immediate yes was easy. How could I do anything but forgive when Jesus has done so much for me? —GRACE FOX

FAITH STEP: *Read Matthew 18:21–35. Note that forgiveness doesn't deny a debt—it releases it. Is there anyone whose debt you must release? Ask Jesus to help you do this.*

THURSDAY, OCTOBER 5

For everything there is a season, and a time for every matter under heaven.
Ecclesiastes 3:1 (RSV)

GROWING UP I WANTED TO BE a schoolteacher. I've always loved kids, books, and learning, and I thought there could be nothing better than a roomful of young, eager pupils. My life took a turn when I became a mom at a young age. Instead of completing college, I started writing during my children's naptime. Jesus used that time when I was a stay-at-home mom of three very young kids to guide me to my passion—to share His truths through the written word. As a bonus He later called me to homeschool my children.

When we are young we often think that there is one purpose for our lives, and it's our job to find it, follow it, and try to bring honor to Jesus while doing so. Instead, I see that Jesus has given me many jobs that have been a training ground for me. I've started a crisis pregnancy center, and I've hosted a radio program. I oversaw a program that educated teens, and I currently work with young moms in the inner city. Yet I never did all these things at once. I walked with Jesus through each season, learning from Him and leaning on Him for wisdom and guidance.

Sometimes when Jesus calls us in a new direction we may think, *That's not what I want to do with my life* or *That's not my dream.* If it's truly Jesus's leading then it's important to know that the areas in which we work and serve today might be a training ground for what Jesus has in store for us later. We might not know what training we need for future work, but Jesus does. —TRICIA GOYER

FAITH STEP: *Make a list of all the seasons you've been through. How has each season prepared you for where you are now? Thank Jesus for your seasons of training. Then thank Him for the seasons to come.*

FRIDAY, OCTOBER 6

"For I have come down from heaven not to do my will but to do the will of him who sent me." John 6:38 (NIV)

MY FATHER DIED when I was in my early twenties, and while the grief and loss grew less sharp over the years, there are still times when a wave of longing pours over me—a deep sense of missing him that can trigger sudden tears.

Today I was finishing a big project at my computer and I ran my hand over the polished wooden desktop. My dad had once cobbled together a slab of wood and mismatched drawers to create a large desk for his den. Years later my husband used that desktop to create a stunning new desk for our office—a lovely connection for me with my father.

As I touched the desk my dad had worked at, I had the wistful thought, *I wish Dad were here. I wonder if he'd be proud of me.*

I heard the quiet prompting in my spirit, *Ask if your heavenly Father is pleased.*

In the beautiful example of love in the Trinity, Jesus lived to please His Father and calls on us to do the same. And because of the redemption of Jesus, we can rest in the knowledge that we have the love and approval of the Father and the guidance of the Holy Spirit.

Whatever our relationship with our human father, because of Jesus we can have a restored and restorative relationship with our ever-present, all-loving Father. Because we live in Jesus, we can join in hearing the words, "This is my Son, whom I love; with him I am well pleased" (Matthew 3:17 NIV). —SHARON HINCK

FAITH STEP: *Dare to hear your heavenly Father's pleasure with you. Thank Jesus that He has restored our relationship with our Father and that we are joint heirs with Him.*

SATURDAY, OCTOBER 7

All around us we observe a pregnant creation. The difficult times of pain throughout the world are simply birth pangs. . . . The Spirit of God is arousing us within. . . . That is why waiting does not diminish us, any more than waiting diminishes a pregnant mother. We are enlarged in the waiting. We, of course, don't see what is enlarging us. But the longer we wait, the larger we become, and the more joyful our expectancy.
Romans 8:22–25 (MSG)

TWENTY MINUTES INTO A ROAD TRIP, I hear from the backseat: "Are we there yet?"

"No, sweetie, we just left."

Two minutes pass.

"It feels like we've been driving forever. How much longer?"

"A really, really long time, honey. We'll be driving forever, so get used to it."

Sound familiar? The agony of "The Wait" is why I love this paraphrase of Romans 8:22–25. For anyone who has chafed waiting for answered prayer, for a longing fulfilled, for a trying season to pass, for relief and rest, this verse is a breather. The waiting time isn't wasted. In fact, it primes us so the fulfillment is even more fulfilling.

Just as an expectant mother grows fuller as she waits for her beautiful baby, we can grow fuller of Jesus while we wait in His strength, trusting that He is working within us. Waiting patiently isn't easy, but we get the incredible opportunity to grow through it, knowing that Jesus is using that time for our good and to complete His purposes.
—ERIN KEELEY MARSHALL

FAITH STEP: *What do you have trouble waiting for? What gifts have been worth the wait? Write a thank-you note to Jesus for how He's working now on an answer yet to come.*

SUNDAY, OCTOBER 8

[Jesus] . . . stood up to read. The scroll of the prophet Isaiah was given to Him, and unrolling the scroll, He found the place where it was written: "The Spirit of the Lord is on Me, because He has anointed Me to preach good news to the poor. He has sent Me to proclaim freedom to the captives and recovery of sight to the blind, to set free the oppressed, to proclaim the year of the Lord's favor."
Luke 4:16–19 (HCS)

IT WAS THE SABBATH, and Jesus, in the synagogue as usual, stood up and read from the scroll. Then He sat down, and everyone stared at Him. It's so cool! Why did they stare? N. T. Wright says, "What Jesus was offering...was not a different religious system. It was a new world order, the end of Israel's long desolation, the true and final forgiveness of sins, the inauguration of the kingdom of God." They stared because they recognized something big was happening. Something huge. Something that would change everything, forever.

Imagine you'd heard those words all of your life. A prophecy that someday, Someone would come from heaven to help you. Maybe you were literally enslaved or maybe, like all of us, you were entangled by certain sins. You could never get free. You spent your life looking for that Savior to come and rescue you, sometimes wondering if He'd ever show up, if He was even real. And now He stands before you with arms outstretched, proclaiming, "I am here!"

It must have been amazing. But you know what? It's not that far-fetched. It still happens to people every day. Can you hear Him speaking to your heart today? —GWEN FORD FAULKENBERRY

FAITH STEP: *Make a list of things that hold you captive, things you need to see with new eyes. Then claim the promise of Jesus over those things, and rip up the list. He has come—you are free!*

MONDAY, OCTOBER 9

She gave this name to the Lord who spoke to her: "You are the God who sees me," for she said, "I have now seen the One who sees me."
Genesis 16:13 (NIV)

HAVE YOU EVER FELT INVISIBLE? I remember standing on the black-top at recess as teams were picked for kickball and no one chose me. Or hovering in the corner at the high school dance, wondering if the guy I liked would notice me. Or pasting on a smile at work while grief shredded my soul and no one knew.

Hagar, Abraham and Sarah's slave, must have felt invisible as she and her child were dying of thirst in the desert. Her life had been full of hardship and injustice, and now she was alone under the blazing sun. An outcast. She likely thought if the God of Abraham existed, He hadn't noticed her.

Yet in a dramatic moment of mercy and love, God intervened. He provided life-giving water and also a promise to bless her. She was no longer forgotten and forsaken. I love Hagar's response. She declared that God is a God who sees.

If you are an empty nester who feels forgotten by your grown chil-dren, take heart. Jesus knows about your pangs of loneliness. If you are an at-home mom facing long days of service that no one notices, take heart. Jesus is aware of your efforts. If you walk through a crowd and feel disconnected and alone, take heart. Jesus sees. And as we remember that, we'll also begin to see Him. His love will show up in unexpected ways. Like Hagar, we'll exclaim, "You are the God Who sees me. I have now seen You!" —SHARON HINCK

FAITH STEP: *Do you ever feel unnoticed or invisible? Invite Jesus to reassure you that He sees your situation and is guiding you and providing for you, today.*

TUESDAY, OCTOBER 10

*The faithful love of the Lord never ends! His mercies never cease.
Great is his faithfulness; his mercies begin afresh each morning.*
Lamentations 3:22–23 *(NLT)*

"I FORGOT." I groaned as I looked in the pantry for the item. Why hadn't I remembered to buy it? A little voice niggled inside: *Write it down next time.* I'd heard that reminder often from my husband, who admits the secret of his memory lies in his lists.

Then one day he hit on a simple idea: put a magnetic notepad on the refrigerator, and when we run out of an item, write it down on the pad. For the most part, that method has transformed my grocery shopping. But not my brain. Invariably, within a few hours of returning home, I'll be hunting in the fridge or pantry for something else. "Oh no, I forgot to write it down!" And I begin a new list.

I've discovered my spiritual life is similar. Each morning as I spend time in Jesus's presence, I invite Him to show me anything in my life that needs changing, is missing, or needs rearranging. As He does, I make a note on my mental list and I can visualize checking off that list.

But before the day ends, I remember a hidden motive, a wrong reaction, a misspoken word, and my list fills up again. That process could bring discouragement until I realize that a faith-filled life is not about a list of dos and don'ts. It's not about what I forget but what I remember: Jesus's forgiveness is complete; His mercies are fresh and new every day. —REBECCA BARLOW JORDAN

FAITH STEP: *Today, put a blank sheet of paper in your Bible. Each time you look at it, thank Jesus that His mercies are fresh and new every day.*

WEDNESDAY, OCTOBER 11

The Lord says: "These people say they love me. They show honor to me with words. But their hearts are far from me...." Isaiah 29:13 (ICB)

ONE DAY MY FIVE-YEAR-OLD GRANDSON wrote a sweet love note to his mom. Unfortunately, he wrote it on the tall wooden slat on the side of his bed. With a permanent marker. In big letters. The bed that his grandpa and uncle had just built for him two weeks earlier. Roman had been sent to his room for misbehaving with instructions to think about what he had done. I'm sure when his mom walked into the room, she would have preferred to find a repentant attitude rather than "I love you, Mom" written across her newest piece of furniture.

The concept that love and obedience go hand in hand is not easy to grasp, even for adults. In the Old Testament, the Israelites got comfortable going through the outward forms of worship, observing the rituals, sacrifices, and feasts. Yet they failed to honor God in their daily lives even though the prophet Samuel told them, "To obey is better than sacrifice" (1 Samuel 15:22, NIV).

The problem was still around in New Testament times. Jesus quoted Isaiah 29:13 to the church leaders of His day (Matthew 15:8–9). He told His followers, "If you love me, show it by doing what I've told you" (John 14:15, MSG).

My church service may be different from those of biblical times, but I can still slip into the habit of merely going through the motions without truly honoring Jesus in my heart. In that case, Jesus may hope for a repentant attitude and change in behavior from me more than a love note. —DIANNE NEAL MATTHEWS

FAITH STEP: *Before you attend your next church service or sing praise songs, ask Jesus to reveal any disobedience in your life that needs to be dealt with first.*

Thursday, October 12

For our present troubles are small and won't last very long.
Yet they produce for us a glory that vastly outweighs them and will last forever!
So we don't look at troubles we can see now; rather, we fix our gaze on things that
cannot be seen. For the things we see now will soon be gone, but the things
we cannot see will last forever. 2 Corinthians 4:17–18 (NLT)

My only sister has struggled with health issues for more than thirty years. Her body reacts negatively to scents and chemicals of every sort—toothpaste, laundry soap, candles, gasoline, even her kitchen cabinets. She's been confined to her house for a year, and that's where she'll stay unless Jesus performs a miracle on her behalf. Every day I ask Him to restore her health, but so far I've only seen her decline.

In the past, I've gone through periods of time when I've felt deeply burdened on my sister's behalf, wishing I could fix her situation and feeling guilty that I enjoy good health while she does not.

The verses cited above have anchored my soul in hope. They remind me that suffering lasts but a moment in the grand scheme of eternity. Jesus uses it to deepen us, refine us, and reveal Himself to us in intimate ways when we open our hearts to Him and trust His wisdom.

Someday suffering will end. I can hardly wait! In the meantime, knowing that Jesus won't waste it brings me hope. He has a purpose for allowing it, and He will bring that purpose to pass. Pain persists for a night, but joy comes in the morning and it will last forever.
—Grace Fox

Faith Step: *Memorize 1 Peter 5:10–11 (NLT): "After you have suffered a little while, he will restore, support, and strengthen you, and he will place you on a firm foundation. All power to him forever! Amen."*

FRIDAY, OCTOBER 13

This is the confidence that we have toward him, that if we ask anything according to his will he hears us. And if we know that he hears us in whatever we ask, we know that we have the requests that we have asked of him.
1 John 5:14—15 (ESV)

FOR YEARS I WANTED TO PLANT a plethora of tulips in my yard, but other priorities kept taking over. And then finally I took the plunge, and fifty-some tulip bulbs went in the ground—a solid start. Now I just need to wait out the winter for the fruits of my labors to push up from the earth to show off their radiance. Sure, some may not turn out as I'd anticipated, but I can believe that planting them triggered a response in each bulb.

Over these next months, I have several prayer requests I'm planning to commit to Jesus. Just like those tulips are designed to respond to being planted, when I plant my prayers with Jesus, I can trust that He will deliver an answer. His answer may sometimes be no, and sometimes it may be wait, and sometimes it may be a different color or variety than I expected.

Planting prayers always yields a response from Jesus because of His promise in 1 John 5:14–15. I pray to connect with Him first of all, and even when I don't see the answer for a long time— sometimes not in this lifetime—I can still trust that every prayer triggers a response from the heavenly throne room where Jesus sits at God's right hand.

Plant a prayer today and trust that each one will yield a response from Jesus...every time. —ERIN KEELEY MARSHALL

FAITH STEP: *Buy a packet of bulbs or seeds and watch them grow, letting your faith grow too, knowing Jesus hears and acts on your behalf, even when all seems quiet.*

SATURDAY, OCTOBER 14

Learn to do right; seek justice. Defend the oppressed. Take up the cause of the fatherless; plead the case of the widow. Isaiah 1:17 (NIV)

SIX OF OUR TEN ADOPTED CHILDREN have been adopted from foster care. To enter foster care there must be significant amounts of abuse, child endangerment, or neglect—or a combination of all three. Children who are raised in an unsafe environment often have trouble trusting those who honestly care for and love them after they've left those fraught situations. They carry around a lot of baggage. They have layer upon layer of offenses against them that they have a hard time forgiving.

Our kids have been through a great deal, and one lesson we're trying to teach them is the lesson of forgiveness. Forgiveness is not saying that what's been done to you—or others—is okay. It's giving the offense to Jesus and asking Him to deal with it. Jesus is a God of grace, but He is also a God of justice. He gives what is due, and we should leave it in His hands to mete it out.

One way to take up the cause of the fatherless is to give them a home, a family, and unconditional love. But another way to care for them is to teach them that forgiveness is not just for the other person; it's for them also. Teaching our kids the truth of forgiveness is like giving them a pass to freedom and peace for the rest of their lives. They don't need to be chained to what was done to them in the past as they hand it over to the Lord to carry on their behalf.

Defending the oppressed can mean bringing them into your home. It can also mean teaching them to turn continually to Jesus, Who will defend and heal them. —TRICIA GOYER

FAITH STEP: *Think about someone you need to forgive. Hand that offense over to Jesus and ask Him to deal with it. Also, if you've hurt someone, ask that person to forgive you.*

SUNDAY, OCTOBER 15

This is how we've come to understand and experience love: Christ sacrificed his life for us. This is why we ought to live sacrificially for our fellow believers, and not just be out for ourselves. 1 John 3:16 (MSG)

I ENJOY HEARING my cousin tell about his first Sunday dinner at his then-girlfriend's home. Raymond had never met Elaine's parents; he was eager to make a good impression. Instead of telling Mrs. Shepherd he didn't like iced tea, he decided to drink the glassful quickly and then request water. But his Southern hostess refilled the glass before he could speak. Then, as soon as Raymond finished his plate of food, Mrs. Shepherd served him a slice of homemade pie before anyone else was ready for dessert.

Raymond didn't think the pie tasted good, but he polished it off as the others finished eating. When Mr. Shepherd took his first bite, he told his wife that something wasn't right. She tasted the pie and looked confused. After a few minutes, the truth dawned on her and she covered her face with her hands. In the Shepherds' compact home, the washer and dryer were in the kitchen. Mrs. Shepherd had used detergent in place of sugar!

The first time I heard this story, I asked Elaine, "How could you *not* love a man willing to eat soap pie for you?"

Sometimes, reading the Bible, I think, *How can I not love a Savior who sacrificed His life for us?* And now Jesus asks us to live lives of selfless service to others. Sometimes this goes against our nature, but considering what Jesus went through for us, nothing seems too much to ask. Fortunately, it probably won't include eating detergent pie. —DIANNE NEAL MATTHEWS

FAITH STEP: *Thank Jesus for the sacrifices He made for you. Then ask Him how He wants you to serve someone today.*

MONDAY, OCTOBER 16

"You will know the truth, and the truth will set you free." John 8:32 (ESV)

I HAVE AN IMPULSE to create an image of perfection—not to show any weakness or tell the stories of my failures. Why? Because it's scary to tell the truth—to be seen and known and sometimes judged and rejected. But I have found that the flip side of fear is freedom. Not only for myself but for other people.

Yesterday something happened that illustrates this real-versus-perfect dichotomy. Our son Harper played in a basketball game and did well. And I did lots of cheering. At the buzzer, he grabbed a rebound in his spectacular, muscular style. Then he went back up strong, just like he's been working on, and scored a basket. "*Woo hoo!*" I cheered louder than ever. The crowd went crazy. The only problem was, it was the opposing team's crowd. Harper closed his eyes and grimaced. He'd just scored a basket for the other team.

I bit my nails as we waited for Harper to come out of the locker room. One by one his teammates appeared, but no Harper. When he finally emerged, I searched his face for signs of stress. To my relief, he grinned. He climbed up in the stands where his father and I were sitting. "I heard you cheering, Mom. The only one as silly as me was you."

I nodded. "You know you can count on me." He hugged me and we had a good laugh.

To those more highly evolved than Harper and me, this may not sound like much of an accomplishment. But for people like us, who tend to place too much value in our ability to not make mistakes, it's a slam dunk. —GWEN FORD FAULKENBERRY

FAITH STEP: *Your value is not in your performance. It's in Jesus's unchanging love. Embrace this truth and live free today.*

TUESDAY, OCTOBER 17

In tight circumstances, I cried out to the Lord. The Lord answered me with wide-open spaces. Psalm 118:5 (CEB)

OUR 112-YEAR-OLD HOUSE, an American Foursquare, is built around a central chimney once meant to ensure that each of the four rooms it intersects on both levels could be kept warm in a Northwoods winter.

With the addition of modern furnaces over the years, the chimney moved from heat producer to stumbling block. It narrows the passageway at the bottom of the stairs to the second floor to a mere twenty inches. And the chimney's central location makes it an obstacle to the main traffic flow through the house, whether we want to go upstairs, into the kitchen, from the kitchen to the dining room, or from the kitchen into my office. Imagine the scene with a houseful of kids and grandkids.

It's in the way. If we choose to put this house on the market someday, we'll have to do some fast-talking to minimize the constant bottleneck that the chimney creates.

Sometimes life closes in on us like that too-narrow opening. We can get through but not easily, comfortably, or efficiently. And if we're limping, on crutches, or using a walker following a deeper trauma, navigating the tight places grows even more distressing.

Is that your story today? Cry out to Jesus who answers "with wide-open spaces." He's a fan of an open floor plan for the human spirit. The hindrance may remain, but the soul can stretch its arms wide when He provides more spiritual elbow room. —CYNTHIA RUCHTI

FAITH STEP: *Does a hospital room, your office, laundry room, or a wayward child's bedroom make you feel like the walls are closing in? Post this truth: "I will walk around in wide-open spaces because I have pursued your precepts" (Psalm 119:45, CEB).*

WEDNESDAY, OCTOBER 18

You will go out in joy and be led forth in peace; the mountains and hills will burst into song before you, and all the trees of the field will clap their hands. Isaiah 55:12 (NIV)

THIS PAST WEDNESDAY, Jack, our thirteen-year-old, was awarded a plaque and a check for one hundred and fifty dollars for winning a patriotic essay competition. One hundred and fifty dollars for an eighth grader is like winning the lottery. He told us, "This is my first payment in my burgeoning writing career." It may be, since he actually knows what the word *burgeoning* means.

When I picked up the boys from school that afternoon, my eight-year-old, Addie, handed me his report card with a huge grin and exclaimed, "Look, Mom! All A's and Bs!" Another reason to celebrate.

Our evening was spent cheering on eleven-year-old Will to victory at his basketball championship game. The joy on the boys' faces when the buzzer went off was beautiful. Will told us afterward, "I was running so hard I thought I was either going to throw up or die." Winning is like that sometimes. Fantastic and difficult at the same time. We headed out to celebrate with friends and milkshakes, a winning combo.

Life is fantastic and difficult too. But Jesus created us for joy. He wants us to celebrate in Him and with Him. He wants you to let out a yell of delight. He is so good! The life He has given you is filled with sweetness. So clap! Jump for joy! Do a funky dance! Share a meal with friends! And know that in Him there are more wins, more joy, and more celebrations on the way. —SUSANNA FOTH AUGHTMON

FAITH STEP: *What are some of the wins that Jesus has helped you to achieve? Take a moment to celebrate them and thank Him for the joy He brings you.*

THURSDAY, OCTOBER 19

"As you go, proclaim this message: 'The kingdom of heaven has come near.'
Heal the sick, raise the dead, cleanse those who have leprosy, drive out demons.
Freely you have received; freely give."
Matthew 10:7–8 (NIV)

EXHAUSTED, I COLLAPSED on the couch. For a week I'd been working extra hours writing newsletters, sending e-mails, answering questions, hosting an event, interacting with readers, and doing interviews to spread the word about one of my books.

The work was fun, and the response was great. The catch? We were giving away the book.

After the rush of the event finished, physical fatigue led to depression.

"Lord, why did You call me to spend years of effort on the book and then give it away? And why should it require all this hard work just to offer a gift?" I felt envy for my friends who worked set hours and received paychecks.

Then I thought of all that Jesus did—the effort He poured into offering a free gift. The miles He walked, the conversations, the rejections, the exhaustion, and the eventual suffering. Not to gain anything for Himself but to give freedom, grace, and salvation.

I want to be Jesus's follower, but I'm often far from ready to walk in His steps. It's only as He lives in me more and more that I can embrace the joy of freely receiving and freely giving. —SHARON HINCK

FAITH STEP: *Ask Jesus to show you something—a possession, a resource, your time—that He would like you to freely give to others. Then give joyfully, remembering all He has given you.*

Friday, October 20

"You will not even need to fight. Take your positions; then stand still and watch the Lord's victory. . . ." 2 Chronicles 20:17 (NLT)

I'VE LEARNED A LOT about myself from my nervous, active puppy. Her foster mom called her a high-drive dog, and I now understand. When we come in from a walk, I can't get her to stop wiggling long enough for me to unsnap the buckle to her leash.

I was a lot like my puppy today. I knelt down to pray before working and immediately thought of something I should do. I stifled it, but before a minute had passed, I thought of another and even made a move to get up.

Hold still, I thought. So I did, taking a deep breath and relaxing again into the silence around me. Finally, after what felt like a long struggle, I *became* still.

I'm not sure how long I knelt there—and I'm not sure that time really matters. I stayed still, in an attitude of prayer, long enough. I got up feeling different, stronger. As if I had been in the presence of the Lord.

I spend a lot of time rushing around from one thing to another, trying to get everything done. In the process of chasing my tail like this, I give up the source of my strength.

In the above verse we see that holding still was a God-given strategy for Judah and King Jehoshaphat when they faced a greater enemy. We can hold still as well.

Jesus told the weary to come to Him for rest (Matthew 11:28–30). Quiet down. Hold still. Wait for the victory.

—SUZANNE DAVENPORT TIETJEN

FAITH STEP: *Try this with or without a timer. Get in whatever position is comfortable for you when you pray. Be still. Be quiet. Breathe. Ask Jesus to help you know when your prayer time is done.*

SATURDAY, OCTOBER 21

Greater love has no one than this: to lay down one's life. . . .
John 15:13 (NIV)

OUR FAMILY TOOK our beloved German exchange student to the airport yesterday. His flight was scheduled to leave at 10:16 a.m. At 9:00 Tim said, "I better go through security at 9:15." Nine fifteen came and went.

At 9:50 Harper said, "Tim. It's 9:50."

Tears started to flow.

When Tim disappeared through security, we stood in a circle and sobbed. Then we made our way to the van, where we waited, eyes on the sky for the plane. Grace, the closest to Tim, lifted her hand when it took off. To me it looked like prayer.

Love is weird. The first Scripture I learned tells me it's God—*God is love*. And the next tells me it's an action I should do—*Love one another* (1 John 4:7–9). These are the simplest concepts of the New Testament. But simple doesn't mean easy. Sometimes it's hard.

C. S. Lewis wrote, "To love…is to be vulnerable. Love anything and your heart will be wrung and possibly broken." That's what it felt like to watch Tim's plane fly away. But in those moments, according to Lewis, heaven is near. "We shall draw nearer to God, not by trying to avoid the sufferings inherent in all loves, but by accepting them and offering them to Him, throwing away all defensive armour."

No wonder it feels like prayer when I see my little girl's arm raised to the sky, open, defenseless. Accepting the pain because to avoid it would mean missing out on the joy. —GWEN FORD FAULKENBERRY

FAITH STEP: *Love hurts. No one knows this better than Jesus. In Him, choose to love anyway.*

SUNDAY, OCTOBER 22

"We also constantly thank God that when you received the word of God which you heard from us, you accepted it not as the word of men, but for what it really is, the word of God, which also performs its work in you who believe."
1 Thessalonians 2:13 (NAS)

I RECENTLY HEARD A RADIO INTERVIEW where the host asked his guest, "Who led you to faith in Christ?" The guest answered, "No one." It turned out he'd found a New Testament discarded in a prison trash can, fished it out, and began to read. Through that little Bible, he came to faith in Jesus. There is power in the Word!

I've been reading my Bible more this year. I'm using a well-known Bible reading system, where I read ten chapters daily, one from each of these categories: Gospels, Pentateuch, Letters to the early Church (divided into two groups), Wisdom, Psalms, Proverbs, Old Testament history, Prophets, and Acts. Because the sections vary in length, the chapter combinations never repeat. It's not detail reading, although you can certainly go back and study a passage later. My mind and heart are being bathed in the Word of God.

With the increased intake, I sense the Word actively working in my life (Hebrews 4:12). I find these newly familiar verses coming to mind, rising as if from a rich reserve, informing the choices I make in my ordinary moments.

The Word is another of Jesus's names. Jesus, the Word-made-flesh, came to save me. He still comes to me in the spoken and written Word. I'm letting the Word of Christ dwell in me richly (Colossians 3:16) so that He can do His work in and through me.
—SUZANNE DAVENPORT TIETJEN

FAITH STEP: *You may want to try a Bible reading system. May be listening to the Bible works better for you. Whatever the means, increase your intake of God's Word, starting today.*

MONDAY, OCTOBER 23

---

*When the cool evening breezes were blowing, the man and his wife heard
the Lord God walking about in the garden. So they hid from
the Lord God among the trees.*
Genesis 3:8 (NLT)

WITH TEN KIDS, one-on-one time with Mom is at a premium. I try
to carve out time during the day for each child, but they especially
enjoy time away together. Recently I took my fifteen-year-old out
for a special lunch. She soaked up the time, and her smile couldn't
be denied. She even took my photo and posted it on Facebook, stat-
ing, "I'm loving this bonding time with my mom today!" I loved
the time as much as she did, and I'm looking forward to when we can
do that again.

Like me, Jesus enjoys spending time with His children. Unlike
me, He is not bound by limited time and resources. He is available
any time, any place. He desires to be with His children. I forget this.
Sometimes I act as if I'm bothering Jesus when I sit down to read
my Bible or pray. Nothing could be further from the truth. Jesus
wants to spend time with us. He wants us to come out of hiding
and come to Him.

Adam and Eve hid. Sometimes this is true for us too. We don't want
to face Jesus with what we've done. (And we try to forget that He
already sees and knows our sins!) Other times we simply put other
things in our lives before Jesus. Yet just like a parent-child relationship, time is needed to build a bond. By the end of your time together
with Jesus, your heart will be full, and you'll be so thankful you made
the time for Him. —TRICIA GOYER

FAITH STEP: *Sit down and figure out a way you can add in more one-on-one time
with Jesus, and remember that He's looking forward to spending this time with you!*

TUESDAY, OCTOBER 24

No man can serve two masters: for either he will hate the one, and love the other; or else he will hold to the one, and despise the other. Ye cannot serve God and mammon. Matthew 6:24 (KJV)

RIGHT NOW I'M WATCHING whitecaps crash against the shore while rain streaks the windows facing Lake Superior. I'm snug and warm, holding a mug of tea, savoring the rhythms of nature. Our friends own this cabin, and they invited my husband and me to use it. Everywhere I turn there are cozy details, beauty, and comforts. Yet they wrote in their guest book that they consider themselves simply stewards of this beautiful home that God provided for them.

Their example inspired me to think about stewardship. How does Jesus want us to view the belongings that have come under our care?

In Matthew 6, the word translated as *mammon* is most likely derived from the Aramaic term for "the treasure a person trusts in." Modern translations use the word *money*, but the original meaning helps me apply Jesus's words more widely. When we look around our home, some possessions were earned by hard work and some items were gifts. However they came to us, Jesus reminds us that if we put our trust in these things, they can become our masters and steal away our service to Him.

That's why the concept of stewardship is so helpful. We can view any item and ask, "How can I use this to serve Jesus?" Our mixer can be used to bake a cake for a sick friend. Our books can be lent to a classmate searching for truth. We could even lend our home—as our friends did— to a couple needing a quiet place to be refreshed. —SHARON HINCK

FAITH STEP: *Walk through your home with new eyes, as a steward rather than an owner. Ask Jesus to show you ways you can serve Him with the array of items under your roof.*

WEDNESDAY, OCTOBER 25

The Lord bless you and keep you; the Lord make his face to shine upon you,
and be gracious to you; the Lord lift up his countenance upon you,
and give you peace. Numbers 6:24–26 (NRSV)

AS WINTER APPROACHED THIS YEAR, I nestled a few of my Gerbera daisies under the patio for protection. One day I noticed a white, powdery mildew forming on the leaves, so I cut away the sick ones. On one plant, all that remained after my pruning was one yellow daisy standing tall in the center.

Weeks passed, including some freezing nights. But each day I looked out the back door, I saw that stoic yellow flower smiling at me. A month later, still that singular, sweet face appeared unchanged, like Jesus Himself was smiling on me. I gazed at it, amazed. Never had I grown a flower whose blooms remained intact for an entire month, especially in cold weather.

I think Jesus knew I needed that simple object lesson. New attempts at improved health in my life were generally working; yet some days, symptoms like joint pain or fatigue reappeared. Like the powdery mildew on those flowers, they tried to sap my joy and energy. In addition, almost daily, e-mails were filling up my in-box from discouraged people asking for prayers. So many needs! What and how should I pray for them?

That's when Jesus reminded me of that little daisy and a simple prayer of blessing in the Bible. I would ask Jesus to bless and keep them, to make His face shine on them, to lift up His countenance on them, to be gracious, and to give them peace. And in my heart, I knew He would because that's what Jesus is doing for me. —REBECCA BARLOW JORDAN

FAITH STEP: *Write down Numbers 6:24–26 on a piece of paper and put it in a prominent place. Make that your daily prayer for others—and for yourself this year.*

THURSDAY, OCTOBER 26

At that time the disciples came to Jesus and asked, "Who, then, is the greatest in the kingdom of heaven?" He called a little child to him, and placed the child among them. And he said, "Truly I tell you, unless you change and become like little children, you will never enter the kingdom of heaven."
Matthew 18:1–3 (NIV)

ONE OF MY GREAT-NIECES—Madison—is three years old. She recently told her parents that she talks with God.

"What do you say to Him?" they asked.

"I tell Him jokes and stuff," said Madison matter-of-factly, "but sometimes He doesn't answer me." The preschooler's attention suddenly turned to her toys, and she ran off to play.

"Wow. Did you hear that?" asked her dad. "She said God sometimes doesn't answer her. That means He sometimes does." The thought of three-year-old Maddy conversing with God left her parents in awe.

Oh, to possess the simple, beautiful faith of a little child. Madison had learned about prayer from her parents and in church, and she took truth to heart. She just talked to God.

But rather than her prayers being one-way streams of conversation, Madison enjoyed two-way engagement with God. Indeed, this child knows Him more intimately than many adults do.

When the disciples asked Jesus who would be the greatest in the kingdom of heaven, He said we must change and become like little children. In the realm of spiritual things, their example teaches us unquestioning faith and trust. Specifically, in the area of prayer, I want to follow Madison's example and learn to listen. —GRACE FOX

FAITH STEP: *What child or children has God placed in your life? Think of one thing you can do or say to encourage that child's faith today.*

FRIDAY, OCTOBER 27

By wisdom a house is built, and through understanding it is established;
through knowledge its rooms are filled with rare and beautiful treasures.
Proverbs 24:3–4 (NIV)

WHEN MY HUSBAND AND I relocated several years ago, we bought a spec house that had just been framed. At that point we could have customized the interior, but the builder had already met with a professional decorator to choose colors, materials, and finishes, with a few exceptions. I was glad I loved what they had already chosen, because it took me many hours and several trips to the store just to settle on cabinet pulls and knobs.

When we finally moved in, I still wasn't able to relax. The large entrance hall needed a table against one wall to look finished; the covered patio called for outdoor furniture. My area rugs weren't the right sizes, and some of my wall art didn't seem like a good fit.

I found myself repeatedly going into the same home decor and fabric stores and browsing the same online sites. Then one morning I read Proverbs 24:3–4 and understood I was obsessing over the wrong things. Instead of worrying over furnishings for a physical house, I would be better off seeking spiritual wisdom and understanding—the kind that fills a life with "rare and beautiful treasures."

Since Jesus is the source of divine wisdom and discernment, I need to be focused on my relationship with Him. If I put Him first every day, everything else will fall into place. And I will have a beautifully furnished life, even if I don't have window treatments or a hall table. —DIANNE NEAL MATTHEWS

FAITH STEP: *Are you obsessing over material things today? Take time to focus on Jesus, asking Him to fill your life with His wisdom and discernment.*

SATURDAY, OCTOBER 28

*"For what does it profit a man if he gains the whole world
and loses or forfeits himself?"*
Luke 9:25 (ESV)

I LOVE TALKING TO PEOPLE and learning about their lives. One of the questions I like to ask a new friend is, "Are you related to anyone famous?" I've met people who are related to presidents, others to outlaws. In our family, my husband is related to Mick Jagger. Mick's father and my mother-in-law's father were first cousins. Crazy, eh? I have great-grandfathers who were pastors and missionaries. One of them founded a Bible college.

Mick Jagger is famous by the world's standards. His songs are still played, and he commands attention wherever he goes. Yet in Jesus's eyes, it's the missionaries, the pastors, and the prayer saints who are famous. Like Hebrews 10:34 (NLT) says, "You suffered along with those who were thrown into jail, and when all you owned was taken from you, you accepted it with joy. You knew there were better things waiting for you that will last forever."

The fame one receives on this earth will last for a lifetime—and sometimes beyond that—but the fame of those who live for Christ goes further still. My great-grandfathers and other family members were never famous on earth. They sacrificed their comfort to serve Christ. They lived on little funds, and they rarely received praise or honor. These faithful saints usually aren't mentioned when someone asks, "Are you related to anyone famous?" Yet they are the ones whom we should most aspire to be like. —TRICIA GOYER

FAITH STEP: *Consider those you are related to. Write down the attributes you appreciate about that person and then write down why his or her example has inspired you.*

SUNDAY, OCTOBER 29

Jesus looked at them and said, "With man this is impossible, but with God all things are possible." Matthew 19:26 (NIV)

I SPOKE AT A MOMS' GROUP the other morning. I never thought I'd be a speaker. The thought of getting up in front of a crowd makes me sweat even now. I am always afraid I will forget my train of thought midtalk. Or that I will embarrass myself. But I keep saying yes when I am asked to speak. It is my leap of faith in my journey with Jesus. I am trusting that He will come through, even though I am completely out of my comfort zone.

Jesus is more than okay with that. He does His best work in impossible situations. He can do more and be more when I am following and trusting Him completely. The journeys that Jesus has for those He loves always seem impossible. Abraham? Sarah? Joseph? Moses? Joshua? Esther? Ruth? David? They faced impossible journeys. They did impossible things. They didn't always get it right. But in the course of their lives, they became more than they could ever have hoped or imagined.

I've found that there are some impossible things in the journey Jesus has for me. I can't complete it in my own strength. Sometimes I'm scared. But I'm learning to take heart because I know that I am in great company. Everyone who journeys with Jesus is. And Jesus doesn't leave me in that place of fear. Instead, He invigorates me, lifts me up, hems me in on every side, gives me thoughts and talents and abilities that I'd never had before. And the greatest joy? I'm becoming more than I could ever have hoped or imagined.
—SUSANNA FOTH AUGHTMON

FAITH STEP: *Read the story of your favorite Bible heroes. Be inspired and uplifted by the amazing way Jesus came through for those heroes on their journeys.*

MONDAY, OCTOBER 30

Moses said to the people, "Fear not, stand firm, and see the salvation of the Lord, which he will work for you today." Exodus 14:13 (ESV)

BACK IN THE DAYS when the Israelites were trying to escape from Egypt, they came to the Red Sea, which was full and impassable for the thousands of men, women, and children who'd been beaten down and demeaned and broken for generations. Their first thoughts must have been terror. Maybe total resignation. They'd been through so much, possibly beyond hope that things could ever improve.

But the Lord was about to show His people His glory and care. To make His point, He hardened Pharaoh's heart, prompting the ruler to chase after the Jewish nation.

And this is where the Israelites were about to see who their Redeemer really was. He was the one Moses spoke of when He instructed the people to stand still and watch the Lord work.

Stand still and watch. Wow, that can be tough. I tend to be a fixer. If something isn't working, or I'm wondering about a direction from Jesus, I tend to search and ask and read and lose sleep until I think I've found a workable solution. Standing still and waiting for the Lord to fix things can feel much harder than stewing about it until I think I've covered all the bases.

The above verse does not say "sit still," as if the Israelites were in a position of resignation, depression, or defeat. And that verse is still the same for me today. It tells me to stand. Honorably. Head held high. No fear. Confident that Jesus will bring the answer.
—ERIN KEELEY MARSHALL

FAITH STEP: *That answer you're searching for? Stand in faith before Jesus, and know that He was working on the solution before you were even aware of the threat.*

TUESDAY, OCTOBER 31

So he [Jesus] got up from the table. . . . He poured water into a washbasin and began to wash the disciples' feet, drying them with the towel he was wearing. John 13:4–5 (CEB)

A WINDSTORM LATE IN THE FALL stripped the last of the leaves clinging to their branches, with the thick woods near our home left exposed. Where in midsummer we could see only a few feet into the woods because of the leaves and underbrush, with the underbrush bare and the trees denuded, our line of sight extended hundreds of feet farther.

What we saw were all of the tripping hazards that had been hidden when the woods were lush with growth. Half-downed trees. Stumps. The litter from those who had used the road nearby. The hazards became much easier to see, identify, and clear away with the leaves gone.

Are there tripping hazards in your life that are hidden when all is at its peak, calm and untroubled? When the wind blows cold and hard, or you enter a dry, bitter, seemingly lifeless season, does the lack of growth uncover those problem areas?

Jesus carries a big chain saw and knows how to use a chipper/shredder. He loves it when we invite Him to clear away the debris—those downed trees, those resentments and past hurts and ungodly affections that can pose a hazard. Rather than shy away from that cleanup task when the wind is howling and you can't see a sign of life, let Him use that time to His and to your advantage.
—CYNTHIA RUCHTI

FAITH STEP: *There's a sweet intimacy in letting Jesus have access to the debris-strewn parts of our lives, the areas not yet yielded to Him. Don't fear the process. Embrace it.*

WEDNESDAY, NOVEMBER 1

God answered Moses, "So, do you think I can't take care of you?
You'll see soon enough whether what I say happens for you or not."
Numbers 11:23 (MSG)

I HAD A FOLLOW-UP VISIT at the Mayo Clinic for my sudden hearing loss and mysterious neurological symptoms. As a nurse, it isn't good to have symptoms that don't fit neatly into an algorithm or textbook picture.

My hearing has improved enough to be helped by a hearing aid, but problems with balance and concentration are making it hard to do my best work in a busy neonatal ICU. Even though I'm thankful to be getting better, I'm also becoming discouraged.

I can identify with the Israelites complaining in the wilderness, glorifying Egypt in their minds, bemoaning what they didn't have while not appreciating the miracle of manna right in front of them every day. And with Moses who couldn't quite believe that God would be able to come up with enough meat to feed six hundred thousand people for a month. Still, he told the people what God said He would do. And God delivered, like He always does. Their problem was that they didn't really know God and how He works.

Jesus knew His Father and tried to get His followers to relax and trust in God's provision. He said, "Steep your life in God-reality, God-initiative, God-provisions. Don't worry about missing out. You'll find all your everyday human concerns will be met" (Matthew 6:33, MSG).

The Father knows what I need. Jesus says I can trust Him. Oh, that I would! —SUZANNE DAVENPORT TIETJEN

FAITH STEP: *So how do we steep ourselves in God-reality? Two of the best ways I know are reading the Bible and spending time in silence before the Lord. Do both today.*

THURSDAY, NOVEMBER 2

In every thing give thanks: for this is the will of God in Christ Jesus concerning you. 1 Thessalonians 5:18 *(KJV)*

NOVEMBER IS NOT my favorite month. It starts to get dark early, and I hate the dark. I also hate the cold. Both of these things make me want to stay in my pajamas all day and cuddle on the couch with my dog, but I must face my life. I have four human beings who depend on me to be sane and kind and responsible and wise. I feel my inadequacy in this child-rearing area every moment of every day. I see my time with them slipping through my fingers and I get scared it won't be enough—I won't teach them enough or give them all they need to navigate life.

Like my kids, my parents are getting older, which I also hate. I don't see or talk to my friends enough and I miss them. My skin is awful. I've gained weight. Then there are my students and my job. And I won't even go into finances—always a fun topic this time of year.

People on social media have started the annoying practice again of posting things they are thankful for each day. *Even though I love Thanksgiving, I'm in no mood for thankful thoughts.* Thus went my grumpy inner dialogue on the way to work today, till I remembered Jesus and the fact that I really am thankful He loves me no matter what.

It seems that one glimmer of thankfulness opened the door to more things I am thankful for. I started to compose a mental list. And guess what? My grumpy anxiety gave way to peace, which was followed by joy. —GWEN FORD FAULKENBERRY

FAITH STEP: *Grab a pen and paper and start writing down things you are thankful for, in no particular order. Don't stop till you feel His peace flowing like a river in your soul.*

FRIDAY, NOVEMBER 3

They will soar on wings like eagles. . . .
Isaiah 40:31 (NIV)

As I WATCHED A BALD EAGLE perched high in a leafless birch tree one day, I noticed how it seemed regal and confident, so unlike the attitude of the carrion-loving turkey vultures in scruffy trees nearby. The vultures were hunched and wary, brooding, needy. The eagle remained alert and poised.

One of the flight dynamics of which eagles often take advantage is obstruction currents. These form when moving air runs into an obstacle—a cliff or mountain. Air is forced up and over the object.

Where we would see a barrier, eagles see an advantage. They ride those obstacle currents high into the air where they can soar for long stretches of time. That high position gives them a better vantage point from which to watch life, stay informed, and find ways to meet their nutritional needs.

The parallel is striking. What if we saw obstacles as gifts, as boosts in our ability to fly higher? What if we appreciated rather than resented the new perspective we gain? What if we followed the pattern Jesus laid out for us? Regal and alert, His confidence bolstered by His heavenly Father, Jesus noted the obstructions in His way—betrayal, rejection, false accusation, imprisonment, the Cross, death—and rode them like flight-boosting currents toward His higher destination.

Obstacles. Eagles approach them with gratitude. And so should we. —CYNTHIA RUCHTI

FAITH STEP: *Stay alert for a visual reminder that obstacles form currents we can ride to catch a Jesus-eye view of our circumstances. Turn to it often when tempted to be discouraged by what stands in your way.*

SATURDAY, NOVEMBER 4

Jesus called the children to him and said,
"Let the little children come to me, and do not hinder them. . . . "
Luke 18:16 (NIV)

"CAN I PLAY with the flour?" My five grandchildren congregate in my small kitchen when they visit. The question from one of them wasn't all that unusual. When they were toddlers, they discovered my three-piece canister set, each one filled with a different kind of flour. On rainy days, they enjoyed opening the canisters' hinged lids, scooping, piling, stirring, and watching how the different types of flour behaved.

Sometimes—with permission—they dusted the countertop with flour so they could draw pictures with their fingers or pretend to be pastry chefs. Messy? Sure. Costly? Far less than an afternoon at the amusement park.

Does Jesus watch us make small messes sometimes—and not stop us—because of the lessons they hold? We make an ill-advised job choice, which makes a mess. But from it we draw wisdom about the kind of job we don't want. We fail to consult Him when looking for an apartment and pay a high price with noisy neighbors until we move. We say something offhandedly, without thinking, which backfires, creating a relationship crisis that needs our attention. Relatively small prices to pay for the lessons learned?

Jesus, please help us learn from the small messes, protect us from the larger ones, and teach us to pay attention when You give us cleanup instructions. We're going to need them. —CYNTHIA RUCHTI

FAITH STEP: *Making the messes doesn't decrease Jesus's capacity for love. Have you carried resentment because He didn't stop you from some of the messes you've made in the past? It's time to let that go and be grateful for the lessons learned.*

SUNDAY, NOVEMBER 5

I waited patiently for the Lord; he turned to me and heard my cry.
He lifted me out of the slimy pit, out of the mud and mire;
he set my feet on a rock and gave me
a firm place to stand.
Psalm 40:1–2 (NIV)

EVER SINCE I HAD postpartum depression with my third little guy, I have realized the importance of filling my mind with good thoughts. Those sullen days can shadow me on occasion. I have had to learn that when life takes hard turns, I don't have to let myself spiral downward. I have a choice...I can turn toward the persistent pull of dark thinking or I can reach for the light. I won't lie. It is a harder thing to choose the light. Some days when grief or health issues or giant bills overwhelm me, I have to work at it. Slipping into the dark pit takes no effort.

Reaching toward the light means moving forward when moving seems impossible. I think that is why I love the Psalms so much. David, before and even after he became king, had some dark days. But he never stopped looking for hope.

Sometimes reaching for the light is beyond us. But when we cry out, Jesus comes to us. In the dark. With His all-encompassing, dark-shattering, hope-filled light. And He begins to set our world aright.

It may take some time to feel the light, but if we ask Him—if we let Him—He keeps coming back, loving us as only He can. Dark day after dark day. Until finally we find we are out in the sun again. —SUSANNA FOTH AUGHTMON

FAITH STEP: *Draw a picture of the sun. Write down the ways that Jesus brings light and hope into your life.*

MONDAY, NOVEMBER 6

Lead me in your truth and teach me, for you are the God of my salvation.
Psalm 25:5 (ESV)

WE'VE BEEN ON a *Star Wars* binge around my house. We watched the complete saga in succession. Stella, who is almost four, loves them. She has totally immersed herself in the story of Anakin Skywalker, trying to wrap her mind around how (spoiler alert) that cute little boy could grow up to become the evil Darth Vader, who is finally redeemed right before he dies.

The other morning she was musing about all of this and she told me, "I like Luke better than Anakin, Mommy."

"Why is that, Stella?"

"Well, Anakin has *hateness* in his brain. That's his problem. That's why he turns bad. But Luke, he doesn't. He only has *loveness* in his heart."

If only we could all be like Luke and just have loveness in our hearts. But I think the reason so many people are passionate about *Star Wars* is because we can all relate to Anakin, just as we relate to Abraham, Isaac, and Jacob. It's the human condition, isn't it? To wrestle with our own fallen nature? Thank goodness Jesus offers us a way out.

The Bible says the truth sets us free. In Anakin's case, the truth was his son's unconditional love, which overcame every lie Anakin believed of the Dark Side. This is actually a great picture of Jesus's love. When we receive the truth that He loves us—really loves us—it sets us free to live the abundant life we were created for. Like Anakin, we can be redeemed. —GWEN FORD FAULKENBERRY

FAITH STEP: *Commit John 8:32 to memory. Whenever you feel your freedom threatened, remind the enemy of this verse. Hold fast to the truth because therein lies your freedom.*

TUESDAY, NOVEMBER 7

After the festival was over, while his parents were returning home, the boy Jesus stayed behind in Jerusalem, but they were unaware of it. Thinking he was in their company, they traveled on for a day. Then they began looking for him among their relatives and friends. Luke 2:43–44 (NIV)

A RECENT NEWS REPORT told of Child Protective Services being called in because a mother allowed her children to play at a nearby park on their own. Society has changed from my childhood days, spent playing unsupervised. These days "helicopter parenting" is more in vogue.

Each time I read the story of Mary and Joseph leaving Jerusalem without Jesus, I try to understand the cultural differences of the time and place. Yet I still shake my head. *How could they leave Jesus behind?* Then the story invites me to confront myself. How often do I leave Jesus behind? I rush into my day full of plans and agendas as if I don't even have a Shepherd to follow. Or I wring my hands as a friend pours out her struggles, feeling helpless, and I don't remember to turn to Christ with my friend's needs. At some point, I look around and think, *Is something missing?*

Even when I'm charging around, self-absorbed and forgetful, my Savior is still with me. Yet in some sense, I can set a course and move onward quite a distance before I realize He's beckoning me to a different way.

When Mary and Joseph returned to Jerusalem, Jesus said, "You should have known I would be about my Father's business." If I glance up from my ministry, activities, or a difficult life situation and have lost sight of Jesus, I need to ask Him to turn my focus back to the Father's work. —SHARON HINCK

FAITH STEP: *Today, thank Jesus that even when we are distracted and forgetful, He never loses sight of us.*

WEDNESDAY, NOVEMBER 8

No more dragging your feet! Clear the path for long-distance runners so no one will trip and fall, so no one will step in a hole and sprain an ankle. Help each other out. And run for it! Hebrews 12:12–13 (MSG)

INEVITABLY, AS I WATCH the wrap-ups from various marathon races around our country each year, I see participants stumbling along with little chance of winning—maybe not even finishing. Yet news clips always zero in on the sidelines, too, where well-wishers hoot and salute the runners on their journey. Occasionally, someone will even rush to a runner and physically help him or her across the finish line.

As I watch these scenarios unfold, I root for the underdogs, cheering them on, even offering a silent prayer that they will finish strong. And then the race is over.

Recently in Hebrews, I read about a race called life that is continual and one in which spectators offer encouragement before—and after—the runners cross the finish line. Only in this race, we are all participants. So how can we help others who may be lagging?

Confident that many have already finished successfully, we can cheer on others by slowing down and running beside them, prodding them to victory. We can pray for them and warn them of any pitfalls and problems we've already encountered. We can help them "run with perseverance" and visualize the goal—Jesus—waiting at the end. And we can encourage them often with words that say, "I care!" "Jesus is with you!" "You can do it!"

No one runs alone. The great thing about life is that all of us cannot only finish, we can win—because of the One who ran before us, and along with us, all the way. —REBECCA BARLOW JORDAN

FAITH STEP: *Review Hebrews 12 and list all of the ways you find to encourage both yourself and others toward life's finish line.*

THURSDAY, NOVEMBER 9

Then Jesus got into the boat and started across the lake with his disciples. Suddenly, a fierce storm struck the lake, with waves breaking into the boat. But Jesus was sleeping. Matthew 8:23–24 (NLT)

I EXPERIENCED A STORM on the night my daughter Kim and her husband drove across the Rocky Mountains from southern British Columbia to central Alberta. They were headed to her occupational therapy convocation ceremony.

That drive takes nearly ten hours in good weather, so they planned to leave shortly after lunch. Unfortunately, car repairs delayed their departure. Then a winter storm blew in and forced a highway closure. Even after the road reopened, the blizzard continued and slowed their pace for hours.

I texted with Kim throughout the evening and prayed for her and her husband's safety. When bedtime came, I texted one more assurance of my prayers, then I crawled into bed. As I lay there, memories of driving that same route—and of sliding on black ice—filled my mind. Fear for the kids' well-being threatened to overwhelm me, but I refused to entertain the what-ifs. Instead, I willed my focus to remain on Jesus.

"Thank You for Your presence with the kids as they drive," I said to Him. "I know they're in good hands." I closed my eyes, and peace eventually lulled me to sleep.

I heard from Kim early the next morning that they had arrived safely.

Storms of life are inevitable, and no one enjoys them. But the good news is this: Jesus is with us in their midst. —GRACE FOX

FAITH STEP: *What storm are you facing today? Fill in the blank: With Jesus in my boat, I can _____.*

FRIDAY, NOVEMBER 10

Commit your activities to the Lord, and your plans will be achieved.
Proverbs 16:3 (HCS)

SOME DAYS JUST DON'T GO RIGHT, like one November morning when my husband and I planned to drive from Texas to Tennessee to visit family. Richard went to work around 5:30 a.m., returning by 11:30 a.m., in time for us to leave. I'd been extrabusy that week, but with six hours to get ready, I was sure I could have everything done.

After cleaning up breakfast dishes, I answered e-mails, gathered work-related items, showered, styled my hair, and started packing. As I filled the toiletry bag, I whipped up a couple of moisturizers. Then I made sandwiches and cut veggies to take for lunch. Not wanting to waste the eggs in the fridge, I boiled them to add to the cooler. I admired my efficiency.

I tidied up the house and finished packing, amazed at how the time had flown. I rushed into the kitchen and mixed dry ingredients for chocolate chip cookies. Then I opened the refrigerator—and remembered that I'd boiled all of the eggs. I walked down the sidewalk and borrowed one from a neighbor. Several minutes later, I stood in the pantry, unable to believe I was out of chocolate chips.

But the one thing I was really out of? Jesus. I'd forgotten to start my day off with Him.

Starting my day with prayer—asking for Jesus's guidance and blessing—doesn't guarantee that I will never have moments of forgetfulness, or be scatterbrained, or have to eat raisin cookies. But it ensures that something will go right with my day.
—DIANNE NEAL MATTHEWS

FAITH STEP: *Begin your morning by telling Jesus your plans for the day. Invite Him to revise them according to His will and purposes.*

SATURDAY, NOVEMBER 11

"My grace is all you need. My power works best in weakness."
So now I am glad to boast about my weaknesses,
so that the power of Christ can work through me.
2 Corinthians 12:9 (NLT)

MY DAUGHTER KIM began submitting résumés for occupational therapy positions in September. It soon became obvious that options in her community were limited, especially for someone new to this field. Our entire family rallied to pray for a breakthrough for her.

In early November, a clinic manager phoned Kim and requested an interview. Then she scheduled a second interview to discuss potential case scenarios. Trouble was, she scheduled it for the same day as Kim's convocation in Alberta, hours away. Fortunately, the clinic manager agreed to talk by phone.

Kim hadn't slept the entire night prior—the white-knuckle ride through the mountains made rest impossible. By the time the interview rolled around, Kim had been awake for thirty-seven hours. The bad news was that her body and brain felt beyond exhausted, and she teetered on the verge of tears. The good news was that Jesus specializes in helping His children in situations like this.

Kim went into the phone interview trusting Jesus to fill her empty tank with His power. And He did. The strength with which He infused Kim enabled her to answer the questions put to her with clarity and skill. The call ended with an offer from the manager for a full-time position. —GRACE FOX

FAITH STEP: *Are you struggling with feeling weak in a specific area? Identify that area and ask Jesus to fill you with His power.*

SUNDAY, NOVEMBER 12

---

*So, because Jesus was doing these things on the Sabbath, the Jewish
leaders began to persecute him. In his defense Jesus said to them,
"My Father is always at his work to this very day, and I too am working."
For this reason they tried all the more to kill him; not only was he breaking
the Sabbath, but he was even calling God his own Father, making himself
equal with God. John 5:16–18 (NIV)*

THOSE LEADERS SURE DID miss the point. Jesus had just healed a
man who had been unable to walk for thirty-eight years. It was
a time to rejoice! Instead, they criticized Jesus for healing on
the Sabbath and for instructing the man to carry his mat and to
walk. Instead of arguing about how many steps were allowed on a
Sabbath day, Jesus gave a powerful response: "My Father is always at
his work to this very day, and I too am working."

I find huge comfort in those words. A common doctrine of our
day is that God made the world and is now letting it unravel without much interest or involvement. As a popular song put it, "God
is watching us—from a distance."

Jesus crushes that lie with His simple words. His very presence in
that dusty town on that particular Sabbath provides the evidence.
He is at work. Always and forever. Drawing people into relationship
with Him. Healing. Saving.

Because we know Jesus continues to work in our lives, we can take
every need to Him. He won't tell us it's the wrong day for miracles or
to figure things out for ourselves or ask us to keep our distance. He is
the Savior who took on flesh to show us God's love close up. He lives
in us. He even offers us the wonderful opportunity to join Him in
His work in the world. —SHARON HINCK

FAITH STEP: *Rejoice that Jesus is still at work in the world. Ask Him how you
can join Him in that work today.*

MONDAY, NOVEMBER 13

Teach us to number our days, that we may gain a heart of wisdom.
Psalm 90:12 *(NIV)*

DON'T ASK ME how it happened, but my online calendar disappeared one day. Initially, I didn't panic. *There's always a way to get it back*, I thought. *I'll "undo" whatever I've done or search for an alternate route into the information.* An hour later, my blood pressure crept higher as I envisioned the impossibility of retrieving much of the information. I could call the clinic and dentist office with little trouble. I could retrace some of the e-mails that contained information. But not all of them.

"How do I retrieve missing information from my online calendar?" I asked the online universe and unearthed a dozen possible solutions, none of which worked.

"Why do I care so much?" I asked the King of kings.

When I changed my prayers from "Fix it! Fix it! Fix it!" to "Jesus, what am I supposed to learn from this?" the stress factor shifted. It became less about losing information and more about regaining priorities.

"Numbering" my days had turned into filling them up and ticking them off, too often letting a calendar dictate my time rather than flowing with the inhale and exhale of the Holy Spirit. The disappearance of my calendar recalibrated my attitude toward it.

My calendar returned. It was as if Jesus waited until He could trust me with it. —CYNTHIA RUCHTI

FAITH STEP: *Do you have a day planner or a calendar that plays a stronger role than it should? Like me, will you work on letting it bow to the Sovereign One Who fills our lives with good things (Psalm 103:5, NLT)?*

TUESDAY, NOVEMBER 14

Behold, I am doing a new thing; now it springs forth, do you not perceive it? I will make a way in the wilderness and rivers in the desert. Isaiah 43:19 (ESV)

IN 2000 I HAD THE CHANCE to visit the Van Gogh Museum in Amsterdam. I wasn't a huge fan of Van Gogh's work as I entered the doors, but by the time I left I was in awe of his talent. Seeing the big canvases with thick paint skillfully applied inspired me. He was a man who knew how to masterfully use the tools of his trade. It's amazing how talented artists create with paint and brush, but even more amazing is when Jesus does something with nothing...or at least that's how it seems at times.

Only Jesus can create a path through a tangle of trees, under brush, and roots. Only He can create a river in a desert. And only Jesus can spark something new in our lives. We never know if today will be the day when Jesus will choose to bring something new to our lives.

I can look back on ordinary days and see where Jesus changed everything. The day when my pastor called and asked if I'd help start a crisis pregnancy center and the day when I saw the first Heart Gallery display of waiting kids in foster care who needed forever homes. Even the day when I walked into an art gallery with a friend and walked out with a new favorite artist.

Sometimes we believe that Jesus can only do something with all the pieces we already have stacked up in our lives, but we must remember that unlike us humans, Jesus can do something with nothing—or at least nothing that we can see currently in the life around us. We simply have to trust. —TRICIA GOYER

FAITH STEP: *Think of a time when your perspective changed in the course of a day. Then pray for Jesus to do something new and wonderful in your life, during His timing.*

WEDNESDAY, NOVEMBER 15

May Jesus himself and God our Father, who reached out in love and surprised you with gifts of unending help and confidence, put a fresh heart in you, invigorate your work, enliven your speech. 2 Thessalonians 2:16–17 (MSG)

I'VE BEEN GOING THROUGH a difficult time in my life and, instead of responding with a good attitude, I've been decidedly grouchy. That makes it worse.

I drop things. I lose my balance without warning. My fine motor dexterity isn't what it once was. My short-term memory is shot. All this after a sudden, one-sided hearing loss. I've been to the best doctors and am glad they've ruled out pretty much every injury or disease that could be causing it. Really, I am.

It's just that they've been able to say what it isn't, but none of them has a clue as to what it *is*. And they can't fix a problem they can't identify.

I'd like to say I've received this news and adjusted to the changes in my new way of living with trust and acceptance. I'd like to, but I haven't. I'm kind of mad about it. Anger is one of the stages of grief, after all. Then, because I know my situation is so much better than that of most other people, I end up feeling guilty in addition to shaking my fist at God—at least some of the time.

Yeah, I'm a mess. The saving grace is—grace. People are praying for me. I'm reading the Bible more than before, and it's coming alive inside me. I'm humbled to realize that even though I'm behaving badly, I am still loved. The way Jesus feels about me never depended on how I acted.

He loves me anyway, and He's helping me in my words and in my work. And in my heart. —SUZANNE DAVENPORT TIETJEN

FAITH STEP: *I'm sure you, like me, want your attitude to please the Lord. When it doesn't, talk to Him about it. Ask Him to put a fresh heart in you.*

THURSDAY, NOVEMBER 16

"Ask, and it will be given to you; seek, and you will find; knock, and it will be opened to you. For everyone who asks receives, and he who seeks finds, and to him who knocks it will be opened. Or what man is there among you who, if his son asks for bread, will give him a stone? Or if he asks for a fish, will he give him a serpent? If you then, being evil, know how to give good gifts to your children, how much more will your Father who is in heaven give good things to those who ask Him!"
Matthew 7:7–11 (NKJV)

SOME DENOMINATIONS OF CHRISTIANITY use these verses to teach that we should ask God for the material things we want. To name those things and claim them as our birthright.

And surely I believe it's okay to ask God for things. We live in a material world and have certain needs. I don't believe He begrudges us things we want either or that people of faith are supposed to be these dour-faced characters who deny themselves every pleasure of the flesh. The above verses are in red in my Bible. They are Jesus's idea.

However, I do believe we must recognize that in all of our desires and petitions for material things, there is the reflection of a deeper longing. François Varillon says they are really a sign of the need to be "invaded and transformed by God."

Have you ever noticed that when a child wants something really badly and asks for it for a present—then gets it—it doesn't take long for the excitement to wear off? In a few days the child moves on to the next thing.

Adults are no different. We are designed this way. The only thing that really satisfies, for the long term, is Jesus. —GWEN FORD FAULKENBERRY

FAITH STEP: *Is there a material thing on your list of wants or needs right now? Something you desire greatly? Ask Jesus to use that thing to reveal your deeper need for more of Him—and to supply it.*

FRIDAY, NOVEMBER 17

"He cuts off every branch in me that bears no fruit, while every branch that does bear fruit he prunes so that it will be even more fruitful." John 15:2 (NIV)

I'M LEARNING TO GROW GRAPES. I pictured myself harvesting and preserving grapes, but, for some reason, I never imagined myself pruning the vines. Then, the other day, when lasting snow was predicted, I walked the lane, clearing downed limbs and branches left from the Upper Peninsula's gales of November. There were a lot of them. Many trees had even fallen before the strength of the storms.

It occurred to me as I walked and pruned that God tends the forest like a vinedresser, but He uses mighty winds instead of hands. Old, brittle branches tumble to the forest floor. What's left is stronger, more ready for the weight of winter and buds of spring. God's winds ruthlessly thin the forest, leaving openings for new growth where an unbroken canopy would have prevented it.

I walked past my little vineyard and realized I hadn't been ruthless enough when the choices were up to me. In the vine passage, Jesus says *all* the unproductive branches had to go. That even the best branches had to be cut back to help them bear all the good fruit they were meant to make. But when I stood in the vineyard holding my pruning shears, I thought, *Really? This much? That can't be right*, and hesitated, afraid I'd kill the plants with all that cutting. In holding back, I didn't do the vines any favors. What seemed ruthless was more right than I could understand.

I'm glad the One who tends my life knows what's best for me, no matter how intense the pruning feels. —SUZANNE DAVENPORT TIETJEN

FAITH STEP: *Are you going through some difficulty? Losing something or someone? Ask Jesus to help you to be more receptive to whatever (yes, whatever) He is doing in your life.*

SATURDAY, NOVEMBER 18

Now to him who is able to do immeasurably more than all we ask or imagine, according to his power that is at work within us, to him be glory in the church and in Christ Jesus throughout all generations, for ever and ever! Amen.
Ephesians 3:20–21 (NIV)

MY FRIEND BETH, a pastor's wife, and her family recently moved to our state, so they could serve a church here. When they arrived, they settled into a small parsonage that had no dishwasher and a smaller-than-normal refrigerator—a challenge for a family of five. Even more challenging, after a few weeks the bottom of the refrigerator kept filling with water.

Beth shared her frustrations with Jesus. "Every time we move, we end up having to buy appliances for the parsonage. We can't afford to do this again. You know we need a working fridge. And it wasn't our idea to move here—it was Your leading. Please help us find something."

Her husband began searching online and soon found someone who was selling a full-size refrigerator. He mentioned that they were buying it for their parsonage. When the man heard that he was a pastor, he got excited. "I'd like to donate it to you. And we're remodeling, so I also have a dishwasher. Would you like that too?"

I love this example of the lavish kindness of Jesus. Beth asked for an affordable fridge and was given a free fridge and a free dishwasher too!

Do you ever hesitate to let Jesus know about a need or longing? Not only does He delight in providing, He is able to do immeasurably more than we ask or imagine. —SHARON HINCK

FAITH STEP: *If you don't have one yet, start a prayer journal. Record your petitions, and leave space to write about the answers. Marvel at the ways in which He gives beyond what we ask.*

SUNDAY, NOVEMBER 19

Jesus also did many other things. If they were all written down,
I suppose the whole world could not contain the books that would be written.
John 21:25 (NLT)

FOR TWO WEEKS I watched my husband grow weaker. He slept most of the time, ate little, and alternated between chills and high fevers. I wished he could see my family practitioner, but this doctor was in such demand that "it would take a miracle to get a new patient appointment."

That Sunday evening I prayed, "Lord, I know it would be impossible to get an appointment with Dr. Hammett, but please let Richard see him or somebody who can figure out what is going on."

Early the next morning I called the clinic and asked if Dr. Hammett had any openings. The receptionist said he was booked for weeks. I asked to see whoever was available. She gave us a 10:30 a.m. appointment. I asked whom we would be seeing. She said, "You'll be seeing Dr. Hammett. The receptionist next to me just took a cancellation."

We normally think of a miracle as something dramatic, but I believe that less obvious miracles happen around us every day. I'm convinced that what some call a coincidence is actually Jesus working out our circumstances for good. During this "impossible" appointment, we had a doctor who diagnosed a viral illness that most doctors never see. This one just "happened" to have treated three cases of it in the past two years.

John wrote that the Bible includes only a tiny fraction of the things Jesus did. I've come to believe that we notice only a fraction of the everyday miracles He performs in our lives.
—DIANNE NEAL MATTHEWS

FAITH STEP: *Tell Jesus what situation in your life needs an everyday miracle, and then watch to see how He works.*

MONDAY, NOVEMBER 20

Give thanks in all circumstances; for this is God's will for you in Christ Jesus.
1 Thessalonians 5:18 (NIV)

THANKSGIVING IS A TIME of gratitude and delicious food. But this year was a different kind of Thanksgiving for me. After a couple of weeks of being so tired I could barely prop my eyelids open, I discovered some weird bites on my left leg that wouldn't go away. Did I have bed bugs? A carnivorous spider living in my bed? I e-mailed my doctor a picture of my leg.

She wrote me back saying, "It looks like shingles. Why don't you come in?"

I went in. My doctor laughed at my spider and bug invasion theories. She gave me antiviral meds and said, "You need to rest… because you are STRESSED OUT."

The fact that she said it would take a month to resolve the shingles may have caused me some stress. But mostly I was thankful. Shingles can be a blessing (because they are not bug or spider bites).

It may seem strange that sickness or heartache or bug bites can bring about thankfulness. But they can. Sometimes Jesus uses hard things to show me how much He has blessed me in other areas of my life. He is constantly showering me with His goodness in spite of the fact that I may be walking through difficulties. He is a loving, caring Savior who has good things for me even in the midst of trouble. And that is something I can truly be thankful about.
—SUSANNA FOTH AUGHTMON

FAITH STEP: *Take a stone and write down something good that Jesus has done for you. Use it as a stone of remembrance that you can be thankful for when you are walking through a difficult time.*

Tuesday, November 21

No test or temptation that comes your way is beyond the course of what others have had to face. All you need to remember is that God will never let you down; he'll never let you be pushed past your limit; he'll always be there to help you come through it. 1 Corinthians 10:13 (MSG)

DURING THE HOLIDAYS LAST YEAR, we were visiting our children several hundred miles away when we heard a familiar *beep-beep-beep*. We immediately recognized the CodeRED weather alert and grabbed the cell phone nearby. But what appeared on the screen was not the flash flood or severe thunderstorm watch we expected. This time it read, "Tornado Warning."

The warning didn't target our area but rather the surrounding counties near our home. There was nothing we could do to prevent a potential disaster. But it was a reminder to pray for those back home.

On our way home several days later, we witnessed firsthand the destruction from one of ten tornadoes that had touched down. Traffic crawled as onlookers gaped at the damage to a large apartment complex near the interstate.

Later I thought how great it would be if Jesus would give us a CodeRED alert every time danger approached. What if He would warn us each time temptation or potential destruction hovered?

Really, He's already done that. His Holy Spirit, Jesus's presence in us, is that constant reminder: *Danger approaching*. He's made a way to escape. We can't eliminate the tests and temptations around us or even the destruction nearby, but no matter where we are, we can trust Jesus to bring us through as we keep alert and prayerful.
—REBECCA BARLOW JORDAN

FAITH STEP: *Every time you hear a siren, a ringing alarm clock, or a weather warning, breathe a prayer of thanks that Jesus is in control.*

WEDNESDAY, NOVEMBER 22

Therefore, He is always able to save those who come to God through Him, since He always lives to intercede for them. Hebrews 7:25 *(HCS)*

MY SISTER AND HER HUSBAND missed our Thanksgiving gathering a couple of years ago. Instead, they shared the holiday in a prison visiting room. My brother-in-law was paying for his crimes. Crimes for which Jesus and our family had long ago forgiven him.

In the middle of the afternoon, I received a text message from my sister, sending us their loving greetings. From the limited offerings in a vending machine, they'd created their Thanksgiving meal with Cheetos and Oreos. After the meal, the two of them played Scrabble.

"New rules," her husband said. He suggested they use the lettered tiles to spell the names of family members. "When we make a name-word, we'll stop and pray for that person." I could feel the joy behind my sister's explanation of how much that tender few hours meant to her. While we feasted on our abundant meal, they spent the day thinking of others and praying for needs known and unknown. From inside a prison. Those of us who heard the story were reduced to tears to have been the recipients of their sacrificial prayers.

Two lessons impressed me that day. We—from our comfortable dining room—should have been the ones stopping everything to remember those who were behind bars. And, we have a Savior Who, the Bible tells us, is "ever interceding" for us before His Father's throne. Our names are constantly in front of Him. And from our perspective, every name He speaks before the Father is our triple-word score! —CYNTHIA RUCHTI

FAITH STEP: *Imagine a Scrabble board in front of you right now. What name or names are the letters forming? Who needs you to stop everything and pray? Jesus already is. Join Him.*

THURSDAY, NOVEMBER 23

*Do everything without complaining and arguing,
so that no one can criticize you. . . . Philippians 2:14–15 (NLT)*

A COUPLE OF YEARS AGO my daughter hosted Thanksgiving. At breakfast, Holly said, "Let's choose to have a good day. No complaining or grumbling all day!" She set out a square glass vase, slips of paper, and a pen and explained that whenever someone complained they'd have to write down their name and one thing they were thankful for.

Within minutes, my two older grandchildren were writing on slips of paper. Eventually, the adults also added slips of paper. I participated, too, even though I considered my comment a statement of fact rather than a complaint.

What I remember most from that day is the dramatic transformation in my grandson's attitude. At first, the "punishment" for complaining made Roman grumble even more. But then he began to ask to fill out slips of paper as he thought of things to be thankful for. "This is fun," he declared.

I used to joke about how I enjoyed complaining, even though the Bible makes it clear it's a serious matter. In Exodus 16:8, Moses warned the people that when they grumbled, they were actually grumbling against the Lord. So I appreciated that a child's example provided the help I needed to fight this unhealthy habit. Now, whenever I start to voice a complaint, I think of something to thank Jesus for instead. And Roman was right. It *is* more fun to focus on what I'm grateful for instead of what I'm disgruntled about.
—DIANNE NEAL MATTHEWS

FAITH STEP: *Guard against an attitude of grumbling today by making yourself jot down something you're thankful for each time you verbally or mentally complain.*

FRIDAY, NOVEMBER 24

Dear brothers and sisters, when troubles of any kind come your way,
consider it an opportunity for great joy.
James 1:2 (NLT)

UNTIL RECENTLY, I'd always connected the word *opportunity* with positive circumstances. For instance, moving to a larger house became an opportunity to host overnight guests more comfortably. Relocating to a neighborhood with a fitness center nearby meant I could attend exercise classes.

Considering negative circumstances as a positive opportunity hadn't crossed my mind until one morning when I read James 1:2. *That's a great concept,* I thought. *Applying it could change my life!*

Twelve hours later I ruptured my left Achilles tendon. Nine days after that, I suffered an injury on the opposite leg and subsequently lost mobility for three months. In the midst of my pain, I asked Jesus to help me apply James 1:2. He answered.

My trouble became an opportunity for me to trust Jesus for daily strength and healing. Through it, I learned to humble myself and to gladly accept others' help with washing my laundry, cleaning my house, and preparing meals. My circumstances were very difficult, but they became an opportunity for changing my life.

I'm learning that everything changes when I view my troubles as Jesus does—as opportunities for personal growth, greater intimacy with Him, and ultimately, for joy. I'm also learning that the key is to pray, "Jesus, what do You want to teach me through these circumstances? Please use them for Your glory." —GRACE FOX

FAITH STEP: *Fill in the blank. My current opportunity for joy is_____.*
Ask Jesus to enable you to view your circumstances through His eyes and thank Him for being faithful in the midst of trouble.

SATURDAY, NOVEMBER 25

"What's the price of two or three pet canaries? Some loose change, right? But God never overlooks a single one. And he pays even greater attention to you, down to the last detail—even numbering the hairs on your head!"
Luke 12:6–7 (MSG)

THE FIRST SNOW of the season arrived yesterday, and early this morning my daughter Calianne and our puppy Paxton were out playing beneath the falling flakes. Now everyone is back inside.

Sitting next to Calianne on a blustery winter day reminds me of when she and Paxton were small and they first discovered the lacy patterns of frost on the windows on cold mornings. What perfect opportunities those pieces of art were to explain to them how Jesus cares about the details of their lives! He is the one Who pays intricate attention to how cold, moist air forms beautifully on a window.

In the dead of winter when it seems all is barren, the Lord shows His care and even sends surprises of beauty in the midst of barrenness.

Jesus cares for His nature. But we have His heart, and as the above Scripture says, He pays even greater attention to us, down to the last detail.

While you slept last night, He was working out that situation you feel stuck in or the unknown ahead that unsettles you or healing your heartache. You may not notice right away the beautiful piece of art He is creating behind the scenes, but trust that He is at work, and sometimes the most wondrous things He does show up in the bleakest seasons. —ERIN KEELEY MARSHALL

FAITH STEP: *Make a paper snowflake like you did as a child. Write "Jesus cares for _____," and fill in your name. Ask a friend to hide it somewhere in your house so you'll find the reminder when you least expecting it.*

SUNDAY, NOVEMBER 26

"Happy are people who are hungry and thirsty for righteousness, because they will be fed until they are full."
Matthew 5:6 (CEB)

WOULDN'T YOU THINK that anyone who writes devotions begins each day with a deep, meaningful quiet time with the Lord? I would think so if I didn't know myself. I've always struggled with maintaining a consistent prayer time. Some days end with the sinking feeling that I've failed to make time for what's most important. I vow to start fresh the next day and make time with Jesus my first priority.

I'd always chalked up my failure in this area to lack of discipline. One Sunday my perspective changed as I sat in my parents' little country church. The guest speaker reminded us that prayer time is not an item to check off from our to-do list. It's not a matter of discipline but a matter of hunger for God. Our actions reveal our appetites. If we say that we ate three meals yesterday, no one is going to say, "Wow, you sure are a disciplined person!"

So I looked at what I've been hungry for lately. I admit that I usually find time to scroll through my newsfeed at least once a day and keep up with the latest episode of *The Voice* on TV—trivial activities that can get in the way of intimate fellowship with the King of kings.

From now on, I won't be praying for more spiritual discipline. I'll ask Jesus to help me get so hungry for Him that my soul's longing outweighs my stomach's growling for breakfast in the mornings. —DIANNE NEAL MATTHEWS

FAITH STEP: *Today watch to see what your activities reveal about your appetite. If you sense the need, ask Jesus to give you a hunger for spending time with Him and His Word.*

MONDAY, NOVEMBER 27

Let us throw off everything that hinders. . . . Hebrews 12:1 (NIV)

WHEN OUR DAUGHTER quit basketball, I wrote her this letter:

Grace,

I am so proud of you. You are brave and strong. You did the right thing.

As your mom, it feels weird to say quitting was the right thing. We are not quitters. Our family is all about hanging in there and facing adversity, whether it's marriage or church or jobs or algebra. Quitting is mostly a bad thing in our vocabulary. And I want it to stay that way.

But I want something else for you, too, something I saw in this situation that was painful but so beautiful and right. You saw something you wanted and went after it. You committed yourself. You worked hard. You faced difficulties and kept going. You prayed. You gave and received grace. You cried. You sought advice from wise people. You did everything you could to make it work. And after a reasonable time, you faced that it wasn't working and there was nothing more you could do. Then you had the courage to walk away. You let it go because to keep holding on was not healthy for you. Bravo!

I hope you remember for the rest of your life that you are too brave and strong to quit unless quitting is the bravest, strongest thing to do. When there's a relationship that's toxic to your soul. When there's a place that's unsafe for you. When there's a decision that takes you down a bad path. Whenever your hard work and commitment are not enough to create what you need for your health and well-being, walk away. Jesus walks with you. And I'll be cheering you on!

—GWEN FORD FAULKENBERRY

FAITH STEP: *Is there something or someone in your life you need to let go of in order to follow Jesus into the fullness of life? Take His hand and walk away!*

TUESDAY, NOVEMBER 28

He will cover you with his feathers. He will shelter you with his wings.
His faithful promises are your armor and protection. Psalm 91:4 (NLT)

I JUST CAME IN from feeding wood to the outdoor boiler and I'm struck by the difference a year can make. Last year we had enough wood dried, racked, tarped, and arranged in a semicircle to give some protection from the north wind. Winter came early, stacking up snow as fast as I could scrape it off. I couldn't keep up and ended up with ice arches hanging over the racks. Then water seeped between the logs underneath. As the season progressed, I crawled over empty racks to get more wood, chipping the logs loose with a crowbar, all the while afraid I'd bring the ice down and be squashed like a bug. It was an experience I vowed never to repeat.

Our beautiful new woodshed not only covers the impressive amount of wood we need to get through an Upper Peninsula winter, but it also covers me. The metal roof extends over the boiler, so I can stand out of the weather when I adjust controls, do maintenance, and feed the fire.

Living in the Northwoods helps me recognize my vulnerabilities. Not just a modern problem: God's people have a long history of rejecting His protection. Jesus grieved over Jerusalem, saying, "How often I have wanted to gather your children together as a hen protects her chicks beneath her wings, but you wouldn't let me" (Matthew 23:37, NLT).

I want to think I have everything under control. Jesus wants me to admit I don't and, instead, nestle safe and warm under His wings.
—SUZANNE DAVENPORT TIETJEN

FAITH STEP: *Think of a time you needed protection. Remember that feeling of vulnerability. Then recall a time you felt safe. Ask Jesus to bring those feelings to mind as you go through your day.*

WEDNESDAY, NOVEMBER 29

Hear this, you leaders of the people. Listen, all who live in the land. In all your history, has anything like this happened before? Tell your children about it in the years to come, and let your children tell their children. Pass the story down from generation to generation. Joel 1:2–3 (NLT)

EVERY DAY LAST WINTER I read a chapter of *The Long Winter* to my youngest kids. My children would use Play Dough or color as I read about Laura Ingalls sleeping in the trundle bed, making snow candy, and watching her pa whisk Ma around the rough-hewn logged dance floor. Sharing this story is like sharing my own childhood and gives me a chance to share important things like home, family, and faith. Their discovery of this young girl's adventures was mine.

As a mom there is so much I want to pass on to my children, yet children don't learn with long lectures or three-point lessons. They learn best when parents share what is meaningful to them. This is true in life. This is true in faith. Just as I share meaningful fictional stories and my kids pay attention, they pay attention when I share meaningful Bible stories too. As I tell them about how Jesus calmed the storm, I also describe how He has brought peace to my life. As I share about David fighting Goliath, I talk about how Jesus gives us strength to face our fears.

When we pass along meaningful stories of Jesus, they become lights within our children's hearts. Lights that may flicker but do not go out. Lights that will warm our children even in the long winters of their own lives. —TRICIA GOYER

FAITH STEP: *Think about a meaningful Bible story. How has that story influenced your life? Now find someone with whom you can share that story and the meaning.*

THURSDAY, NOVEMBER 30

*The voice of the Lord is over the waters; the God of glory thunders,
the Lord thunders over the mighty waters. Psalm 29:3 (NIV)*

JESUS SPEAKS TO US in many different ways. Within the Scriptures
we find a range of parables, instructions, laments, encouragements,
rebukes, and promises. I get a sense that Jesus communicated in
various ways so that each individual could find a way to hear Him.

In Psalm 29, our Lord's voice is depicted as booming and powerful. Yet He spoke to Elijah in a still, small voice (1 Kings 19:12).

This week I found myself praying, "Jesus, why can't You be louder?
I need direction and I'm not hearing You. A booming megaphone
voice from the sky would be lovely."

As I prayed, I realized that Jesus has plenty to share with me. My
problem is that I don't open my heart to listen to all the ways in
which He might choose to speak.

The voice of loud thunderstorms can remind me of His creative
power and strength—strength I need to face the challenges of the
day. Other times I hear Him during a tender conversation with a
friend—His compassion whispering to my heart. When I seek Him
in the Bible, His Spirit brings new life to familiar words. The rustle of
dry leaves speaks of death and new life. The warble of birdsong reas-
sures me that He knows each sparrow. A piercing siren in the distance
declares that we live in a world of suffering, and He calls me to serve
the hurting. The range of instruments in a praise band shows me how
each unique person brings a valuable sound to the whole.

Instead of complaining to Jesus that He isn't speaking to me, I
asked Him to open my ears to hear. —SHARON HINCK

FAITH STEP: *Close your eyes and listen. What might Jesus speak to your heart
through the sounds you hear?*

FRIDAY, DECEMBER 1

"Come with me. We will go to a quiet place. . . ." Mark 6:31 (ERV)

I WAS ASKED TO WRITE a piece for a blog about things that warm my heart. When I thought about it, it was easy to see that my greatest "heart-warmers" are my kids. They are great at testing my patience, and I don't want to paint some picture of perfection here, but they are also really good at melting my heart with their sweetness and love. Just this week my teenage daughter spent her Christmas money on gifts for others. My teenage son walked his sister to the car, holding an umbrella over her in the rain. My eight-year-old daughter hugs me every morning before she leaves for school and says, "'Bye. I love you. See you after school. Thanks for everything!" Every. Single. Day. And my three-year-old waddles in pajamas out of bed and into my arms.

I've come to believe there is no shortage of heartwarming moments in my life, but sometimes I have a shortage of the good sense to stop and appreciate them. Socrates said, "Beware the barrenness of a busy life." We get so busy that we don't take time to notice, much less savor, the moments that matter most. When we do this, our lives become barren.

Jesus knew how to avoid this pitfall, even in the midst of His intense public ministry. He issues His invitation to us just as He did to His disciples: *Come with Me to a quiet place.*

It doesn't have to be a physical place. It can be a state of mind, a quiet place in your spirit where you can commune with Jesus, where He helps you keep the right perspective, no matter how busy you are. —GWEN FORD FAULKENBERRY

FAITH STEP: *Keep a quiet place in your spirit, and look out for heart-warmers today. When they come along, stop and savor the moment.*

SATURDAY, DECEMBER 2

Make a careful exploration of who you are and the work you have been given, and then sink yourself into that. . . . Don't compare yourself with others. Each of you must take responsibility for doing the creative best you can with your own life.
Galatians 6:4–5 (MSG)

FOR THE LAST THREE YEARS, I've attended a retreat for Christians who are artists (some who aren't artists come because they love beauty and appreciate its various forms). We talk, listen, laugh, learn, and eat delicious food. Some names are in the brochure, planned in advance; while many share work in quiet corners or at meals.

It's easy to be awestruck by the talent around me, but not because anyone acts important. Still, in the presence of all those gorgeous songs and words, I tend to wonder what I have to offer. When I'm brave enough to admit those doubts, I find the people around me feel the same way.

Too often, we see what we make or what we do as ordinary. We wonder why we even bother. Occasionally our courage stirs and we think we just might play in that jam session, give away a copy of a CD, or read a poem—but then we decide not to. We leave our instruments or sketchbooks in our tote bags. After all, we might not measure up.

Here, in this safe place, we gently nudge each other to share. Our work is our work. No one can do it but us. Out of Christ's abundance we have *all* received "gift after gift after gift" (John 1:16, MSG).

Jesus, the Living Word, came giving gifts. Sink into that.

Tear into those presents! —SUZANNE DAVENPORT TIETJEN

FAITH STEP: *Take some time to think about your own gifts. Write one on an index card and put it where you'll see it often. Ask Jesus how He wants it shared.*

FIRST SUNDAY IN ADVENT, DECEMBER 3

We have this as a sure and steadfast anchor of the soul, a hope that enters into the inner place behind the curtain, where Jesus has gone as a forerunner on our behalf. . . . Hebrews 6:19–20 (ESV)

A HUSH FELL as the lights dimmed to near darkness and the speaker described the condition of the world the Baby Jesus would be born into.

God's people had long been oppressed by the Roman government. Those were dark days back then, full of hopelessness for the Israelites. The somber mood in the worship center deepened the sense of hopelessness. It seemed we could feel a fraction of what the Israelites had felt.

And then into the darkness a small flame erupted. The flicker of light came from the Advent wreath at the front of the church, a tiny glow that shattered the darkness. Darkness cannot exist where light is, and when darkness is extinguished, hope is born.

How fitting that hope is the theme for the first of the four weeks of Advent. Hope comes first, hope for the peace and joy and love we cannot find on our own and never in real and lasting measure apart from Christ.

Each year as December rolls along, my spirit simply wants to be quiet and digest Advent's themes, the realities of each of the weeks, instead of hurrying through the chaos. I long to reflect and finish the year with the messages of Advent on my heart.

Advent is for filling up on hope; what a refreshing thought!

As today's verse says, Jesus is the forerunner of our lives. And with Him in the lead, we can welcome the days ahead full of hope.

—ERIN KEELEY MARSHALL

FAITH STEP: *Remind yourself of H.O.P.E. with these responses to Jesus for being our great hope:* **H**allelujah **O**verflowing in **P**raises **E**ternal.

MONDAY, DECEMBER 4

He has granted that we would be rescued . . . so that we could serve him without
fear, in holiness and righteousness in God's eyes, for as long as we live.
Luke 1:73–75 *(CEB)*

WHEN THE PRIEST ZECHARIAH realized through his wife, Elizabeth, that the Christ Child had been conceived and was on the way, carried in the young girl Mary, he remained silent. In fact, he'd been rendered silent, unable to speak, by an angel months before when he doubted the angel's words that his then-barren wife would conceive a son, John, who would pave the way for Jesus.

Zechariah spoke again when his son was born and he insisted on naming him John, as the angel had said. A radical transformation happened within Zechariah during his months of silence. After his tongue was loosened, he delivered a Spirit-inspired prophecy about both Jesus and John. Zechariah used key action words to inform the people about what God had done and was about to do through the birth and life of Jesus, the Messiah. From Luke 1:68–79 (CEB), Zechariah reminds us that, through Jesus, God has "come to help," that He has "delivered his people," that He "raised up a mighty savior." Zechariah told those listening, "He has brought salvation from our enemies . . . shown the mercy promised . . . remembered his holy covenant . . . granted that we would be rescued."

Let those truths, uttered by a man after a long, silent period of waiting, fill you with hope that God sees, He knows, and He will respond to your need. —CYNTHIA RUCHTI

FAITH STEP: *Do you welcome silence or rush to fill it with something, anything? Profound words for you and others are waiting in the silent places with Jesus. Get comfortable being silent before Him. Make it a daily habit!*

TUESDAY, DECEMBER 5

*Then I saw heaven opened, and there was a white horse.
Its rider was called Faithful and True, and he judges and makes
war justly. His eyes were like a fiery flame, and on
his head were many royal crowns. . . .*
Revelation 19:11–12 (CEB)

SOMEONE SUGGESTED A DRIVE through nearby neighborhoods to look at Christmas lights. The group included my husband's two sisters, our daughter, granddaughter, and grandson. As we eased down one street, Roman leaned forward in his car seat and said, "Hey, I'm the only boy in the car!" Then he sat back, looked straight ahead, and nodded. "Don't worry," he assured us, "I will protect you and keep you safe."

Oh, how I loved that Roman saw himself as a protector and defender at age three. Maybe that's why he was always dressing up as a super-hero. I still remember the night he insisted on going to bed in his Batman costume. Superhero movies seem to be growing more popular with children *and* adults; maybe that's because our world seems to be more in need of being rescued.

The evening news paints an increasingly depressing picture. Conflicts between groups of people erupting into violence. Terrorists committing barbaric acts of cruelty. Widespread injustice and brutality. It's good to remember things aren't always this way.

At Christmas we focus on Jesus as a newborn; at Easter we concentrate on His Crucifixion and Resurrection. I find courage to face dark days by remembering that Jesus came for us, to be our protector and defender. —DIANNE NEAL MATTHEWS

FAITH STEP: *Read John's vision of Jesus in Revelation 1:9–18 and 19:11–21. Write down how this image of Jesus comforts you in light of current news.*

WEDNESDAY, DECEMBER 6

"If you love me, you will keep my commandments." John 14:15 (CEB)

I REMEMBER WHEN I got the world's worst Christmas present.

That's how I saw it through my immature, middle school, overly dramatic eyes. My best friend and I exchanged gifts at a youth group gathering where we'd drawn names. With the cost limit per gift, it took creativity to find something affordable but meaningful.

I tore open the paper, knowing my best friend would have surely chosen something perfect for me. I ripped through the plastic wrapper to find what special treat she'd put inside the box. But it was what the box said—chocolate-covered cherries.

Some would find that gift a delight. But she and I had talked about how much I hated chocolate-covered cherries.

Today I'm wiser and know that sometimes a gift-giver simply guesses wrong.

During this gift-giving season, we don't have to wonder if what we offer Jesus will please Him. He left us His wish list. He made it very clear when He said:

"If you love me, you will keep my commandments" (John 14:15, CEB).

"Jesus answered, 'Whoever loves me will keep my word'" (John 14:23, CEB).

And this passage: "This is how we know that we know him: if we keep his commandments.... The love of God is truly perfected in whoever keeps his word" (1 John 2:3–5, CEB).

This Christmas let's give Jesus the gift He desires most—our obedience. —CYNTHIA RUCHTI

FAITH STEP: *Take inventory of the kinds of "gifts" you've been offering to Jesus—the places you serve, the time you spend on projects you hope will bless Him. Are they on His wish list?*

THURSDAY, DECEMBER 7

Friends, this world is not your home, so don't make yourselves cozy in it.
1 Peter 2:11 (MSG)

FOR THE LAST FEW WINTERS, stray cats have found their way to our back porch. This year was no different—except one day, an entire family showed up.

On a cold morning in December, we looked at the back patio and saw a black mama cat with her four multicolor kittens, all snuggled in our wicker chair. Each time we tried to approach them, they'd run away. But the next night they'd return and sleep until morning. We'd bought new cushions for the chair earlier in the spring, and they must have provided an extra measure of warmth.

I never fed the cats, but still they'd return. Recently, we had to remove the cushions in preparation for some renovations. I remember times when Jesus allowed the cushions in my life to be pulled out from under me, and my safe resting place seemed suddenly scratchy and uncomfortable. In His kind, patient way, Jesus let me know that some renovations were necessary in my life. Would I remain or look for a new shelter in which to place my trust and faith?

I ultimately decided that *home* meant more than a temporary, cozy place on earth. Like the Psalmist, I chose to stay and make the Lord Himself my home (Psalm 73:28, MSG). There, even with uncomfortable renovations, I find not only warmth but safety in the cushion of His love. —REBECCA BARLOW JORDAN

FAITH STEP: *Where do you run when your earthly "home" becomes uncomfortable? Today, rest in Jesus, your real home.*

FRIDAY, DECEMBER 8

God, who said, "Let light shine out of darkness," has shone in our hearts to give the light of the knowledge of the glory of God in the face of Jesus Christ.
2 Corinthians 4:6 (ESV)

AS A NURSE PRACTITIONER, I worked twelve-hour night shifts. I drove to work after sunset and followed my headlights home in the morning. I went days without seeing the sun.

I'm grateful I didn't struggle with seasonal affective disorder (SAD) like some of my friends. Our bodies need light and are made to react with sunlight in intricate ways to manufacture vitamin D, which not only helps us to have strong bones, but also plays an important role in preventing and treating disease. I got my vitamin D in capsules during that season.

When the power's out, we bump into furniture and trip over obstacles, fumbling for flashlights and candles. "If you walk in darkness, you don't know where you're going" (John 12:35, MSG). As much as we need light to see and to be healthy, there's one Light we need more.

Prophets from Isaiah to Zechariah spoke of the Light that was coming, not only to shine on us, but *in* us. What love and grace!

Every year during Advent, we light one more candle every week as the darkest days of the year approach, along with Christmas. I love the image of light overcoming gathering gloom as we celebrate the birth of our Savior, announced by angels blazing with brilliance.

Sent because we were lost in the dark.

—SUZANNE DAVENPORT TIETJEN

FAITH STEP: *Light a candle today during your quiet time. Look up "light" with a concordance and read what Jesus had to say about it.*

SATURDAY, DECEMBER 9

For to us a child is born, to us a son is given, and the government will be on his shoulders. And he will be called Wonderful Counselor, Mighty God, Everlasting Father, Prince of Peace. Isaiah 9:6 (NIV)

EVERY TIME I GET ON FACEBOOK (or open a newspaper), I read complaints about governments, crimes against humanity, and stories of horrific violence. I think, *If the world is like this now, how will it be when my children are adults?* Will things be worse? I hope not.

It's hard to think of my children as adults, facing the hardship this world serves up. As a mom I try to create a home and an environment that feels loving and safe, knowing that someday my children will leave our protected haven. Thankfully, they won't have to face the future alone.

Why? A babe in a manger. A man arrested, killed, and risen, just as He said. Jesus witnessed the corruption, violence, and evil of the world as He walked this earth…and then He stepped forward and offered Himself in an unexpected way. Love offered up unconditionally.

No matter what our children face, Jesus, the Prince of Peace, will be there.

We will never have a perfect government. And as long as there is envy and greed and brokenness, crimes will be committed. Seeds of hatred will grow into violence, and we will never have peace on earth. That's why Jesus came. Only He reigns with a pure heart and loving, perfect motives. Only in Jesus's kingdom will we find all that our hearts hope for. And only in a relationship with Him will we discover the safety and peace we long for in this broken world.

—TRICIA GOYER

FAITH STEP: *Next time you read about a crime or hardship somewhere, think about those closest to the event and pray for Jesus to give them a glimpse of Himself— and His peace.*

344 | MORNINGS WITH JESUS 2017

Second Sunday in Advent, December 10

The peace of God, which surpasses all understanding, will guard your hearts and your minds in Christ Jesus. Philippians 4:7 (ESV)

WHEN HOPE BREAKS THROUGH DARKNESS, we taste the peace of Jesus that passes understanding. If hope is the light that inspires us to take the chance and believe Jesus is who He claims and follow His sure lead into the future, then peace may just be hope's calming byproduct.

Philippians 4:6, coming immediately before today's verse, says, "Do not be anxious about anything, but in everything by prayer and supplication with thanksgiving let your requests be made known to God." That verse speaks of hope—when we hope, we pray and reject anxiety.

Then comes peace.

At times I've been comforted in the calm of the Advent season while I prayed through a concern until His peace settled me.

But peace isn't just passive; it's also a defender. Jesus's peace that passes understanding is a power-packed arsenal against the uncertainties in our lives so that we don't have to be derailed by the troubles that do come up. We don't have to worry about whether we'll have peace next week or beyond this holy season; Jesus is already there, setting up His defenses in and around us. Our faith is strengthened and grown through *peace* that follows in the light created by hope.

This second week of Advent, peace can be yours and mine. But it must be maintained by drawing close to Jesus for security, by turning our minds to Him, who is our hope. In Him our thoughts are guarded, our thoughts that play a mighty role in our level of peace.
—ERIN KEELEY MARSHALL

FAITH STEP: *Buy a gingerbread house kit, and decorate it as a fortress. With icing, write Peace across the roof or on the door. Throughout the Advent season, remember that drawing close to Jesus keeps us in His fortress of peace.*

MONDAY, DECEMBER 11

Two are better than one, because they have a good return for their labor:
If either of them falls down, one can help the other up. . . .
Ecclesiastes 4:9–10 (NIV)

DRIVING NEAR DOWNTOWN for a family gathering, we passed a homeless man holding a sign asking for help. We had no money with us, and I shook my head in frustration. "I keep forgetting to buy granola bars to keep in the car, so we'd have something to offer."

Later, a friend from our small group Bible study e-mailed. "Next time we meet, we're going to assemble care kits to keep in our cars for when we come across someone in need. Sign up for which items you want to bring."

Thanks to her getting us organized, the next Sunday night we stacked her table with the items we brought: granola bars, bottled water, a gift card to a local fast-food eatery, a bus pass, warm socks, and more. We walked around the table with a bag, gathering one of each item to create our care kits. Then we kept the kits in our cars and watched for opportunities to share.

A simple idea, yet I'd had a hard time getting around to it—until receiving the support of fellowship. Partnering made all the difference.

Jesus sent out His disciples with partners, and after His ascension, the early church continued to serve in pairs and small groups. Together, the body of believers can do more than each of us can do alone. Each individual's gifts can merge with others to feed the hungry more effectively, encourage the downhearted more consistently, and support the lonely more intentionally. —SHARON HINCK

FAITH STEP: *Ask a friend to partner with you to create care kits to keep in your car. If you don't live in an area with many homeless people, give one to anybody you know who is in need.*

TUESDAY, DECEMBER 12

And it came to pass in those days, that there went out a decree from Caesar Augustus, that all the world should be taxed. Luke 2:1 (KJV)

THIS IS WHERE we traditionally begin retelling the birth of Christ. Rudely. With taxes.

But one December, I'd been studying the book of Luke and realized that if we back up a few verses, we gain a more complete picture of who this Baby is and why He came.

Moving back just three verses, we read, "Because of our God's deep compassion..." What a starting point!

"Because of our God's deep compassion, the dawn from heaven will break upon us, to give light to those who are sitting in darkness and in the shadow of death, to guide us on the path of peace" (Luke 1:78–79, CEB).

Deep compassion. Dawn. Heaven. Light. Darkness and the shadow of death. Path of peace.

Then, with that setup, that declaration from the prophet Zechariah, that answer to the human condition, we're eventually introduced to the journey from Nazareth to Bethlehem so Joseph could be taxed, the Baby born in a stable, light dawn for shepherds, kings see a star, shadows disappear, and peace reign. We were given hope that outshines stars, and offered a place at the table with Jesus.

Jesus came because God had compassion for us. Now that is the way to begin the Christmas story. It's certainly going to be our family's new reading tradition for the holidays. —CYNTHIA RUCHTI

FAITH STEP: *Jesus in human form is a product of compassion. Consider posting this companion verse on your mirror or another prominent spot: "Certainly the faithful love of the Lord hasn't ended; certainly God's compassion isn't through!" (Lamentations 3:22, CEB).*

WEDNESDAY, DECEMBER 13

The Lord is my strength and my song. He is my Savior. . . . Exodus 15:2 (GW)

DURING MY HUSBAND'S EXTENDED ILLNESS, I survived on quick prayers and adrenaline. I didn't have time to think about anything other than taking care of Richard. Getting nutrition into him. Trying to keep the fever at bay. Trying to find the reason for his symptoms. Sometimes I felt surprised by the strength and stamina I displayed. That changed one night in the third week of our ordeal.

The doctor had sent us to the hospital for treatment. He suspected a certain virus, but the results for the blood culture would take several days. In the meantime, the doctors at the hospital ran every test they could think of to rule out other possibilities. When our overnight stay stretched into days, I reached a low point one night. I'd been up with Richard several times already, in addition to aides frequently coming in. I felt exhausted. Sleeping on the love seat in the hospital room had aggravated my spinal problems. I was in pain. Suddenly I felt very lonely. We had no family members nearby and we hadn't yet made friends in our new location.

"I can't do this anymore," I whispered in the darkness. And Someone whispered back: "I am able to do all things through Him who strengthens me" (Philippians 4:13, HCS). I remembered reciting it when overcoming my fear of water in an adult swim class, preparing for my first speaking engagement, and racing to complete my first book.

That night I recited the verse again as I settled down to wait for morning, knowing that Jesus would fill me with the strength and courage I'd need for the coming days. —DIANNE NEAL MATTHEWS

FAITH STEP: *In what area of your life do you need strength from Jesus today? Memorize Philippians 4:13, if you haven't already. Pray this verse whenever you need a boost.*

THURSDAY, DECEMBER 14

That energy is God's energy, an energy deep within you, God himself willing and working at what will give him the most pleasure. Philippians 2:13 (MSG)

I WAS HAPPY TO SEE the lights of that gas station.

I'd driven for hours through December rain heading for the Mayo Clinic and buzzed through LaCrosse, Wisconsin. I didn't check the gas gauge until the mighty Mississippi was many miles behind me.

Big mistake. The arrow was barely above the red, so I started looking for fuel. All I saw was prairie. And more prairie. I passed several exits. None had service stations. I was running on fumes when I finally pulled into a station in St. Charles, Minnesota.

Cars have gauges and alarms to make drivers aware of the need to refuel. Hunger and thirst tell us to refuel our physical bodies. But what alerts us to the fact that we're spiritually empty? Sometimes, nothing. We often don't notice. The noise of the twenty-four-hour news cycle, our many devices, and overcommitment prevent quiet contemplation that might show us the depth of our need.

Rest was mandated in Bible times, but today's Sundays are filled with football games and catch-up work.

In my experience, the further I drift from spiritual disciplines and the Shepherd Who feeds me, the less I long to draw close to Him. Prone to wander, indeed. Truth is, I'm nothing but needy. An empty tank.

Jesus invites me to come to Him for rest (Matthew 11:28). If I take Him up on that offered yoke, I'll pull shoulder to shoulder alongside the Source. I'm so grateful I'm not alone in this.
—SUZANNE DAVENPORT TIETJEN

FAITH STEP: *Try turning off everything for several hours today. Spend some time in the Word. Ask Jesus if you need to make any changes. Gently consider what He's telling you and then do it.*

FRIDAY, DECEMBER 15

Because you know that the testing of your faith produces perseverance.
James 1:3 (NIV)

I FEEL OVERWHELMED as a mother most of the time. I've even concluded that motherhood is a series of tests I'm not prepared for.

That was the feeling I had one Christmas when I traveled with my one-year-old daughter to my hometown. I brought gingerbread, her favorite, and the glowworm she loved.

At first, everything seemed fine. She ate the bread and sat peacefully. The moment we leveled off she started to squirm. I checked her diaper and offered her water. She cried. I got up, apologizing to those around me. We marched up and down the aisle with me pleading for her to be quiet, and I prayed, "What should I do?"

Then came the tantrum. She head-butted me, kicked her cup to the floor, and threw her glowworm. I was mortified.

"Give me the baby," the woman behind me said.

"No, I'm okay," I lied.

"Try singing," another passenger said.

I hummed. It didn't work.

After enduring the four-hour flight, we landed. The woman behind me patted me on my shoulder. The man next to us returned the glowworm and handed me a twenty-dollar bill. "You're a good mother," he said. "Buy her something nice. Merry Christmas."

Sighing, I collected my daughter. I could only thank God for the patient passengers and for His faithfulness in helping me survive another test of motherhood. —TARICE L. S. GRAY

FAITH STEP: *Recognize that some things are beyond your control. Find solace in reading and reciting a favorite Scripture.*

SATURDAY, DECEMBER 16

"Praise be to the Lord, the God of Israel, because he has come to his people and redeemed them. He has raised up a horn of salvation for us in the house of his servant David . . . to rescue us from the hand of our enemies, and to enable us to serve him without fear." Luke 1:68–69, 74 (NIV)

ZECHARIAH KNEW ALL ABOUT FEAR. As he stood by the altar of incense one day doing his priestly work, Gabriel appeared. Zechariah was "startled and gripped with fear," and I don't blame him one bit. After Gabriel's message, Zechariah responded with more fear and doubt. Yet months later, Zechariah's song rings with rejoicing and asserts that God enables us to serve Him without fear.

What caused the change? It wasn't just months of silence or witnessing the impossible birth of baby John by his aged wife that deepened Zechariah's faith. The clue is in the early verses of his song that tell us Jesus is coming. It's because of Him that Zechariah's heart changed from feeling fear and disbelief to reveling in joy and trust.

I long to serve without fear, but I find I'm often like Zechariah. Even in the small places Jesus has called me to work, I hold back. My hand hesitates over the phone, because even though my friend is hurting, I'm afraid I'll say the wrong thing and be a nuisance. When doubt swirls around me, giving myself a pep talk doesn't have enough power to change my heart.

But Jesus does. He has come. He has rescued us from our enemies—including the enemies of doubt and failure. Through Him, we can change like Zechariah did. We no longer need to wonder if God can accomplish what He promises or worry that our humble service is useless. We can serve without fear. —SHARON HINCK

FAITH STEP: *Pick one area of service, and ask Jesus to enable you to lend a hand without fear today.*

THIRD SUNDAY IN ADVENT, DECEMBER 17

*So you have sorrow now, but I will see you again; then you will rejoice,
and no one can rob you of that joy. John 16:22 (NLT)*

MY FAMILY HAS GREAT MEMORIES from the eight years we lived by a lake. It was where we brought our newborns, and where a winter ice storm knocked out our power for a week when we had a toddler and a seven-week-old baby. The roads were slick, and hundred-year-old trees had snapped under the ice's weight and fallen across the pavement, so we couldn't risk driving back to town. We were stuck.

Before long the "adventure" grew old, and we longed for electricity and warmth and space to stretch out. Trapped far from medical care with two little ones, I felt robbed of my sense of security.

We want the security of knowing what we value is protected and safe, whether people we care about or property we own. We don't often think of our joy being rendered powerless, but how tragic would that be if Jesus didn't secure lasting joy for us! His joy never yields to ice storms or any other disaster.

"The joy that Jesus came to bring is from outside this world. It is the very joy that Jesus himself has in God the Father—which he has had from all eternity and will have forever," writes author Jon Piper. In this third week of Advent, we celebrate the joy Jesus ushered in. Jesus is Immanuel, "God with us," at all times, in all things.

Today we look back with wonder that God came into the world, and we look forward to His return, expecting the great unceasing joy He has promised us, joy that cannot, not ever, be taken away!
—ERIN KEELEY MARSHALL

FAITH STEP: *Look up Romans 15:13 for more on joy. Memorize it and John 16:22.*

MONDAY, DECEMBER 18

Behold, a virgin shall be with child, and shall bring forth a son, and they shall call His name Emmanuel, which being interpreted is, God with us.
Matthew 1:23 (KJV)

ONE DAY IN MY OFFICE, as I was wrapping up classes for Christmas break, I received an e-mail from an old friend. She mentioned it had been a rough week. Her loved one was one of the Marines murdered in Tennessee, and just now she had finally gotten news of the autopsy report. This slashed open her wound, adding more trauma to a hurt that already seemed impossible to heal. "The holiday should be joy," she wrote, "but all I want to do is cry."

I searched for the right words, a way to respond that might bring some comfort. But I found nothing. I started to spiral down into the darkness, all of the junk in the world, the pain we humans inflict on one another, the mess it all is. I cried when I thought about my friend's family huddled together to try to have Christmas. And then, through my tears, it began to dawn on me. This is what Christmas means.

I wrote to my friend: *If ever there was a picture of our need for a Savior, for the hope that was born into the mess, the poverty, the pain of our lives, surely this is it.* I imagined her family gathered for Christmas with Jesus in the middle of them, because He will be. He is Emmanuel. God with us. Jesus here. Not waving a wand that makes the bad stuff go away. Not a crutch for the weak-minded. But a Savior Who comes to us in our mess. That's what Christmas is. —GWEN FORD FAULKENBERRY

FAITH STEP: *As you prepare for Christmas, ask Jesus to show you a person who needs to hear about the hope you have found in Him. Think of a creative way you can reach out and share what Christmas means to you with that person. It's the best gift you could ever give!*

TUESDAY, DECEMBER 19

*Every good and perfect gift is from above, coming down from
the Father of the heavenly lights, who does not change like shifting shadows.
James 1:17 (NIV)*

CHRISTMAS MORNING AT OUR HOUSE is a time of kids in pajamas with
bedhead, gobbling breakfast and then listening to the Christmas story
before opening presents. The celebration of Christ's birth is a time of
excitement. It has also become a time of transformation for our family.
Six years ago at Christmas we'd just met a birth mom who was considering our family for her soon-to-be born baby girl. (She chose us!)
Three years ago this Christmas we were waiting for a call from DHS
(Department of Human Services) and praying for the child(ren) Jesus
had for us. A few weeks later we were matched with two siblings. Last year
at Christmas we were praying about four sibling girls. This Christmas
we have a FULL HOUSE with seven adopted children around the tree!

Not everyone's family grows exponentially like ours, but everyone
can look to Christmas as a time to consider not only what we can
buy but what we can offer: a welcoming hug, an understanding
heart, even a place to belong.

God gave us His Son, Jesus. For my husband and me, His Son
changed our hearts and opened our eyes to the needs of orphans.
Those former orphans are transforming our Christmases. There is
more noise around our house but also more life. The pile of presents is bigger, and the joy over every little gift is bigger too.

Jesus truly is the gift Who keeps on giving. As we follow Him,
He teaches us to give, love, serve, embrace, and welcome. Just like He
did. —TRICIA GOYER

FAITH STEP: *Thank Jesus for all the people—the perfect gifts—He's given to
you. Say a prayer for each one as a special Christmas gift. Or write down your
prayer and present it to everyone in your life on Christmas Day.*

WEDNESDAY, DECEMBER 20

And so we know and rely on the love God has for us. God is love.
Whoever lives in love lives in God, and God in them.
1 John 4:16 (NIV)

I NEVER REALIZED that I had three boys who considered themselves fashion savvy until they started commenting on my appearance.

This past Christmas, I wanted to look festive. I had on a red shirt and tried on a gold necklace with lots of charms on it. I thought it was fun. There was a general outcry when I walked into the living room. Will said, "Wow. That's a lot." Addie hid his head in shame. Jack took one look at me and said, "I pity the fool who wears that necklace." So since I didn't want to look like Mr. T, I took off the necklace and wore something more subdued.

Sometimes I let other people influence how I see myself. That's not always a bad thing. I am sure that I will be thanking the boys in the future for stepping in and saving me from looking like Mr. T. They are keeping me classy. I am going to keep listening to them.

But the most influential voice I've learned to listen to is that of Jesus. He has the best view of me. He sees me... warts and all. He knows the ins and outs of my heart: my strengths and weaknesses. And still He says, "Love-ly."

Jesus views each of us through His lens of unconditional love. He sees us, not just for who we are at the moment but for the person He created us to be, and is helping us to become, moment by moment. What joy that we can lean into His grace and find freedom!
—SUSANNA FOTH AUGHTMON

FAITH STEP: *Look at yourself in the mirror. Who do you see? Who do you think Jesus sees when He looks at you? Lean into Him and rest in His love today.*

THURSDAY, DECEMBER 21

"For God so loved the world that he gave his only Son, so that everyone who believes in him will not perish but have eternal life." John 3:16 (NRSV)

MY HUSBAND AND I WORKED with a mission organization in Nepal for three years. Back then, Nepal was officially a Hindu kingdom and didn't recognize Christmas, let alone the traditions we're accustomed to in North America. We celebrated minus decorated trees, colored lights, cards, cranberries, and turkey.

One Christmas Eve, about forty villagers filled our courtyard. We'd invited them for a special evening, and curiosity drew them. As they sat cross-legged on the cold ground, a Nepalese woman from a neighboring village stood on our front step and called for their attention. She welcomed them and told the story of Mary, Joseph, and Jesus, using a flannel-graph board to illustrate her words. A lantern flickered a foot away, lighting the board and her face.

I'll never forget the crowd's wide-eyed wonderment. They listened in silence, absorbing the account of angels, shepherds, the virgin birth, and Jesus—God in flesh—come to earth in the form of a helpless baby. That night they heard, for the first time, the life-giving story I knew by rote. And I received a memorable gift—the reminder that Christmas is all about the Good News.

Familiar traditions warm our hearts, but sometimes we can't enjoy them due to conditions beyond our control. No matter. The truth and the power of the Christmas message endure: God so loved the world that He gave His only Son. Now that's cause for celebration! —GRACE FOX

FAITH STEP: *Today, somewhere in the world, people are hearing the Christmas story for the first time. Ask Jesus to help them understand its truth and its relevance to their lives.*

FRIDAY, DECEMBER 22

He does everything just right and on time,
but people can never completely understand what he is doing.
Ecclesiastes 3:11 (NCV)

THINGS SEEMED TO BE falling into place. For four years, my husband had worked as a field engineer, living in temporary housing near his current job assignment. Now he had been laid off and was at home job-hunting. My son-in-law had served four years in the army; he'd decided to take off two years to complete his bachelor's degree.

It all made perfect sense. Since my daughter would be working, I could help with their six-year-old daughter and newborn son. I would get the chance to be part of my grandchildren's lives. My husband would be able to make up for some of the time he had lost being with his kids and grandkids. Best of all, our entire family would be in the same area for the first time in years.

A few weeks later, nothing made sense. My husband found a job; unfortunately, it was 1,500 miles away. Leaving my family proved to be one of the hardest things I've ever done. And ever since that move, I always wonder what Mary thought of the timing of Jesus's birth. Did she think about the inconvenience of traveling to Bethlehem in her state? About the wisdom of delivering her baby in a stable?

Sometimes I look back and see the purpose of events in my life, but some things may not make sense until I see Jesus face to face. I can still choose to trust Him even when His timing seems confusing. Mary modeled the best attitude when Gabriel announced she would deliver the Messiah: "I am the Lord's servant. Let everything you've said happen to me" (Luke 1:38, GW). —DIANNE NEAL MATTHEWS

FAITH STEP: *Think back to a time when you questioned God's timing. If you still struggle to understand those circumstances, repeat Mary's words as a prayer.*

SATURDAY, DECEMBER 23

"I bring you good news of great joy which will be for all the people."
Luke 2:10 (NAS)

DEPARTMENT STORES WHISK PRODUCTS off the shelves earlier each year to make room for Christmas. Advertisements offer discounts as they push back the dates for shopping. "Black Friday" sales began on Thanksgiving, and one ad caught my attention more than any other.

A company offered the clever phrase "thanksgetting" to represent its great offers. Not only did it attempt to steal the true meaning away from a national holiday, but it also satisfied selfish whims: more stuff, more getting, more happiness. The company had found a way to merge Thanksgiving and Christmas into prolonged, empty celebrations.

As I reflected on the holiday season and read the Christmas story again, I saw anew how God had also pushed back the celebration of Christmas long before the actual event. Hints of the Savior's coming began in the Garden of Eden—and even before the foundation of the world (Genesis 3:15, John 1:1–14). Prophets foretold the event, and the intent of God's heart and early messages were not based on consumer "getting" but on divine giving.

In the fullness of time, God gave His best, incomparable gift— His Son, Jesus—to the world, not to offer temporary happiness but lasting joy.

And on that Christmas Eve, Jesus whispered to me in those still, sweet moments, "I did it for you." So I gave thanks again from a truly joyous heart. —REBECCA BARLOW JORDAN

FAITH STEP: *Take time to read the Christmas story in different translations. Give thanks once again for the greatest gift of all, Jesus.*

FOURTH SUNDAY IN ADVENT, CHRISTMAS EVE, DECEMBER 24

You love him even though you have never seen him. Though you do not see him now, you trust him; and you rejoice with a glorious, inexpressible joy.
1 Peter 1:8 (NLT)

LOVE IS THE REASON behind creation and salvation. Divine love so encompassing that it had to be shared.

We've been reminded of hope in Jesus as the forerunner who goes ahead of us into the unknown. And we've thought again of the peace that guards hope when we stay close to Jesus. And we've looked with fresh eyes at the joy in Christ that cannot, not ever, be taken away.

Love binds us together. It's the fulfillment of a promise and the force that guarantees the completion of promises still to come.

We can relate to the ancients who waited on the Lord's timing for the Messiah. Two thousand years ago Jesus was born, and one long wait ended for generations who looked for His birth. Thirty-three years passed. He died, rose, and returned to the Father with the promise that He would be back. They waited, and now we wait for Him to come again.

Waiting would become impossible if we didn't know the One Who holds the promise. We don't see Him face-to-face; still, we know enough of His love and what He has already done to trust that He is in the process of making all things new.

Through Jesus we learn that love does the hard best thing. Love sacrifices and challenges. Love leads with hope and guards peace and protects joy. And love rejoices in faith as it waits well. This love is ours because of Jesus. —ERIN KEELEY MARSHALL

FAITH STEP: *Ask Jesus to show you His love in new ways as you draw closer to Christmas Day and time spent with family, some who may not know Him.*

CHRISTMAS, MONDAY, DECEMBER 25

*It is to your advantage that I go away, for if I do not go away,
the Helper will not come to you. But if I go, I will send him to you.*
John 16:7 (ESV)

CHRISTMAS AT LAST! The majesty of it has finally arrived.

It's a beautiful holy day, and I love it. But sometimes as the hours of Christmas tick by, they begin to feel anticlimactic, as if I'm searching for *What now?* I don't want to let go of this day for another year. It comes and goes too quickly, a reminder of how Jesus came to earth, died, rose, and returned to heaven. And what then?

He promised to come back someday, and now humanity is in waiting mode again. However, that first Christmas changed all of our future days of "What now?" After Jesus returned to His heavenly Father, He sent His Spirit to abide throughout the earth, and even better, directly within His believers.

How much difference does His spirit's presence in us make for life, for all the days that are not December 25? It's all the difference.

Before Jesus was born in Bethlehem, His spirit didn't abide within believers. Now that He does live in us, every day of this fallible, messy life holds the glory of Christmas because He is still here.

Jesus, in the midst of any old everyday day, fills each one with His glory, like Christmas. Even if a day holds sorrow or disappointment or health scares or relationship troubles, it is still full of the Christmas miracle. We can look forward to tomorrow, knowing it'll be as glorious as the one when Jesus came to us all those generations ago.
—ERIN KEELEY MARSHALL

FAITH STEP: *Put a daily alert on your phone or a note on your kitchen window-sill to remind yourself to revel in the truth of Christmas every day.*

TUESDAY, DECEMBER 26

*"I, the Lord, have called you in righteousness; I will take hold of your hand.
I will keep you and will make you to be a covenant for the people
and a light for the Gentiles, to open eyes that are blind, to free captives
from prison and to release from the dungeon those who sit in darkness."*
Isaiah 42:6–7 (NIV)

I USED TO THINK CHRISTMAS was all about joy, hope, and peace on earth. I stayed away from reading news stories filled with pain and despair. But the older I get, the more I realize that Christmas may have more to do with chaos than anything else. Because the people of this earth, in a million different ways, are sitting in the dark, afraid. Hoping beyond hope that someone will protect them, hold them, keep them safe, and lift them out of their fear. We have been in desperate need of a Savior. You and I and our families and the billions of others dotting the globe.

Jesus hears our cries. He sees us all. And He is working out His plan. At great detriment to Himself, Jesus came into the darkness of this world. He saw us down in our fears, our pain, our sin, and our despair. And cracked the sky with His light and great love and said, "I am here with you in the middle of this mess. And even better, if you just hold on to me, I will save you."

Knowing we are not alone, that we are caught up in His love and light, and that He came to save us? That is life-altering-hope-filled-we-will-never-be-the-same-again kind of news that we celebrate with great joy at Christmas and all year round.
—SUSANNA FOTH AUGHTMON

FAITH STEP: *Light a candle and pray for those in the world that need Jesus in the midst of their darkness to bring them hope and joy this holiday season.*

WEDNESDAY, DECEMBER 27

Now it happened that as he was praying alone, the disciples were with him.
And he asked them, "Who do the crowds say that I am?"
Luke 9:18 (ESV)

FOR MANY YEARS I had a daily quiet-time routine of Bible reading
and prayer, and it was actually quiet. My older kids were in high
school and college, and my husband was working. I enjoyed the
alone time with Jesus. Then we felt Jesus's tug to adopt and things
changed. With first a baby, and then lots of little ones, there was not
much alone time. I tried getting up even earlier, but when I did, the
kids did too. And when I tried to read and pray after they went to
bed, I found myself falling asleep.

It was my oldest daughter, Leslie, who pointed out the irony of
Luke 9:18. Jesus was praying alone and His disciples were with
Him. I think it's a fallacy that we need quiet time to truly connect with Jesus. These days I often read my Bible while the kids
sit around me watching cartoons. I pray as I'm folding laundry. I
sing praise songs as I'm cooking spaghetti. Like Jesus, I pray alone
while my children are with me. If we wait for the perfect circumstance before we meet with Jesus, we'll never find it. Jesus is with us
always. We can find Jesus at the kitchen sink, under a blanket fort,
and while sorting socks.

José Lozano is quoted as saying, "I don't pray for God to take
my problems away, I pray only for God to give me the strength
to go through them." And these days I don't pray for Jesus to take
the noise away, I simply ask that He be with me in the midst of it.
—TRICIA GOYER

FAITH STEP: *The next time you're in a noisy, busy place, take a moment to*
connect with Jesus. Turn your heart to Him and ask Him to meet with you there.

THURSDAY, DECEMBER 28

You are the light of the world. A city set on a hill cannot be hidden. Nor do people light a lamp and put it under a basket, but on a stand, and it gives light to all in the house. In the same way, let your light shine before others, so that they may see your good works and give glory to your Father who is in heaven.
Matthew 5:14–16 (ESV)

I CAN LOOK OUT my office door and see a Himalayan salt lamp glowing yellowy-orange on a table near the living room.

Healthy living is one of my favorite fascinations, and I recently discovered the benefits of these lamps for clearing air of toxins and allergens. I look forward to seeing how much they work, but even if only a little, their glow contributes to an inviting and relaxing environment.

Each of us affects the atmosphere, for good or bad, with our attitudes, actions, words, expressions, tone, and body language. No doubt we know someone we'd consider a toxic person. If we're honest, we all have had times when we've contributed more negativity than positivity.

Not only do the lamps soothe and help the air, they also remind me to live on the healthy, healing side of life instead of contributing to the world's brokenness. The only way to live that way is to soak up the glow of Jesus through studying His Word, praying, and relying on His Holy Spirit for empowerment.

If we live on our own power, our brokenness will come to drain us and those around us, just as my salt lamp cannot last forever. On our own, our power will evaporate. But Jesus's holiness lights us within and flows out for the benefit of others—and ourselves. —ERIN KEELEY MARSHALL

FAITH STEP: *Himalayan salt lamps come in a variety of sizes and prices. Try finding one today, and enjoy its benefits and the reminder to get your glow from Jesus.*

FRIDAY, DECEMBER 29

Then Caleb silenced the people before Moses and said, "We should go up and take possession of the land, for we can certainly do it." But the men who had gone up with him said, "We can't attack those people; they are stronger than we are." Numbers 13:30–31 (NIV)

STICKY NOTES COVERED MY DESK with reminders of all the steps in my big project. I had thought I had weeks to do all the work, but an unexpected deadline threw me into a panic. My temples pulsed, and my breathing grew tight.

I e-mailed a few friends and asked them to pray, venting about feeling overwhelmed and frustrated—especially as I was preparing for a vacation and I'd anticipated a few days of peace.

Friends replied with compassion but also encouraged me to cry out to Jesus in my need. As I remembered His greatness and His sufficiency, my little stress hurricane blew out to sea.

The Israelites also felt overwhelmed by the task ahead. Enemy territory was terrifying and loomed large. But Caleb didn't focus on the size of the problem. He focused on the greatness of God. Whether our enemy territory is a tough conversation we're afraid to initiate, a pile of work that crushes us, or a bad habit we want to conquer, we often must acknowledge that the problem is stronger than we are.

What a gift that on the heels of that realization comes an even more important truth. Jesus is bigger than any challenge. He doesn't leave us to fight battles alone; knowing that, we can say with Caleb, "We can certainly do it." —SHARON HINCK

FAITH STEP: *On a large sheet of paper, draw a huge cross. Then write some of your most pressing problems in as tiny letters as possible at the foot of the cross, praying for a fresh perspective.*

SATURDAY, DECEMBER 30

Peace I give to you; not as the world gives. . . .
John 14:27 (NAS)

IN PREPARATION FOR a cross-country flight, we passengers boarded the plane, only to sit at the gate, unmoving. The captain reported a small malfunctioning part with big consequences. An hour and a half later, we were told to deplane and wait at the gate. Many got in a painfully slow-moving line to rebook their flights. Still later a baggage handler wordlessly brought our carry-ons off the plane into the gate area. Another hour later, an attendant announced that the airline was sending a new plane, a new gate, and we would likely miss our connecting flights, even those with a four-hour layover. I stayed relatively calm. Inconvenienced but confident Jesus hadn't left the building.

One man, all alone, spoke almost no English. The panic on his face must have been even more crippling in his mind. What was happening? He couldn't understand. Eventually, an attendant took him to airport headquarters where an interpreter could ease his fears.

When a crisis hits, some of the people in our day-to-day lives are as confused as that man in the airport because they don't speak the language that Jesus speaks. They catch a word here and there, but because of the language barrier, they don't understand concepts such as trust, hope, secure, protected, Holy Spirit, Comforter, peace. . . .

We learn the language that helps us navigate life through God's Word, the Holy Spirit, and by communication with Jesus through prayer. Without that connection, the panic is real.
—CYNTHIA RUCHTI

FAITH STEP: *If you've felt confused, lost in the frenzy of what's going on around you, consider Jesus language lessons. Or, you may be the one to step forward and steer a fearful traveler toward the language help he or she needs.*

SUNDAY, DECEMBER 31

God is our refuge and strength, always ready to help in times of trouble.
Psalm 46:1 (NLT)

OUR FAMILY LIVED in Kalispell, Montana, for fifteen years, at the foot of the Rocky Mountains. There, the Columbia range of mountains shoots up from the valley floor. Every time I looked at the mountains, Psalm 121:1–2 (NAS) came to mind: "I will lift up my eyes to the mountains; From where shall my help come? My help comes from the Lord, Who made heaven and earth."

A couple of years after we moved to the valley I rode to the top of a local ski park, and what I saw shocked me. Behind the huge Columbia mountain range was another range, just as large. And behind that, another. And behind that, another. As far as I could see.

Now, when I read these verses from God's Word I know that Jesus is not only available for my present help, but all the challenges to come. When we see the problems in our lives, God's Word reminds us that with His help we can overcome even more than we can currently see. That's why turning to God's Word is so important. It reminds us of Jesus's help.

Pastor Richard Blackaby says, "If Jesus could speak and raise the dead, calm a storm, cast out demons, and heal the incurable, then what effect might a word from Him have upon your life? The possibilities should cause you to tremble! The next time you open God's Word, do so with a sense of holy expectation." Know that Jesus is your help for today's challenge and the next one and the next one to come. God's Word promises that. —TRICIA GOYER

FAITH STEP: *What challenge is a mountain in your life right now? Turn to God's Word and look up one of your favorite Scripture verses to strengthen you. Read it with an expectation of what Jesus is going to do.*

ABOUT THE AUTHORS

 SUSANNA FOTH AUGHTMON is the mother of Jack, 14, Will, 12, Addison, 9, and the wife of Scott, the lead pastor of Pathway Church in Redwood City, California. Susanna has led worship, worked in children's ministry, and done the odd janitorial job here and there during their ministry. She loves connecting with fellow readers through her books and speaking engagements, using humor and focusing on how God's grace intersects with our daily lives. You can find Susanna on Facebook and at tiredsupergirl.com.

 GWEN FORD FAULKENBERRY lives in the mountains of Ozark, Arkansas. Her passions are Jesus and the family He has given her. She loves to travel the world with Grace, 15, ride the range with Harper, 13, bake with Adelaide, 8, and read books with Stella, 3. Gwen holds a master's degree in liberal arts and enjoys teaching literature at a local university, writing, running, and playing the piano at her church. She is the author of novels and devotional books and loves to connect with readers. You'll find her at gwenfordfaulkenberry.com, where she blogs about everything from raising chickens and goats to the spiritual symbolism of Dostoyevsky.

 GRACE FOX is a global worker, international speaker, and author. Some of her books are *Morning Moments with God: Devotions for the Busy Woman* and *Moving from Fear to Freedom: A Woman's Guide to Peace in Every Situation*. She lives with her husband of thirty-five years in British Columbia, close enough to their six grandkids to babysit as often as they get the chance. Grace would love to hear from you at gracefox.com and fb.com/gracefox.author.

TRICIA GOYER is a homeschooling mom of ten, grandmother of two, and wife to John. A best-selling author, Tricia has published more than fifty books and written more than five hundred articles. She is a two-time Carol Award winner, as well as a Christy, Christian Retailing's Best, and ECPA Award nominee. Tricia is on the blogging team at TheBetterMom.com, volunteers around her community, mentors teen moms, and leads a teen MOPS (Mothers of Preschoolers) group in Little Rock, Arkansas.

TARICE L. S. GRAY has had her work published in various forms over the past two decades. She's written for *Gospel Today* magazine and *The Huffington Post*, among other publications. She earned a master of fine arts in creative nonfiction writing from Fairleigh Dickinson University and is an associate editor at Guideposts Books. The married mother of a busy seven-year-old, Tarice is also an associate member of the Writers Guild of America, West.

SHARON HINCK writes "stories for the hero in all of us," about ordinary people experiencing God's grace in unexpected ways. Her novels have won three Carol Awards and a Christy finalist medal, and all of her books explore the challenges and joys of following God's call. Her most recent novel is *The Deliverer*. Sharon and her husband enjoy spending time with their children and grandchildren and make time for gardening, remodeling, and laughter-filled conversations with friends. She interacts with readers at sharonhinck.com.

REBECCA BARLOW JORDAN is a best-selling inspirational author who has penned eleven books and more than two thousand greeting cards, articles, and devotions. She is a devoted follower of Jesus and is passionate about home, family, and helping others find intimacy with God. She and her minister-husband have two children and four grandchildren and live in northeast Texas, where she loves gardening and reading great fiction. Read her blogs at rebeccabarlowjordan.com.

ERIN KEELEY MARSHALL is the author of *Tea Rose* (book two of Guideposts Books' latest fiction series Tearoom Mysteries), *Navigating Route 20-Something,* and *The Daily God Book.* She spent the early years of her career as an editor and lives in Arkansas with her husband, Steve, and their kids, Paxton and Calianne. She calls erinkeeleymarshall.com her home on the Web and can also be found on Facebook and Twitter @EKMarshall.

DIANNE NEAL MATTHEWS is the author of daily devotional books, including *The One Year Women of the Bible* and *Designed for Devotion: A 365-Day Journey from Genesis to Revelation,* and writes for periodicals, Web sites, and blogs. She and her husband, Richard, have been married for forty-two years and live in southeast Texas, too far away from their three children and three grandchildren. She loves to connect with readers through DianneNealMatthews.com and Facebook and Twitter @DianneNMatthews.

CYNTHIA RUCHTI tells stories hemmed in hope through her award-winning novels, novellas, devotionals, nonfiction, and speaking events for women and writers. She and her husband live in the heart of Wisconsin, not far from their three children and five grandchildren. Visit her at cynthiaruchti.com.

SUZANNE DAVENPORT TIETJEN is the author of *The Sheep of His Hand* and *40 Days to Your Best Life for Nurses*. She and her husband, Mike, live in a cabin deep in the forest where they enjoy breathtaking beauty and an outdoor way of life. A former shepherd, neonatal nurse practitioner, and transport nurse, Suzanne misses the lights and sirens as well as her beloved sheep, but she is now working hard on two writing projects. You can find out more at suzannetietjen.com or follow her on Twitter @suzishepherd.

SCRIPTURE REFERENCE INDEX

TOPICAL INDEX

waiting and, 105
of water, 207
fellowship, in suffering, 41
firstfruits, 81
flight, physics of, 247
flooding, 166
flying, 171, 247, 307, 364
focus
    on the future, 32
    on God, 363
    on Jesus, 3, 123, 133, 186,
        196, 207, 223, 250, 251,
        293, 300, 311, 313
    on love, 45
    memory and, 65
    on others, 153
    trying to maintain, 11
fog, 139
forgetfulness, 283, 314
forgiveness, 31, 48, 53, 102,
    146, 221, 277, 283, 287
fostering children, 6
fostering/foster children,
    287
fraud, 220
freedom, 38, 289, 310
friends/friendship
    admiration for, 74
    gratitude for, 205
    making new, 301
    making time for, 172
    problems within, 67
    sharing burdens and, 84,
        243
    support within, 41, 351
frustration, 132, 322

G
galaxies, observing, 219
gardening, 39, 82, 133, 150,
    186, 286, 321
generosity, 81, 153, 205, 208,
    322
gifts
    giving and receiving, 152,
        153, 222, 292, 340,
        353
    from Jesus, 159
    talent and, 336
glory, 8, 197, 236
God
    compassion of, 346

dedication to, 50
gift from, 357
love from, 45, 137, 216,
    256, 282, 294
relationship with. see rela-
    tionships
sign from, 59
strength from, 50, 174, 215,
    276, 361
talking to, 299
trust in. see trust in God
God's Call, 174
God's Peace, 265
God's Plan, 200
God's Power, 54, 350
God's Word, 55, 72, 114, 162,
    186, 190, 211, 212, 216,
    260, 266, 295, 364, 365
Good Friday, 104
good health, maintaining, 12,
    342, 362
Good Shepherd, 57
grace, 134, 166
grandchildren, 72, 184, 192,
    209, 229, 233, 251, 255,
    261, 284, 308, 339
grapes, growing, 321
gratitude, 13, 93, 107, 128, 152,
    205, 229, 255, 307
grief/grieving, 7, 149
guidance, 261, 273, 278
    from Jesus, 2, 4, 17, 28, 62,
        91, 126, 139, 166, 171,
        172, 189, 193, 238, 314
    from others, 142
    through prayer, 42

H
harvest, 82
Hayford, Jack, 4
healing, 67, 73, 77, 136, 316
health. see also good health
    challenges, 4, 34, 58, 118,
        262, 264, 285, 305, 319,
        323, 328, 347
    program for, 129
hearing problems, 305
heartbreak, 67
heaven, 141
help
    asking for, 227
    Jesus providing, 95

helping others, 37, 52, 63, 74,
    80, 98, 128, 134, 170,
    172, 174, 176, 203, 227,
    228, 238, 242, 243, 252,
    272, 287, 345, 347, 352
hiking, 62, 168
Himalayan salt lamps, benefits
    of, 362
hoarders, 49
hobbies, 20, 244
Holcomb, Jack, 218
Holy Week, 99–105
home
    building a, 95
    downsizing a, 66
    moving, 38, 157, 300,
        322
    sanctuary and, 160
hope, 6, 99, 106, 142, 259, 285,
    309, 337, 344, 358, 360
    dashing of, 110
household chores, 70, 179
housesitting, 181
Hurston, Zora Neale, 161
hurt, dealing with, 201, 287,
    294
hybrid cars, 224

I
impressions, making good, 288
inconvenience, 52, 364
insomnia, 123
inspiration, 232, 301, 302
interviews, 315
irritation, 132, 223

J
joy, 4, 8, 10, 179, 187, 204,
    229, 291, 351
judgment, 88, 316
justice, 166

K
Kim, Yongsung, 207
kindness, 74, 80, 111, 149, 158,
    203, 227, 228, 322
Kingdom of Christ, 138

L
Lawrence (Carmelite lay
    brother), 63
leadership, 57

A NOTE FROM THE EDITORS

We hope you enjoyed *Mornings with Jesus 2017*, published by the Books and Inspirational Media Division of Guideposts, a nonprofit organization that touches millions of lives every day through products and services that inspire, encourage, help you grow in your faith, and celebrate God's love.

Thank you for making a difference with your purchase of this book, which helps fund our many outreach programs to military personnel, prisons, hospitals, nursing homes, and educational institutions.

We also create many useful and uplifting online resources. Visit Guideposts .org to read true stories of hope and inspiration, access OurPrayer network, sign up for free newsletters, download free e-books, join our Facebook community, and follow our stimulating blogs. To delve more deeply into *Mornings with Jesus,* visit MorningswithJesus.org.

You may purchase the 2018 edition of *Mornings with Jesus* anytime after July 2017. To order, visit Guideposts.org/MorningswithJesus, call (800) 932-2145, or write to Guideposts, PO Box 5815, Harlan, Iowa 51593.

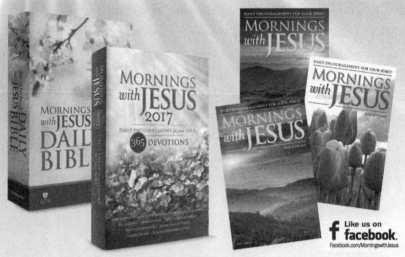